A Guide to Writing for Human Service Professionals

A Guide to Writing for Human Service Professionals

Morley D. Glicken

ROWMAN & LITTLEFIELD PUBLISHERS, INC.
Lanham • Boulder • NewYork • Toronto • Plymouth, UK

ROWMAN & LITTLEFIELD PUBLISHERS, INC.

Published in the United States of America
by Rowman & Littlefield Publishers, Inc.
A wholly owned subsidary of The Rowman & Littlefield Publishing Group, Inc.
4501 Forbes Boulevard, Suite 200, Lanham, Maryland 20706
www.rowmanlittlefield.com

Estover Road
Plymouth PL6 7PY
United Kingdom

British Library Cataloguing in Publication Information Available

Library of Congress Cataloging-in-Publication Data

Glicken, Morley D.
  A guide to writing for human service professionals / Morley D. Glicken.
    p. cm.
  Includes bibliographical references and index.
  ISBN-13: 978-0-7425-5947-9 (cloth : alk. paper)
  ISBN-10: 0-7425-5947-5 (cloth : alk. paper)
  ISBN-13: 978-0-7425-5948-6 (pbk. : alk. paper)
  ISBN-10: 0-7425-5948-3 (pbk. : alk. paper)
  1. Human services—Authorship. 2. Social service—Authorship. I. Title.
HV41.G53 2007
808'.066361—dc22   2007004889

Printed in the United States of America

♾ ™ The paper used in this publication meets the minimum requirements of
American National Standard for Information Sciences—Permanence of Paper
for Printed Library Materials, ANSI/NISO Z39.48-1992.

This book is dedicated to my father, Sam Glicken, who loved the written word and believed that English was the poet's language, and to my daughter, Amy Glicken, whose writing blesses this book and my life.

Contents

Acknowledgments

It takes a certain amount of ignorant bliss to write a "how to write" book. Not until I began writing it did I realize how little I knew about the rules of writing and the complexities of the English language. Helping me progress throughout, thankfully, was my wonderful significant other, Patricia Fox, who corrected many bad sentences and looked at me sympathetically while taking into consideration that a guy who grew up in Grand Forks, North Dakota, and dreamed of playing professional hockey probably slept through every English class he ever took. Thankfully, Patricia stayed awake and I'm the beneficiary of her diligence. Thanks, Pat! You are the best!

Arthur Pomponio, my editor on three prior books was, as always, gracious, supportive, and enlightened. Thanks, Art, and thanks to Rowman & Littlefield for publishing my book and recognizing that good writing is an important part of being a human service professional.

You can't write a book without going to other sources. Thankfully, I found some lovely people who allowed me to use their material. They include Robert Harris, whose terrific book *When Good People Write Bad Sentences* helped immeasurably, a book that should be bought by everyone interested in good writing; Russ Dewey, professor emeritus at Georgia Southern University Department of Psychology; Bill Scott of the College of Wooster; Doc Scribe; Owen Williams, director of the University of Minnesota, Crookston Library; Perfesser Cumber and his sidekick Bert, whose website on incorrect word use helped so much; Yana Parker for her work on resumes and cover letters; Dr. Cecilia Julagay, writing instructor at California State University, San Bernardino, for sharing her work on expository writing; a cast of people who made writing this book such fun including Taco and Bell, Macho and Mann, Short, Brutish and Surly, and everyone else whose material gave me ideas or clarified questions I had about writing. Thank you folks. I couldn't have written this book without you.

Finally, thanks to the reviewers of my book who gave me such valuable feedback and helped me organize the material in a more logical and readable way.

Preface

Most human service professionals speak clearly and understand the need for effective verbal communication. But when it comes to effective writing, many of us have difficulty. I think the reason is that somewhere along the line we've been taught to mystify writing by making it much more complicated and difficult than it really is. In this book, I've simplified the entire process. I've explained when certain punctuation marks are needed and why the choice of certain words gives incorrect or vague meaning. I've given many examples of correct writing to help you write client reports, psychosocial histories, evaluations, professional papers, papers for mass audiences, and the many other uses of writing by professionals. I've cautioned you not to use psychobabble, slang, or bureaucratic language—that most insulated and vague form of writing preferred by public agencies. And I've tried to keep my writing clear and concise.

I've been a social work practitioner, educator, and administrator for over 40 years. During that time, I've published nine books (including this one) and many professional and nonprofessional articles. I've written for *Wall Street Journal* publications. I gave a paper in Israel on the way children learn about death to members of Kibbutzim who deal with death everyday. That experience and others like it have led to a strong belief that all of us in the human services have a responsibility to write well. Our reports and how clearly and precisely they are written often affect the clients we serve. The outcomes of child abuse and domestic violence cases may hinge on our evaluations. Parents who are otherwise competent and effective may lose custody of their children because we've done a poor job of advocacy in our written reports. What we do is important. Our clients deserve nothing but the very best from us.

Having taught a variety of courses over the years, I've come to believe that bad writing is often the norm for many students in the human services. To reinforce that belief, Alter and Atkins (2001) found that 60% of the graduate social work students in their sample wrote at less than graduate school level (see references in chapter 1). Only 20% of the sample who wrote badly sought help from writing centers or took tutorials or special writing classes, largely because the writing courses and tutorials were not practical and failed to help them with the nuanced writing required of professionals.

I've written this book to reduce common writing problems so that human service professionals write clear, concise reports, documents, scholarly papers, and records that benefit our clients.

Much of the material in this book has been tested in the classroom where I taught expository writing courses to undergraduate and graduate students. Since I am familiar with a number of human service work settings, I've made the examples of professional writing as true to real life as possible. Because I believe that most of us learn best when we are in our child ego states, I hope you won't mind a joke or two, or a bit of silliness.

If this book improves your writing and helps you say whatever is in your heart and mind with elegance and joy, then I will have written a book that matters. In the scheme of things, that's really all that counts.

With Warmest Regards,
Morley D. Glicken, DSW

1

Writing Is Just Talking With a Few Rules

WRITING ISN'T DIFFICULT

I don't want to mystify writing by giving you so many rules that it makes your head spin. Writing is simply talking and using simple punctuation and a few grammar rules that allow you to write just as if you were speaking. Writing is speaking, with guidelines provided for the reader so that when we read something, we know exactly how the writer would present the material if he or she were speaking it out loud. Because writing allows us to think about what we are going to say, it is often much more creative and descriptive than speaking.

The rules of writing are very simple. Throughout this book, the simplicity of writing will be stressed. The few rules of writing we need to use will be so concrete and easy to remember that, with some practice, your writing should flow. As just several examples of the simple rules of writing, or what we have come to call punctuation, a period (.) tells us that a specific thought or idea is completed. If we were talking, the listener would know this because there would be a short break at the end of a statement. A comma (,) tells us to pause, so when we write and include a comma, it's nothing more than saying to the reader, "If I were speaking to you, I would have paused for a split second." There are some authors, like Cormac McCarthy, who punctuate when they feel like it, or my father, Sam Glicken, whose punctuation broke every rule in the book but who still wrote beautiful, expressive, wonderful letters that I could understand because I had grown up with his immigrant English. Obsessing about correct punctuation often inhibits our writing. In this book you'll be encouraged to write and to learn, in the process, to use the few necessary grammar and punctuation rules that will help make your writing informative, descriptive, and engaging.

You also need to know that the more you write, the better you become. While I wrote many professional articles and columns for *National Business Employment Weekly*, a Dow Jones publication that also publishes the *Wall Street Journal*, it wasn't until I was 60 years old that I wrote my first book. Between the ages of 60 and 66, I wrote nine books. The more books I've written, the better I've become as a writer, and the easier it's been for me to write. The simple fact is that, much like the development of any skill, writing takes a lot of practice.

One other thing to keep in mind is that I read and correct my work more than 5 times and sometimes 10 times. No one writes well in the first draft, even the best of writers. The great novelist Ernest Hemingway didn't think he could write more than 500 useful words a day. A famous poet, Dorianne Laux, once told me that 80% of a wonderful poem of hers, "After Twelve Days of Rain" (1990), was written in a week, but that the rest of the poem took a year to complete. It's a wonderful poem about loneliness and the imperceptible pain caused by early life traumas. Whenever she reads it in public, she wants to sit down and change it. Good writing requires practice and revision.

Many of us have noted a serious decline in the ability of students to write well. In an article by Alter and Atkins (2001), the authors report that 60% of the graduate social work students in their sample wrote at less than graduate school level. Of the 60% of the students who wrote badly in their sample, only 20% sought help from writing centers, took tutorials, or attended special writing classes. Something fundamental is not working when students can't or won't write well. In the human services, children are taken from parents, elderly people have their savings placed in receivership, and people go to jail based on the reports we write. If our writing is poor, imagine the harm we can do.

You can become a good writer. In this short book, I'm going to show you how. I'm not going to give you a lot of useless rules or talk about dependent and independent clauses. I think that type of book turns most of us off. It certainly turns me off. What I *am* going to do is to tell you why we do something, using very simple terms and examples. When you're done with the book, you'll hear sentences in your head and you'll dictate what you hear to your hands so that writing becomes automatic. You will know the correct punctuation marks to use, how to paraphrase quotes, and how to use APA style in research papers. Although many people find the *Publication Manual of the American Psychological Association* (2001) unwieldy and sometimes difficult to use, the wise student and practitioner should own a copy.

You will also know when to begin a new paragraph and how long a sentence should be. You'll know about correct word choice and why we should never use slang or psychobabble in professional writing. Most important, you'll write with confidence. You will never wonder why you speak so clearly but write so badly. That's a promise. So let's get to it.

A FEW RULES FOR BETTER WRITING

Here are some rules that certainly have helped me in my writing. I will provide a hopefully humorous example of the rule followed by a more complete explanation. Future chapters will go into much more detail about each of the following rules.

1. **Prepositions are not words to end sentences with.** A preposition is a connecting word such as *with*. If you read a sentence ending in *with*, it sounds awkward. The better way to write this sentence would be: "A sentence ending in the word *with* sounds awkward and should be avoided."
2. **And don't start a sentence with a conjunction.** Conjunctions are words that connect ideas in a sentence such as *and, but,* and *therefore,* and should generally not be used to begin a sentence.
3. **Avoid clichés like the plague. (They're old hat.).** Clichés are trite sayings that tend to reduce an idea to, well, a cliché. Clichés are particularly poor choices in the human services because they fail to show the uniqueness of people.
4. **Also, always avoid annoying alliteration.** Alliteration occurs when a string of words start with the same letter. Alliteration tends to annoy the reader. It certainly can cause continued cloying consternation. See what I mean?
5. **Be more or less specific.** Vague terms such as *more or less* lack concise meaning and should be avoided in professional writing.
6. **Parenthetical remarks (however relevant) are (usually) unnecessary.** Parentheses look like this ( ) and usually contain information that can be easily included in a sentence. For example, the initial sentence might read, "However relevant, parenthetical remarks are usually unnecessary."
7. **Also too, never, ever use repetitive redundancies.** A redundancy is using a word or idea repeatedly. Once, perhaps twice, is often enough. This sentence might read, "Try not to say the same thing twice in a sentence."
8. **No sentence fragments.** This example is an incomplete sentence and should read, "When writing a sentence, the idea you intend to convey should be complete."
9. **Contractions aren't necessary and shouldn't be used.** Using contractions such as *aren't, won't,* and *shouldn't* in our writing conveys a lack of

formality. Professional writing generally eliminates contractions by using complete words such as *will not* for *won't*, and *should not* for *shouldn't*. In my view, contractions are permissible if used occasionally.

10. **Foreign words and phrases are not** *apropos* **(appropriate).** In professional writing, being understood is very important. For that reason, we usually do not use foreign words or phrases even though they may be appropriate and have greater meaning than a word in English because the reader may not be familiar with the word or phrase. If using a foreign word is necessary, place the English meaning next to it in parentheses. For example: "The *alte cocker* (old fool) sat at his computer early in the morning and drank his *café* (coffee) in a big *azur* (blue) mug."

11. **One should NEVER generalize**. A generalization is a statement made without factual evidence. For example, "Poor people always have school-related problems." It's true that some people living in poverty have school-related problems, but not all of them. This rule suggests that presenting generalizations without factual information weakens an argument.

12. **Don't use no double negatives**. Need I say more?

13. **Eschew ampersands (the character "&" instead of** *and*)**, & abbreviations (first letters of a name such as** FBI **for** Federal Bureau of Investigation)**, etc.** This isn't always true and in the coming chapters I'll discuss ampersands and abbreviations in more detail. In professional writing, too many abbreviations can be confusing, particularly if you fail to define them in the first place. Using the character "&" in the body of a professional document makes the document appear informal and implies to the reader that you are in a rush.

14. **Eliminate commas, that are, not necessary. Parenthetical words (words such as however and therefore) however should be enclosed in commas.** This example shows how commas can be incorrectly used to the point of affecting the meaning of a sentence. The sentences should read, "Eliminate commas that are not necessary. Parenthetical words, however, should be enclosed in commas."

15. **Never use a big word when a diminutive (small) one would suffice.** As a rule, we try to use words that are familiar to all readers. Lesser used words, or words that may be unfamiliar, are generally not chosen because they may cause confusion or lack clarity.

16. **Kill all exclamation points!!!** Only use exclamation points when the sentence requires a great deal of emphasis and, then, be very cautious. An explanation point suggests very strong emotion.

17. **Use words correctly, irregardless of how others use them.** As you probably know, the correct word is "regardless." I have an entire chapter (chapter 4) on word choice that includes incorrect words.

18. **Understatement is always the absolute best way to put forth earth-shaking ideas.** You can see that this sentence is about overstatement. A sentence about understatement might read, "Understating an idea by using neutral language is the best way to write about important ideas."
19. **Eliminate quotations. As Ralph Waldo Emerson said, "I hate quotations. Tell me what you know."** Of course, we do occasionally use quotes, particularly when we're quoting a client or another author, but professional writing is best when we summarize what others say. Too many quotes can give the impression that we haven't written a paper ourselves but have simply strung together what other people have said.
20. **If you've heard it once, you've heard it a thousand times: Resist hyperbole (exaggeration); not one writer in a million can use it correctly.** Exaggeration is sometimes used in the human services with little evidence that we are even close to being correct about an issue. Know your facts, share them in an objective way, and try not to exaggerate even if you feel strongly about a subject. The statement "All children who have been abandoned by their parents suffer from attachment problems" is an exaggeration. A better way to say this is that "Some children (indicate estimates) experience attachment problems when abandoned by their parents."
21. **Puns are for children, not groan (should be grown) readers.** As you can see, a pun is a play on words. Puns are fun to use in our personal correspondence, but they really haven't a place in professional writing, and they can be very annoying to those of us who find puns childless. Sorry.
22. **Go around the barn at high noon to avoid colloquialisms.** Many everyday expressions that we use are not as universal as we think. They may be popular, but only locally. An example might be the old North Dakota colloquialism, "Life is a just a slice of lefsa without any ludafisk to make it tasty." What can I say? The problem with using colloquialisms is that a diverse population of practitioners might not be familiar with certain expressions.
23. **Using slang ain't cool.** It certainly isn't. Slang has no place in professional writing unless you are accurately quoting another person. For example: The client said, "I ain't got but one life to live, and so far, it ain't rock 'n' roll."
24. **Psychobabble should never be used in written reports unless you want the report to generate transparent feelings of love and existential bliss.** Psychobabble includes expressions commonly used in the human services that are familiar but have very vague meaning. Sentences such as, "The client is experiencing transparent feelings

of love for his wife and is now in a state of existential bliss" are so vague that they have little place in professional writing. Wouldn't this be clearer? "The client has reached a point in his relationship with his wife where he can openly express his love for her. The ability to openly express love for his wife has resulted in strong feelings of happiness and contentment with his life."

25. **Never overwrite by using jaded words that tell the reader you are inconsequential in the vocabulary area.** In other words, don't use words you think will impress others when, in reality, they are incorrectly applied.

APPLYING THE RULES: SOME EXAMPLES

OK, so there's more to writing than these 25 rules, but they are a good place to start. Let's take **Rule 11** about generalizing. We often generalize in the human services by making statements that seem set in concrete. For example, "Joe is a 44-year-old bipolar who has been deteriorating over the past 10 years and has a poor prognosis for improvement." What's wrong here? Well, Joe can't be defined as a bipolar. He's a human being with many strengths and some problems, including suffering from bipolar disorder. How can we possibly know that the prognosis is bad, and how do we know for certain that during the past 10 years he has been deteriorating? Wouldn't a better statement about Joe be: "Joe is a 44-year-old former university professor who was diagnosed with bipolar disorder 10 years ago. While he is unable to teach, he has written two well-received books and seeks help now for a severe problem with writer's block, which he believes is related to the progression of the illness. He is optimistic about the future but worried about his ability to write and remain self-sufficient." A positive statement offers the reader optimism and makes Joe a human being rather than a disorder.

How about **Rule 17** regarding the need to use words correctly? Chapter 4 is all about word choice, but we often use words that are overly negative and stigmatizing, and may not even be accurate. The use of the words "personality disorder" or "psychosis" are red flags in the human services because they describe people who may be very difficult, if not impossible, to treat. Markowitz (1998) reports that people diagnosed with a mental illness are "more likely to be unemployed, have less income, experience a diminished sense of self, and have fewer social supports" (p. 335), in large part because of the discriminatory experiences they've had with others who treat them as if a mental illness is akin to a contagious disease and not because of the illness.

The evidence is that most people with an initial diagnosis of mental illness overcome the problem and are symptom-free and well-functioning in time. Carpenter (2002) reports that the majority of people with a diagnosis of schizophrenia or other serious mental illnesses experience "either complete or significant remission of symptoms, and work, have relationships, and otherwise engage in a challenging and fulfilling life" (p. 89). In a 40-year follow-up study, Tsuang, Woolson, and Fleming (1979) found that 46% of those diagnosed with schizophrenia had no symptoms or had only nonincapacitating symptoms. The Vermont Longitudinal Study (Harding, Brooks, Ashikaga, Strauss, & Breier, 1986a, 1986b), a 20- to 25-year follow-up study of former state hospital patients, found that 72% of the people diagnosed with schizophrenia had only slight or no psychiatric symptoms.

Despite these very optimistic findings, Carpenter (2002) writes "the premise of chronicity continues to be widely accepted in the mental health system, and dismal prognoses continue to be communicated to people with psychiatric disabilities (Kruger, 2000). These prognoses leave little room for a sense of hope on the part of those labeled with mental illness and, as such, may become a self-fulfilling prophecy (Jimenez, 1988)" (p. 89).

Why then would we ever use the terms *psychosis, mental illness,* or *schizophrenia* to describe anyone who has overcome the illness? Aren't there better ways of describing a problem? For example:

Jane is a 36-year-old computer programmer who seeks help for difficulty in making important life decisions because her thinking is sometimes confused. The problem of confused thinking was first noted by the client when she was attending college at age 18 and led to her being hospitalized for 6 weeks. With some therapy and medication, the problem went away but has resurfaced in the past 6 months. Jane believes the problem has returned because of the stress of her work and the recent unexpected death of her mother, with whom she'd had a strained relationship for much of her life.

Not using the term "psychotic" paints a very different picture of Jane. She works, she thinks she knows why she's having the problem now and, more importantly, she hasn't had the problem in more than 15 years.

Rule 20 about hyperbole (exaggeration) is one we should all understand when we write reports about client improvement. Take, for example, this statement: "Andrew lacks the social skills necessary for everyday life and should remain under supervision in a halfway house for the long-term future. He has bouts of anger that frighten the residents." That sounds awfully negative, doesn't it? How about this instead:

Andrew has made some very good gains in his ability to cope with life on his own. He knows how to use the bus system, can give accurate amounts of money for services, is learning to cook by himself, and can generally interact with others without losing his temper. Andrew believes that there are still many skills he needs to learn, including better relationships with others and anger management. For the time being, he would prefer to stay in the halfway house and be a part of the treatment program. He has agreed to help keep the halfway house clean, to attend all meetings, and to seek help from staff when his anger becomes troublesome. We have agreed to review his status in six months, and have encouraged him to think about independent living. He increasingly believes that he will be able to live independently with our continued help and seems motivated, but fearful. It would be the first time in 40 years that he has ever lived away from an institution and by himself. Needless to say, the idea is worrisome to him.

WHEN ENGLISH IS A SECOND LANGUAGE

No one ever said that English is an easy language. My parents were both from Europe and they spoke, if not perfect English, very acceptable English. Writing was another matter. My father never understood punctuation. I'm convinced that no one taught him the elements of punctuation, so he used his own version. It was readable, but only if you understood his system. My suggestion to the reader whose second language is English is to write simple sentences and to edit and get feedback from others. Writing centers in universities and colleges can be a big help, and practice will help you improve. Don't turn in first or second drafts, but keep trying to find the rhythms of your writing. If you listen to yourself speaking on a tape recorder, you will hear where sentences end and you'll know when it's time to pause and put in a period. Remember that sentences are about a single idea. A paragraph is about that idea in an expanded way. Choose words carefully. Use words you know, try to understand professional words that may be unfamiliar, and use them in the proper context.

I go to Mexico frequently to practice Spanish. I know many words, but I just don't know how to put them together into a coherent sentence. Writing Spanish is very difficult for me, and I've been trying to write in Spanish for years. My heart is with you in learning to write English. I hope this book is written in a clear and concise way so that you benefit.

A STARTING POINT: EVALUATING YOUR WRITING

Many universities require that all students pass an expository writing course, either to graduate with their bachelor's degree or to enter a graduate program. A former colleague, Cecilia Julagay (personal correspondence, April 22, 1998), sent me the following questions she asks her students to consider in evaluating their own papers and, when asked to evaluate the work of others, the papers of their classmates.

1. Can you identify a main point (thesis) or purpose in this paper? Has this point been thoroughly examined?
2. Does the subject matter and the style of writing reflect depth, fullness, and complexity of thought? Indicate any areas that need improving.
3. Does this paper demonstrate a clear, focused, unified, and coherent organization? Indicate any areas that need improving.
4. Are there enough details in the paper to identify the person, place, group or event being profiled? Make note of any sections where vague or general statements fail to hold your interest. Indicate at least two examples of vivid detail. How appropriate are the details included in this paper?
5. Evaluate the mechanical aspects of this paper. Look for grammar, punctuation, paragraph formation, variation, and the use of transitions. Indicate any obvious areas needing improvement, but do not spend an excessive amount of time on this aspect.
6. Is the information presented in an entertaining way that is easy to follow? If not, what suggestions would you offer to make it more interesting or easier to follow?
7. Reread the beginning and decide whether or not it is effective. Did it capture your attention? Is there any quotation, fact or anecdote elsewhere in the paper that might make a better opening? Did the opening adequately represent the rest of the paper?

In using the above questions, Julagay also applies a scoring guide developed at her university to grade papers (White, 1996). The guide should help you evaluate your own writing. In getting feedback from others, it might help to share this scoring guide with them so that you have consistency in feedback. She writes:

What follows is a copy of the scoring guide that is used as the criteria for instructors to follow when grading papers. I give it out to students and we talk about why these items are important. In particular I point out the importance of "fully answering the question" and "complexity of thought." The "answer question" issue is important because it is often used as dividing point between a score of 3 (fail) and 4 (pass) for the common exam. The "complexity of thought" is important because it often can mean the difference between a just pass (4) and a better (5) or best (6) paper. These two points are also issues that students do not "see" in their own or others' writing.

I have also kept all sample essays that were used before grading the common exam. I put students together in groups of 4–5 and have them read prior papers, the question, and the sample essays. They then discuss why some essays were 6, 5, or lower. I rotate among the groups and sit in on the various discussions. This exercise helps students to see other writing styles and to implement the criteria. (Julagay, personal correspondence, April 22, 1998)

A Scoring Guide to Evaluate Your Writing

Score of 6: Superior

- Addresses the question fully and explores the issues thoughtfully
- Shows substantial depth, fullness, and complexity of thought
- Demonstrates clear, focused, unified, and coherent organization
- Is fully developed and detailed with ideas supported by apt reasons and well-chosen examples
- Evidences superior control of diction, syntactic variety, and transitions; may have a few minor flaws

Score of 5: Strong

- Clearly addresses the question and explores the issues
- Shows some depth and complexity of thought
- Is effectively organized
- Is well developed, with supporting detail
- Demonstrates control of diction, syntactic variety, and transition; may have a few flaws

Score of 4: Competent

- Adequately addresses the question and explores the issues
- Shows clarity of thought but may treat the topic simplistically or repetitively
- Is adequately organized
- Is adequately developed, with some detail
- Demonstrates adequate facility with syntax, mechanics, and usage but may contain some errors

Score of 3: Weak

- May distort or neglect parts of the question
- Lacks focus or demonstrates confused, stereotyped, or simplistic thinking
- May not provide adequate or appropriate details to support generalizations, or may provide details without generalizations
- May show patterns of errors in language, syntax, or mechanics

Score of 2: Inadequate

- Indicates confusion about the topic or neglects important aspects of the task

- Lacks focus and coherence, or often fails to communicate its ideas
- Has very weak organization and/or little development
- Is marred by numerous errors in mechanics, usage, and syntax

Score of 1: Incompetent

- Suggests an inability to comprehend the question or to respond meaningfully to the topic
- Is unfocused, illogical, incoherent, or disorganized
- Is deliberately off topic
- Papers so incompletely developed as to suggest or demonstrate incompetence
- Papers wholly incompetent mechanically

SUMMARY

This chapter discusses the ease with which competent writing can be mastered. The chapter includes a general discussion of the writing process and explains some rules of writing and how those rules may apply to the documents written by human service professionals. In future chapters, issues including punctuation, grammar, APA style, and other important issues will be explored.

FIND THE MISTAKES

1. I tried to help the client over the hump of his emotional problems but he steadfastly stuck to his old behavior which always got him into an astonishing amount of crap.
2. It is a tough row to hoe for the client but as we continue the treatment its becoming easier and the client isn't fighting the process so much any more.
3. Ezra Pound who wrote the *Cantos,* the best poetry anyone has ever written was also certifiable and spent a lot of time in a loony bin for doing Nazi radio programs where he lambasted America when he basically should have been sent to the joint.
4. If you think music tell us a lot about the human condition then Madonna's superb new song going Mental is really where it's totally at.
5. I happen to believe cognitive therapy is better than anything around although I'm also fond of behavioral therapy and while I can't think of why I wouldn't be a cognitive therapist there are certainly times I'd want to be behavioral.

REFERENCES

Alter, C., & Atkins, C. (2001). Improving writing skills of social work students. *Journal of Social Work Education*, 3(7), 493–505.

American Psychological Association. (2001). *Publication manual of the American Psychological Association*, 5th ed. Washington, DC: American Psychological Association.

Carpenter, J. (2002). Mental health recovery paradigm: Implications for social work. *Health & Social Work*, 27(2), 86–94.

Harding, C. M., Brooks, G. W., Ashikaga, T., Strauss, J. S., & Breier, A. (1986a). The Vermont longitudinal study of persons with severe mental illness: I. Methodology, study sample, and overall status 32 years later. *American Journal of Psychiatry*, 144, 718–725.

Harding, C. M., Brooks, G. W., Ashikaga, T., Strauss, J. S., & Breier, A. (1986b). The Vermont longitudinal study of persons with severe mental illness: II. Long-term outcome of subjects who retrospectively met DSM-II criteria for schizophrenia. *American Journal of Psychiatry*, 144, 727–735.

Hemingway, E. (1987). *The complete short stories of Ernest Hemingway: The finca vigia edition*. New York: Simon and Schuster.

Jimenez, M. A. (1988). Chronicity in mental disorders: Evolution of a concept. *Social Casework*, 69, 627–633.

Kruger, A. (2000). Schizophrenia: Recovery and hope. *Psychiatric Rehabilitation Journal*, 24, 29–37.

Laux, D. (1990). After twelve days of rain. *Awake*. Brockport, NY: BOA Editions LLT.

Markowitz, F. E. (1998). The effects of stigma on the psychological well-being and life satisfaction of persons with mental illness. *Journal of Health and Social Behavior*, 39(4), 335–347.

Tsuang, M. T., Woolson, R. F., & Fleming, M. S. (1979). Long term outcome of major psychoses. *Archives of General Psychiatry*, 36, 1295–1301.

White, E. (1996). *Guide to scoring papers in the university expository writing course*. San Bernardino: California State University.

2

Getting Started

WRITING FOR A PURPOSE: TYPES OF WRITING

Writing papers in the human services is much like writing papers in any other discipline. One major difference is that human service papers are often application-oriented. That is, their purpose is to help you understand how to work with clients by recognizing certain troubling behaviors and by using research evidence to show how those behaviors can be modified. Nevertheless, there are a number of different types of papers you may be required to write. Many of the chapters in this book go into much more detail about the type of writing you will do for various audiences. The following discussion provides a brief description of the five types of papers (DeLamarter, 2006) you will probably be asked to write.

1. **Reports:** In a report, a student is expected to accurately indicate the contents and arguments contained in a book or article(s) read. The goal is to summarize what the author has said.
2. **Reviews:** In a review, you will be asked to evaluate a work written by someone else. You will generally be asked to take a position that is either in agreement or disagreement with the position taken by the author. In the opening paragraph, you will provide a brief overview of the book or article ending with your evaluation. The body of the paper justifies your point of view.
3. **Critical Analyses:** A critical analysis might also be called a literature review, a policy paper, or even a term paper. You will be asked to include a number of works by different authors on a specific topic or issue. In many ways, a critical analysis combines and extends the type

of writing done in reports and reviews. You must accurately present the positions of others and evaluate those positions. You must also interpret the research and theory of other authors rather than simply report them. Interpretation means that you need to help the reader understand how a research finding, theory, or method is relevant to your argument. For example, if you were to try to show that children who are abandoned by their parents suffer from attachment problems, which make intimacy difficult, then you would need to find relevant material to support that belief. However, in making the argument, you must also include counterarguments and the conclusions of others who disagree, and yet hold true to your original thesis that children abandoned early in life have intimacy problems.

To help you understand how to develop a critical analysis by using the research data in the literature, I'm including a small section of a chapter I wrote for an introduction to a social workbook (Glicken, 2007, pp. 288–289) explaining posttraumatic stress disorder (PTSD) and the treatment approaches used by human service professionals with clients who experience traumas. I've only used a portion of that material, but you will hopefully see how a question is posed asking whether large numbers of people will develop PTSD if we experience another terrorist attack and reporting that, based on actual research, it's unlikely to occur. This may also be called "critical thinking" because you are asked to make a logical argument that includes a series of statements you can defend.

You might run across the concept of critical thinking in your work. Astleitner (2002) defines critical thinking as "a higher-order thinking skill which mainly consists of evaluating arguments. It is a purposeful, self-regulatory judgment which results in interpretation, analysis, evaluation, and inference, as well as explanations of the evidential, conceptual, methodological, or contextual considerations upon which the judgment is based" (p. 53). In another definition of critical thinking, or what Gambrill (1999) calls, "Ways of Knowing," Gambrill writes that "different ways of knowing differ in the extent to which they highlight uncertainty and are designed to weed out biases and distortions that may influence assumptions" (p. 341). Let's see if the following discussion critically approaches the issue of whether another terrorist attack in the United States, such as 9-11, will have a large-scale impact resulting in high numbers of people experiencing PTSD.

The Question: If America experiences another large-scale terrorist attack such as 9-11, will large numbers of traumatized people relive the traumatic experience and develop PTSD?

Data to Help Answer the Question: To answer this question, the author considered the developing research literature on PTSD and natural and man-made disasters. To report just one of several studies, Gist and Devilly (2002) wonder if PTSD is being predicted on such a wide scale for every tragedy that occurs that we have watered down its usefulness as a category of emotional distress. The authors suggest that many early signs of PTSD are normal responses to stress that are often overcome with time and distance from the event. Victims often use natural healing processes to cope with traumatic events. Interference by professionals could make the problem more severe and prolonged. In determining whether PTSD will actually develop, people must be given time to cope with the trauma on their own before we diagnose and treat PTSD.

Additional Data to Help Answer the Question: To emphasize this point, Gist and Devilly (2002) report that the immediate predictions of PTSD in victims of the World Trade Center bombings turned out to be almost 70% higher than actually occurred four months after the event. Susser, Herman, and Aaron (2002) interviewed 2,000 New Yorkers by telephone between January 15, 2002 and February 21, 2002. The interviews found a significant decrease in the stress-related symptoms subjects experienced during and after the World Trade Center bombings only several months earlier. This finding prompted the authors to write, "Many affected New Yorkers are clearly recovering naturally, a tribute to the resilience of the human psyche" (p. 76). Although symptoms of PTSD may develop later than four months after a trauma, people often heal on their own and a diagnosis of PTSD made too early may be inaccurate.

The Answer: In explaining the potential for developing PTSD, the *Diagnostic and Statistical Manual of Mental Disorders*, 4th ed. (DSM-IV) (American Psychiatric Association, 1994), notes that "the severity, duration and proximity of an individual's exposure to the traumatic event are the most important factors affecting the likelihood of this disorder" (p. 426). Additional factors that may contribute to PTSD, according to the DSM-IV, include the absence of social support networks, traumatic family histories or childhood experiences, and preexisting emotional problems. There may be other factors determining whether PTSD develops following a trauma. A review of studies predicting the impact of traumatic experiences found in the *Harvard Mental Health Letter* (2002) suggests that "the people most likely to have symptoms of PTSD were those who suffered job loss, broken personal relationships, the death or illness of a family member or close friend, or

financial loss as a result of the disaster itself" (p. 8). Several additional studies reported in the *Harvard Mental Health Letter* indicate
that a person's current emotional state may influence the way he
or she copes with the trauma. Environmental concerns (living in
high crime areas, for example) and health risks (disabilities which
make people vulnerable, as another example) raise the likelihood
of repeated traumatization that may increase the probability of
developing PTSD. Stein (2002) suggests that one significant event
influencing the development of PTSD is the exposure to violence
including serious fights, domestic violence, child abuse, mug-
gings, sexual molestation and rape, and other forms of traumatic
violence. Stein believes that vulnerability to repetitive acts of violence greatly increases the probability of developing PTSD. The
potential to develop PTSD in response to another terrorist attack
seems moderate and then is usually dependent on the presence of
preexisting factors unrelated to the attack itself.

  The answer to the question seems to be no, that most people have
self-righting capabilities that inhibit the development of PTSD, although some people are more easily affected by traumas. You could
make the opposite argument, for example, that large numbers of people are affected by terrorist attacks, but you would need to convince
the reader with evidence and logical arguments. One way to do this
would be to show the impact of other nonterrorist traumatic events
such as natural disasters and war. There is ample evidence that soldiers
returning from the war in Iraq experience PTSD at rates as high as 20%
(Elias, 2004). You might also use the evidence gathered from Hurricane Katrina that many people suffered from PTSD as a result of that
traumatic event. But does the use of data related to two very different
events explain whether a terrorist attack will result in large numbers
of people experiencing PTSD? Not really. The data are interesting, but
they relate to very different experiences.

4. **Research Proposals:** Some courses require research proposals. In
   chapter 11, I suggest an outline for writing research proposals. Research proposals are just that: proposals that indicate what you plan
   to do. Some instructors believe that writing the proposal will help
   you go to the next step in actually doing the research study, since a
   competently done proposal provides the theory, supportive data, and
   the methodology needed to complete a research study.
5. **Lab Reports:** A lab report contains a research proposal with the results
   of your study and a discussion of the implications of the data that support or reject your initial predictions about the findings of your study.
   This prediction is also called a hypothesis. In the above example of

PTSD, the hypothesis would be that large numbers of people experiencing a terrorist attack will develop PTSD. As we discovered from the research, that hypothesis is very likely incorrect.

CHOOSING A TOPIC: GUIDELINES

While there are a number of different ways to choose a subject for reports, the following might help you move from the larger issues, which may be difficult to write about given the limited time you may have to complete an assignment, to something more manageable:

1. **Special Meaning:** The topic should have special meaning to you, but it should not cause you to be so emotionally involved that it could affect your objectivity. If you are going through a divorce, for example, it may not be a good idea to write about divorce. If you've gone through a divorce and have successfully resolved the issues, then it may make sense to do your report on divorce if it's an issue you want to pursue and feel strongly about. Remember that all reports should be objective. If you can't approach a problem without becoming overly emotional, I suggest that you move on to something less emotionally troubling. Writing, unless it's propaganda or fiction, starts with the premise that your report writing is factual, objective, and logical.

   The problem of emotionality versus objectivity is a difficult one. Feminist researchers correctly suggest that one has to feel strongly about the way women have fared in our society in order to effectively study the subject. This deep concern for women provides a way of viewing your research and the motivating reason for doing it. It is difficult to be dispassionate about issues in the human services since they may include racism, sexism, violent treatment of women and children, and other problems that beg for solutions. Two role models of compassionate objectivity are psychotherapists and social service providers who work with people suffering from emotional pain. These helping professionals are compassionate and caring while maintaining objectivity and sufficient control over their emotions to help others. You may want to talk to practitioners you respect about how they can be compassionate and objective at the same time.

2. **Availability of Information:** The problem you choose to write about should have a considerable amount of available literature on which to base your report. If you have very limited literature to draw from, even after an extensive literature review, you may want to consider another topic. There are usually two ways to determine the availability of sufficient research. You can do your own literature review (time

consuming and often frustrating), or you can look for outstanding articles or books on the subject, and find out what those authors have to say. If the experts in the field say that the literature is limited, it's a good sign that you'll have a very small pool of research studies to draw from for your report.

As a personal example of limited research, I wrote a book on the strengths perspective (Glicken, 2004), a treatment approach that focuses on what works for people rather than on their pathology. I think the book does a good job of explaining the approach and giving underlying evidence that people often change dysfunctional behaviors because they have self-righting abilities. However, because of an absence of research evidence to support this belief, I could never show that the strengths perspective is a superior approach to treating clients over other approaches. Yes, I had many opinions from others that it is better to approach people by focusing on their strengths, but I found limited research to support that notion. Should I have not written the book? No, I'm glad I did, but having research data to support the effectiveness of the approach would have made it a much better book.

3. **Time Constraints:** You should be able to complete your report in the amount of time you have available. It may be helpful to consider Glicken's third law of using back roads: on a map, it looks like a quick ride, but once you've committed yourself, it takes forever to get there because the map doesn't show the windy roads and hairpin turns you encounter. Don't be shy about asking reference librarians for assistance, and use the Internet services and virtual libraries available at most universities to speed up your literature review.

4. **Relevant Problem:** The problem should be relevant to the human services and should include current research. You may also want to consider the political ramifications of writing about certain problems. A Caucasian student or professional writing about African American issues is not always felt to have sufficient objectivity to do an unbiased piece of work. Findings may therefore be considered questionable. Even when the researcher is of the same race, ethnicity, or gender, findings that deviate from those normally held by most people may cause strong negative reactions within the professional community, and from other researchers. In a recent example, several researchers, Rind and Tromovitch (1997), reviewed a number of studies of the long-term impact of child sexual abuse. It is almost universally believed that child molestation has a long-term negative impact on children and adults. However, the authors found this not to be the case. Their finding is contrary to the experiences of most therapists who work with the results of child abuse. The outcry from the therapeutic community was so fierce that the journal editors were forced to issue a retraction citing methodologi-

cal weaknesses in the article. Science is not without its political side and taking on politically sensitive issues may result in ill will.

I'm telling you this as a cautionary tale, but actually I think that political correctness has no place in the human services and that no topic, if explored ethically and with good intentions, should be prohibited. Social and political sensitivity is a requisite attribute for all of us in a free society. Political correctness, however, is a form of censorship. It has no place in the academic world where curiosity and the quest for knowing should form our intellectual agenda.

5. **Your Level of Expertise in Research:** The problem you intend to study should suggest research designs and sampling procedures that are realistic given your current level of expertise. If this is your first attempt at writing a research-oriented report, don't be too hard on yourself. Choose methodologies that you understand and that aren't so difficult that you'll end up with a large amount of data that, in the final analysis, you don't understand. Clichés are sometimes wise and "keep it simple" is one of the wiser clichés I know.

6. **The Audience:** Before you begin to write, you need to understand your audience. Academic papers are read by your instructor and possibly by other students. More ambitious writing has a much larger and diverse readership. Articles I wrote for the Dow Jones publication *National Business Employment Weekly* had a readership of over 3 million people. My audience was large, sophisticated, and intelligent, and they often disagreed with me. It was a humbling experience but it prepared me to write books. It also taught me to write in a very clear and concise way. In the articles I wrote, I had 1,200 words to say what would normally take me 10,000 words in a report. Think about the audience you're writing for and adjust your writing accordingly.

IT'S TIME TO GET STARTED

The first activity in writing is to get your ideas down on paper. We might call this a rough draft since it's your first attempt to write something. Don't worry if the ideas are incomplete in your rough draft. Once you have your ideas down, you can concentrate on making them clearer and finding supportive information to validate your ideas. Raibert (1985) says that "incomplete sentences, streams of consciousness, lists of ideas, and outlines are all good ways of getting started. These methods will help you to figure out what you want to say. You don't have to worry about the writing being bad because you will revise it later" (p. 1). When I wrote the first draft of this book I focused on getting my ideas down so that I could then organize the material and clarify the writing. It's important for me to write what I think should be said. Even though I have an outline for the book, I don't know for certain where the material will turn up in the book and I may, in time, discard it or replace it with something else. That's the wonder of computers and the process of cutting and pasting. As you edit your writing, you have the power to place material wherever you want it to go. Never discard ideas since they may be useful elsewhere in your writing project or in another assignment. I suggest the following process as you revise your work:

1. Evaluate every sentence and paragraph and revise it until it is concise, clear, and logical. Use one main idea for every paragraph. For example, if I'm writing about aging and the problem of therapists assuming that older adults are not good candidates for therapy, I would build an argument for that position in the following way:
   a) **The Problem:** Kennedy and Tannenbaum (2000) suggest the existence of compelling evidence that older adults experience a variety of emotional problems including depression, anxiety, and extended bereavement.
   b) **Continuation of the Problem:** However, large numbers of anxious and depressed older adults often go undiagnosed and untreated because underlying symptoms of anxiety and depression are thought to be physical in nature and professionals frequently believe that older adults are neither motivated for therapy nor find it an appropriate treatment. This often leaves many older adults trying to cope with serious emotional problems without adequate help.
   c) **The Solution:** The authors believe that many elderly clients can benefit from psychotherapeutic interventions and suggest that adjustments for clinical practice with elderly clients should include consideration of "sensory and cognitive" problems, the need for closer collaboration with the client's family and other care providers, and a belief by the clinician, shared with the elderly client and his or her family, that treatment will result in improved functioning and symptom reduction to offset stereotypes that elderly clients with emotional problems are untreatable, or unlikely to improve.
2. Get to the point immediately, in the title of your work, in the abstract, in the opening sentence, and in the first paragraph. This is called "spilling the beans" and you should spill them immediately. On spilling the beans, Raibert (1985, p. 3) says:

> When you are spilling the beans at the beginning of your paper, don't just refer to your results, *give* your results. Use simple summaries of your most important points. For instance:

Wrong way: In this paper I will give you my formula for good writing.

Right way: My formula for good writing is simple—once you decide that you want to produce good writing and that you can produce good writing, then all that remains is to write bad stuff, and to revise the bad stuff until it is good.

3. Don't get too attached to what you've written. Most of us fall into this trap, but it makes editing almost impossible. I've discarded some of my most lovely prose because it didn't fit and, after letting it sit for a while, I also decided it wasn't very good.
4. Don't overwrite. Use words that convey clear meaning and are normal everyday words that almost anyone can understand. This includes not using psychobabble and slang. Words like "enmeshed" should be used sparingly and only when they absolutely describe a situation. Words like cool, bad dude, bad actor, crazy, babe, sexy, and so on have no place in professional writing unless you are quoting a client. Those words often suggest that you have hostile or superior notions of others.
5. When you're stuck and you can't seem to write what you'd like to say, it usually means that your thinking about a subject hasn't gelled. I use several tricks to overcome being stuck. One is to go to another section of a paper and work on that section. If you were to watch me put a book together, you'd be struck by how illogical the process seems. If I'm working on chapter 1 and having trouble with it, rather than trying to fix it, I move on to something else. In time, the book comes together. I've learned to never fight my writing. When it's not going well, I do other things, such as searching for references or reading more material to clarify my thinking.
6. Have others give you feedback about your writing. It's painful, even for me, but it's essential. When I turn this book in, a professional editor will edit the material. I can tell you that almost every paragraph will either have a mistake I didn't catch, or it will include some unclear writing. I fight the edits like mad, but ultimately I know the edits have made my book better. Give up your ego and get feedback and help from others. Bad writing can inhibit the quality of your work and will never be unnoticed.

A friend who works for a large law firm tells me that most lawyers can't write. She spends much of her time editing their work. When she's unavailable and an attorney is left without her editing help, the work is often so bad that the court makes note of it and returns the work with an expectation that it be rewritten. How painful for the lawyer, and how troubling for the client who may be charged up to $800 an hour.

7. Write so that an eighth grader can read and understand your work. You can write complex ideas using simple, expressive language. I've developed surveys for numerous research projects. The directions on a questionnaire can destroy the data if they are unclear. Many of us try to impress others by overwriting or by using words that are much too complex. It tends to tax the reader. Consider this sentence from a former student: "I'm cognizant of the boisterous opposition to Freud's thesis of the Oedipal Complex and how it creates problems in men because of the notion of castration anxiety which, however bold and innovative, seemed superfluous to people in the 1890s." Well, I think this means: "Many people in Freud's time were strongly opposed to his theory of the Oedipal Complex." Maybe we could also say that, "The opposition to the theory came at a time when Victorian society in Europe had difficulty with frank discussions of sexuality."

8. Look at other writing. There are many people who write well and whose style might suit you. I read a short story in college by Ernest Hemingway (1987) that, in three pages, said more than most books do. The story, "Hills Like White Elephants," is about a man and woman meeting in a small-town train station in Spain where the woman has come to get an abortion. Nothing much happens and the word abortion is never used. Instead the man says, "It's an awfully simple operation. It's not really an operation at all. . . . It's the only thing that makes us unhappy" (p. 212). The woman wonders if everything will remain the same after the operation and the man assures her it will. He says, "We can have the whole world" (p. 213). To which the woman replies, "No we can't" (p. 213). You know that the abortion is going to destroy the relationship and the writing, while always restrained, leaves you feeling as if someone has put a knife in your heart. It's a chilling story because the dialogue is so civilized and proper. The man knows what's best for the woman and keeps telling her that nothing will change after the abortion when the reader knows that *everything* will change. Because the story was written in the 1920s, we also know that there is a high probability that an abortion might seriously harm the woman, and even kill her. The story is about 1,000 words long, but it packs a wallop so strong that I could never think about the issue of abortion from a man's point of view again. From then on, I've tried to keep my sentences short and to the point. Hemingway is my model of great writing. The famous American writer William Faulkner was heard to tell someone that Hemingway's writing never forced anyone to use the dictionary. It's true, but it's also true that his simple use of language touched many people in a way that Faulkner's more complex writing never did.

9. When you're stuck, try talking into a tape recorder to say orally what you can't say in writing. This is particularly important if writing is a chore because of concerns about punctuation and grammar. Listen to yourself. The natural pauses in your speech will almost always tell you the correct punctuation mark to use.
10. Although the American author Hunter S. Thompson wrote wild and funny books while high on drugs and alcohol, and stayed up for days without sleep to meet deadlines, most of us can't write when we're tired, drinking, drugged, or ill. Give yourself plenty of time to write papers. Papers written the night before an assignment is due are almost always full of spelling and punctuation errors and are, at best, first drafts.

SUGGESTIONS TO SIMPLIFY YOUR WRITING

Outline Your Report: When I write books, I must first write a book proposal justifying the need for the book I want a publisher to accept. In that proposal, I also outline the book in a table of contents. I'm going to show you what some of that proposal looked like when this book was accepted. You will find many differences between the proposal and the final product. Once you begin to write something, it has a life of its own and goes in directions you may not imagine when you organized the material in an outline. The proposal I'm including should help you know that rather than winging it one sunny southern California day, I actually had a plan in mind. Here's a shortened version of the proposal. The actual proposal ran 20 pages.

OUTLINING: A BOOK PROPOSAL

Book Title: *A Simple Guide to Writing for Human Service Professionals*

I. Project

[*Author's note:* This section helped me understand what I wanted to say. Ultimately, much of what I wrote here ended up in the book's preface. I knew I wanted to write an easy-to-read book for students and professionals in the human services, but until I wrote the introduction, I wasn't quite sure how I would organize the book or the material I wanted to include.]

Brief Description: Accurate and effective professional writing is extremely important because it can drastically affect people's lives. Social workers, psychologists, physicians, nurses, probation and parole officers, public health professionals, and counselors have a responsibility to write well since our reports and how clearly and precisely they've been written may affect legal outcomes in child abuse and domestic violence cases. Medical treatment may be affected by our reports. Parents who are otherwise competent and effective may lose custody of their children. Referrals for medical, social, educational, and emotional help may be so badly written that needed help is not provided at the expense of someone's health. Every day, professionals write reports related to competency, child abuse, medical treatment, court adjudications, and a long list of other important life events. It is important that professionals know how to write. The lives of our patients, clients, and their families often depend on it.

But you wouldn't know that from the documents we see in the files of our clients and patients. Many of those documents are so badly written that judges can't understand them. Parole review boards wonder what they mean. Social workers and doctors picking up on existing cases haven't a clue about what a prior professional did with a client and find the case reports singularly misleading and unhelpful. Many documents written by professionals contain a jargon that has become a substitute language used by bureaucrats, with hidden meanings and misleading conclusions that are more political and self-protective than professionally helpful. As a result, people get hurt.

To further reinforce how badly professionals write, Alter and Atkins (2001) found that 60% of the graduate social work students in their sample wrote at less than graduate school level. Only 20% of the sample sought help from writing centers or took tutorials or special writing classes, largely because the writing courses and tutorials were not practical and failed to help them with the nuanced writing professionals are required to do.

Professionals should be able to write well. That's why I'm writing this book: To help professionals write clear, concise reports, documents, scholarly papers, and records, so that people benefit from the creative ways we explain the behavioral, legal, and health problems of our clients and patients and suggest how certain forms of assistance will affect their lives.

II. Market Considerations

A. Primary Markets

[*Author's note:* This section helped me understand my audience. I've taught expository writing courses before and I was very aware that most of the students didn't read the books I'd assigned, even though they were admirable books. I analyzed those books, found them a bit too complex, and decided to write a really simple book—a book that didn't use the terms of grammar or the exotic examples contained in many of these other books that seemed to confuse my students.]

College: This book could be used as a companion book on writing for all undergraduate and graduate college programs in psychology, counseling, social work, public health, psychiatric nursing, marriage and family counseling, applied sociology, and criminal justice. It could be a required book for all students in the helping professions since poor student writing is considered a serious problem in many, if not all, of the disciplines mentioned.

Professional Reference: The book would have a large audience among helping professionals who are often asked to write a variety of reports, evaluations, and recommendations as well as professional papers to be given at workshops and conference. The book includes many of the possible ways professionals will be asked to use their writing with examples and explanations of why the examples contain all the elements of well-written reports.

B. Secondary Markets

The book could certainly be used for the expository writing courses many universities and colleges require before a student can graduate. This is particularly true of universities and colleges that have an expository writing course taught within an academic program such as psychology or social work where enrollments tend to be quite high. It could also be used in extended education courses where professionals with writing problems can be taught to improve their writing. I teach these courses in California and enrollments are always high.

III. The Table of Contents

[*Author's note:* This section helped me organize the content. Naturally, I looked at other writing books and found some material I needed to include. For the most part, the table of contents (TOC) was the most difficult part of the book, since it had to include material I wanted to include but also the material the publisher wanted. That's why this TOC is actually longer than the one I ended up using. In the end, I was asked to write a book of about 75,000 words. The original version of the proposal suggested 100,000–125,000 words. I had 22 topics in the original. For illustrative purposes, I've reduced the number to two topics.]

Title: *A Simple Guide to Writing for Human Service Professionals*
Preface
Acknowledgments
Dedication
Chapter 1: Why Writing Is So Important

1. Professionals need to know how to write well.
2. Examples of the type of writing professionals do and how it affects people's lives:
   a) Medical reports (physicians and nurses).
   b) Psychological profiles and evaluations.
   c) Psychosocial histories (social workers).
   d) Deficits in learning evaluations (educators) .
   e) Court reports (all professionals).
   f) Committee reports.
   g) Workers' compensation reports.
   h) Professional papers and research reports.
   i) Worker evaluations and period reviews.
3. Why other people can't substitute for professionals when written communication is required.
4. Choosing the right words to communicate your ideas, thoughts, and beliefs: Words have power.
5. Summary.
6. Useful websites.
7. References.

Chapter 2: The Writing Process

1. Organizing your thoughts.
2. Critical thinking.
3. Initial drafts: Organizing and limiting the topic.
4. Revising your work.
5. Editing: The mechanics of editing and some tips about editing when writing on a computer.
6. Using feedback from others. This is not a time for ego to get in the way.
7. Professional editing.
8. Knowing when a draft is a completed piece of work.
9. Ready to let go or keep it until it's perfect: Why perfectionism is the opposite side of the same coin as sloppy writing.
10. A few choice words about using other people's work: Plagiarism and the rules regarding quotations and paraphrasing.

11. Writing suggestions for professionals using English as a second language.
12. Summary:
13. Useful websites.
14. References.

IV. Length and Timetable

[*Author's Note:* This section helped me decide how quickly I could write the book and how long it would be. I wrote it quickly but, luckily for you, the length turned out to be almost 50,000 words shorter than I imagined it would. You can do a word count automatically within most word processing programs.]

The book can be completed in nine months from the point of signing the contract. I have always been able to get books done on time and, in many instances, well before the deadline. A book on men for Lawrence Erlbaum Associates and a book on evidence-based practice for Sage Publications were completed a year ahead of schedule. Length will be about 100,000–125,000 words plus the index and any references and websites.

1. **If You Get Stuck:** There may come a point in writing your report when you get stuck. It happens to all of us. If you use the suggestions I gave earlier in the chapter about getting unstuck (move to another section of the report, go back and do an additional literature search, edit what you've written, or move material around) and they don't work, call it a day and go play tennis. No kidding, exercise is a good way to get the creative juices going again. The point is, give yourself enough time to write the report. If you wait until the last minute, trust me, you will not be able to write well, and if you get stuck, I hope you have a sympathetic instructor.

2. **Have Others Read Your Writing:** In my writing classes, we break into small groups of five. At the end of the class, everyone passes out the assigned writing for the day. Students in the group must read and write a critique of the papers for the next class. The critique is graded. This helps students give proper feedback and helps the writer know how others view his or her work. No one learns to write without feedback. Writing is, after all, generally done for others. If you have a tough time getting feedback or feel that you're being attacked, get over it or write nasty words on your tongue with your teeth and grin, bare it, and learn.

3. **Edit and Rewrite:** Ernest Hemingway wrote 500 words a day but he endlessly rewrote those 500 words so they were true words that moved the reader. John Updike writes 1,000 words a day. If you're turning in

your first draft, it will very likely have many errors. I spend most of my time correcting writing errors when I grade papers. I always mark papers down that are badly written, not only because it's insulting to be handed a paper with spelling, punctuation, and grammatical errors, but because it is often difficult to know what the writer is trying to say. Unless you think the instructor's job is to read your mind, edit your work a few times, eliminate the rough spots, and watch your grades increase. Here's an example of the editing process:

First Draft (225 words): Tjaden and Thoennes (1998) report that approximately 1.5 million women are sexually or physically assaulted every year in the United States. Serial battering by men may also be a serious problem in which one man batters between multiple victims. One-third of all pregnant women report physical abuse by men. In a number of studies, a third to a half of all women seeking therapy as adults have been abused by men, many before the age of 18 (Bagley, 1990; Hale, Duckworth, Zimostrad, and Scott, 1988). Dewhurst, Moore, and Alfano (1992) note that sexual and physical assaults are identified as the two major crimes by men against women in our society. Victimization rates for both types of offenses have been estimated at between 10% and 30% of all women. In national surveys, Dutton (1994) reports that 72% of all men surveyed are not violent in their homes and that the remaining 28% use violence occasionally to frequently. Of those who do use violence, Dutton notes that 55% are stifled men who have poor impulse control and do not know how to control anger, while 20% of those surveyed have, "borderline personalities and are prone to intensive anger in intimate relationships. A quarter of the remaining abusers are so entrenched in their violent behavior that they are considered untreatable by current technologies to help reduce abusive behavior" (p. B1).

Second Draft (199 Words): Tjaden and Thoennes (1998) report that approximately a million and a half women are sexually or physically assaulted every year in the United States. Serial battering is also a serious problem and describes a single man battering multiple victims. One-third of all pregnant women report physical abuse by men. A third to a half of all women seeking therapy as adults have been abused by men; many before the age of 18 (Bagley, 1990; Hale, Duckworth, Zimostrad, and Scott, 1988). Victimization rates for sexual and physical assaults have been estimated at between 10% and 30% of all women (Dewhurst, et al., 1992). In national surveys, Dutton (1994) reports that most men surveyed (72%) are not violent in their homes and that the remaining 28% use violence occasionally to frequently. Dutton notes that 55% who use violence in the home are stifled men who have poor impulse control and do not know how to control anger. Twenty percent of those surveyed have, "Borderline personalities and are prone to intensive anger in intimate relationships. A quarter of the remaining abusers are so entrenched in their violent behavior that they are considered untreatable by current technologies to help reduce abusive behavior" (Dutton, 1994, p. B1)

Third Draft (177 Words): A million and a half women are sexually or physically assaulted every year by men (Tjaden and Thoennes, 1998). Male violence is the reason for a third to a half of all women seeking therapy, many before the age of 18 (Bagley, 1990; Hale, Duckworth, Zimostrad, and Scott, 1988). An average of four women a day are killed by men who batter (Tjaden and Thoennes, 1998) making domestic violence the single largest cause of violence to women in America. Dewhurst (1992) estimates that between 10% and 30% of all women have been physically or sexually abused. Although 72% of all men are nonviolent in their homes, Dutton (1994) found that the remaining 28% use violence occasionally to frequently. Fifty-five percent of the violent men are stifled men with poor impulse control and difficulty controlling anger. However, a dangerous 20% of those surveyed have, "Borderline personalities and are prone to intensive anger in intimate relationships. A quarter of the remaining abusers are so entrenched in their violent behavior that they are considered untreatable by current technologies to help reduce abusive behavior" (Dutton, 1994, p. B1).

Fourth Draft (142 Words): A million and a half women are sexually or physically assaulted every year by men (Tjaden and Thoennes, 1998). Violence accounts for the reason one-third to one-half of all women seek therapy, many before the age of 18 (Bagley, 1990; Hale, Duckworth, Zimostrad, and Scott, 1988). Dewhurst (1992) estimates that between 10% and 30% of all women have been physically or sexually abused.

[*New paragraph because the subject changes from the number of abused women to male perpetrators.*] Although 72% of all men are nonviolent in their homes, Dutton (1994) found that the remaining 28% use violence occasionally to frequently. Fifty-five percent are stifled men with poor impulse control and have difficulty controlling anger. However, 20% of those surveyed have "borderline personalities and are prone to intensive anger in intimate relationships. A quarter of the remaining abusers are so entrenched in their violent behavior that they are considered untreatable by current technologies to help reduce abusive behavior" (Dutton, 1994, p. B1).

4. **Wanting to Write Well:** As Raibert (1985) says, writing well is all about writing the first draft (the bad stuff) and editing until the bad stuff is good. In other words, you need to be motivated to write well, go through the steps of editing that will produce good writing, and practice writing. Writing well is a matter of motivation and hard work, and not some innate ability God gave us. All writers write badly in the beginning and edit their material until it's acceptable.

SUMMARY

This chapter includes the types of writing you will be asked to do, choosing topics, and examples of editing and abstract writing. It concludes with a truism that all writers know: Writing well takes time, practice, feedback from others, and a great deal of motivation. There is no other way to write well than to write often and to edit, edit, and then edit some more.

FIND THE MISTAKES

1. A research study by Manly and Strong (2006) indicates that while men are physically stronger than women, women live longer and are generally less likely to die from 15 of the 16 major causes of death than men. This proves that women are more likely than men to survive a terrorist attack and not develop PTSD.
2. I told my professor that I'd written my paper during the night and that it wasn't a rush job and I'd been thinking about it for weeks before I wrote it. Once I started writing it all came to me and I didn't need to edit I was so sure that I'd done it right but he was very picky and gave me an "F." He said it was unreadable. I didn't have any trouble reading it.
3. If the author is right that you change much of what you intended to do when you outline a report than why outline in the first place?
4. When a teacher says a paper has to be like 5,000 words long than why would I want to edit it to make it shorter? It just makes sense to write 5,000 words and forget trying to edit it down to say 3,000 words. That means you just have to write another 2,000 words which is pretty dumb if you ask me.
5. This whole thing about paragraphs containing a single idea strikes me as pretty confusing given that the author sometimes writes paragraphs with more than one major idea. I thought a paragraph should be about a half page long and the rule was not to write more than three sentences in a paragraph. No?

REFERENCES

Alter, C., & Atkins, C. (2001). Improving writing skills of social work students. *Journal of Social Work Education*, 3(7), 493–505.

American Psychiatric Association. (1994). *Diagnostic and Statistical Manual of Mental Disorders*, 4th ed. New York: American Psychiatric Association.

Astleitner, H. (2002). Teaching critical thinking online. *Journal of Instructional Psychology*, 29(2), 53–77.

Bagley, C. (1990). Development of a measure of unwanted sexual contact in childhood, for use in community mental health surveys. *Psychological Reports*, 66, 401–402.

DeLamarter, W. A. (2006). Writing papers in psychology. Retrieved July 6, 2006, from www/webpub/alleg.edu/dept/psych/psychInfo.htm

Dewhurst, A. M., Moore, R. J., & Alfano, D. P. (1992). Aggression against women by men: Sexual and spousal assault. *Journal of Offender Rehabilitation*, 18, 41–65.

Dutton, L. (1994). Domestic violence. *Los Angeles Times*, Aug. 11, p. B1.

Elias, M. (2004). Many Iraq veterans fighting an enemy within. *USA Today*, July 1, p. D10.

Gambrill, E. (1999). Evidence-based practice: An alternative to authority-based practice source. *Families in Society: The Journal of Contemporary Human Services*, 80(4), 341–350.

Gist, R., & Devilly, G. J. (2002). Post-trauma debriefing: The road too frequently traveled. *Lancet*, 360(9335), 741–743.

Glicken, M. D. (2007). *Social work in the 21st century: An introduction to social welfare, social issues and the profession*. Thousand Oaks, CA: Sage Publications.

Glicken, M. D. (2004). *Using the strengths perspective in social work practice*. Boston: Allyn and Bacon/Longman.

Glicken, M. D. (in press). *Competency based supervision for the human services*. Thousand Oaks, CA: Sage Publications.

Hale, G., Duckworth, L., Zimostrad, N., & Scott, D. (1988). Abusive partners: MMPI profiles of male batterers. *Journal of Mental Health Counseling*, 10, 214–224.

Harvard Mental Health Letter. (2002). What causes post-traumatic stress disorder: Two views. *Harvard Mental Health Letter*, 19(4), 8.

Hemingway, E. (1987). *The complete short stories of Ernest Hemingway: The Finca Vigia edition*. New York: Simon and Schuster.

Kennedy, G. J., & Tannenbaum, S. (2000). Psychotherapy with older adults. *American Journal of Psychotherapy*, 54(3), 386–407.

Manly and Strong. (2006). Fictitious source.

Raibert, M. H. (1985). Good Writing. Retrieved May 17, 2006, from www.alice.org/Randy/raibert.htm

Rind, B., & Tromovitch, P. (1997). A meta-analytic review of findings from national samples on psychological correlates of child sexual abuse. *Journal of Sex Research*, 34(3), 237–255.

Stein, M. B. (2002). Taking aim at posttraumatic stress disorder: Understanding its nature and shooting down myths. *Canadian Journal of Psychiatry*, 47(10), 921–923.

Susser, E. S., Herman, D. B., & Aaron, B. (2002). Combating the terror of terrorism. *Scientific American*, 287(2), 70–78.

Tjaden, P., & Thoennes, N. (1998, November). Prevalence, incidence, and consequences of violence against women: Findings from the National Violence Against Women Survey. Atlanta: Centers for Disease Control and Prevention and National Institute of Justice.

3

Punctuation and Grammar

SIMPLE WRITING MAKES COMPLEX
PUNCTUATION UNNECESSARY

Writing should be simple. Punctuation is nothing more than a few rules to help readers understand what you've written as if you were speaking. The longer the sentence, the more complicated the punctuation becomes. For that reason, write short sentences or you'll be writing like this:

> Michel, the protagonist of the Houellebecq's previous novel, "Platform"—the rather bleak and enigmatic English rendering of "Plateforme: Au Milieu du Monde," possibly an allusion to global politics, or a pun on "flat style," a characterization that most French critics find apt—helps promote, in conjunction with the ideally compliant and lewd travel agent Valérie, a momentarily booming chain of Asian vacation resorts for European sex tourists. (Updike, 2006a, p. 76)

John Updike is a major American novelist. His books are wonderful books about the difficulty of life for ordinary Americans. When Updike writes fiction, it flows. His criticism, as you can see from the above example, can be too complex for the reader to follow. I went to a lecture by John Updike as I was writing this chapter. His new novel *Terrorist* (2006b) had just been lambasted by a critic in a major U.S. newspaper and yet, gracious and generous, as he told the audience about his novel, he glowed. I wanted to read it badly. It's a beautiful book and as much as his reviews annoy me, his fiction is wonderful.

The same thing that Updike takes such pains to make complicated could have been written more simply in the following way:

> In the new novel by French author Michel Houellebecq, the main character of the novel, Michel, and his compliant travel agent friend, Valérie, promote a briefly booming chain of Asian vacation resorts for European sex tourists. Michel was also the main character in the author's previous novel, *Platform*. Much like his prior novel, the author's writing style is flat and unemotional.

COMMON PUNCTUATION MARKS AND RULES

In the following section of the chapter, I'm going to provide a few examples of punctuation marks you would normally use in writing. Once again, if you keep your writing simple you should not need more complex forms of punctuation. Additional information on punctuation is included in chapter 5 (on APA style). Here are some common punctuation marks and how to use them.

1. **A period (.)** ends a sentence. It tells us that a thought is over.

   I'm going to the store.

2. **A question mark (?)** is used when a question is asked.

   Did you go to the store?

3. **An exclamation mark (!)** is used when we want to emphasize something or suggest strong emotion. In normal professional writing it would be unusual for us to use an exclamation mark, since the writing we do is normally controlled and formal.

   The prices at the store were outrageous!

4. **A comma (,)** is used to separate ideas within a sentence.

   The old store, which had gone to ruin in the past 10 years, was now making a comeback as a shelter for homeless people.

5. **A comma (,)** is also used to separate items in a list.

   I went to the store with my client to help him buy shoes, socks, underwear, and a coat.

6. **A comma (,)** is generally used to separate conjunctions (words such as *and, but, yet, or, nor, for*), but not always. Statements like "Jim and I went shopping" do not require commas because there is no break (or pause) in the sentence. On the other hand, a sentence that reads "I went to the store to help my client buy shoes, but we only bought underwear" does require a comma. Try reading this sentence without a comma (or pause) and you'll see it begs for a comma. My best advice is to put a comma in when the sentence sounds unclear without one. Read the sentence out loud when in doubt.

7. **Quotation marks (" ")** are used when reproducing someone's words, whether those words have been spoken or written.

> "Getting up early to work is a good way to get books written" (Ambien, 2007).

8. **Quotations fewer than five lines** in your paper should be set off with quotation marks (" ") and should be incorporated within the normal flow of your text.

> While riding my bicycle to work, it dawned on me that Jackson (2007) was right when he said "The taller the person, the higher his or her IQ." It supported my own belief that, because I am seven feet tall, I must be very smart.

For material exceeding that length, omit the quotation marks and indent the quoted text one-half inch (or one tab space) from your left-hand margin. If an indented quotation is taken entirely from one paragraph, the first line should be even with all the other lines in that quotation; however, if an indented quotation comes from more than one paragraph, indent the first line of each additional paragraph an extra tab space.

> Male bashing is one of those serious problems in America we tend not to take very seriously. But just as women and ethnic and racial minority groups have been bashed in the past and often continue to feel the sting of pejorative jokes and name calling, bashing is a harmful and insensitive way of responding to any group because the essence of bashing is hostility and a feeling of superiority. (Glicken, 2005a, p. 52)

If quotation marks appear within the text of a quotation that already has the usual double-quote marks (" ") around it (a quote-within-a-quote), set off that inner quotation with single-quote marks (' ').

The gender debate has primarily been about women's problems and men's faults. As a result, male bashing flourishes, not only in the feminist movement, but in popular culture, from sitcoms to greeting cards. As a good example of the way men are portrayed, Goldfarb (2004) writes, "I agree with Alkon (2003) who wrote, 'Let's take a moment and read the average man's mind: Sex, sex, sex, red meat, sex, sex, sex, beer, sex, sex, sex, Cheetos, sex, sex, sex, baseball, football, sex, sex, sex.'" (Alkon, 2003, p. 17)

9. **Quotations can indicate a dialogue**. Start a new paragraph for each person's lines of dialogue to make it easier for the reader to follow.

> "I can't read this writing book by this Glicken guy," John said. "It must be that I'm bored with the subject."
>
> "Yes," Elaine replied, "what's the big deal about writing, anyway? I mean, duh."
>
> "I think you're both wrong," Jackson said, rising from his chair, shaking his fist vehemently, and speaking in very short sentences. "Glicken is a genius! His book is brilliant!"

10. **Paraphrasing** occurs when you don't directly quote someone, but in different words say what he or she would have said in a direct quote. This is tricky because there is a fine line between paraphrasing and plagiarism. You must do more than change a few words. Let's take what Jackson said in the prior example: "I think you're both wrong," Jackson said, rising from his chair, shaking his fist vehemently, and speaking in very short sentences. "Glicken is a genius! His book is brilliant!" By paraphrasing what Jackson said, it might read, Jackson thinks that Glicken's book on writing is a first-rate book that could only have been written by a very talented writer.

11. **A semicolon (;)** is used instead of *and, but, yet* or *for*, often using connecting words such as *however* or *therefore*. There must be two closely related ideas in a sentence whenever a semi-colon is used. The first idea is therefore connected to the second idea by a semicolon. Each part of the sentence must be complete and could stand alone as a sentence.

> The store was being renovated to assist hundreds of homeless men; however, there were protests from the community in opposition to a homeless shelter in the heart of the downtown area.

> The store is being renovated to house the homeless; they will certainly need many more shelters.

12. **A colon (:)** is used to "create an abrupt pause in your writing or to introduce a word or phrase that deserves special notice" (Harris, 2003, p. 170).

> I realized that I had to change my approach to treatment and that the following approaches would provide the best results: cognitive therapy and solution focused therapy.

13. **A dash (—)** gives a sentence dramatic appeal.

> I read Glicken's book on writing—every annoying word—and I still can't write.

14. **Parentheses allow you to interject a brief aside, often a clarifying remark**.

> Reading Glicken's book (what an odd name) made me realize that I know more about writing than he does.
>
> PTSD is a misused diagnostic category (when will the next DSM ever come out?) and should only be used when a person has actually experienced a trauma.

15. **The titles of plays, novels, magazines, newspapers, and journals are underlined or *italicized*,** as in, <u>A Simple Guide to Writing for Human Service Professionals</u> or *A Simple Guide to Writing for Human Service Professionals*. The titles of poems, short stories, and articles should be contained in quotation marks. The usual practice is to place periods and commas inside quotation marks. For example, the Hemingway story that taught me a great deal about gender inequity is "Hills Like White Elephants."

16. You can write an entire essay on literature without **using the first-person singular** *I*, but it's also OK if the first-person singular enters into your review. Generally, the more objective your paper sounds, the better. When I began writing books, rather than using the word *I*, I used the word *we*, as in, "We believe psychoanalysis is a valid approach to treatment." A copy editor reminded me how dotty that sounded. Since then I've used *I* instead of *we*. It's always a good idea to discuss the use of "*I, we, or neither word*" with your instructor. Some people still use neutral terms such as, "This writer, the clinician, the author, or the researcher."

> By interviewing children arrested for voyeurism (looking in windows of children and adults to see them naked), the researcher found that the

average age when these children began to molest younger children was 10 years of age. The children who were being molested were almost always younger siblings or friends of siblings.

SOME EASY GRAMMAR RULES

The Paragraph

A paragraph contains several sentences that make a point. Generally, it takes two or more sentences to form a paragraph because a paragraph starts with a central concept, develops that concept, and then summarizes it. In a well-written paragraph, each sentence focuses on the same subject, and the ideas presented in each sentence should relate to those contained in the sentences before and after. I like short paragraphs, but if you read magazines like the *New Yorker* you'll find paragraphs that go on for a page or more. Bad stuff, in my view, since it's hard for the reader to remember the original point made in the beginning paragraph. Here are two examples of paragraphs:

> ***Wrong:*** My name is Dr. Morley Glicken and I'm a writer. A writer's life is pretty darn good. Yesterday, I went to the store to buy roses for my girlfriend. She hated them. I took the roses back, but they wouldn't accept them. Used goods, they said. *[This paragraph meanders. First it's about being a writer, and then it's about roses. Let's rewrite it correctly.]*

> ***Right:*** My name is Dr. Morley Glicken. I'm a writer. I've always wanted to be a writer. It wasn't until later in life that my skills and motivation came together. Since that time, I've published eight books. With this book on writing and a book on supervision, I will have published 10 books in four years. I have also self-published a guide to men and women in relationships entitled, *Ending the Sex Wars* (Glicken, 2005b). I have plans to write mystery novels about a handsome, tennis playing, dashing, semi-retired social work educator having no resemblance to me." *[This paragraph is about one thing and one thing only: writing.]*

The Proper Tense

The basic rule is to keep tenses the same in a sentence and, if possible, in a paragraph. Since we often write about events or ideas that take place in the past, we usually write in the past tense. Seldom do we write about the future unless it's to predict something (always dangerous in our line of work). In the human service fields, in keeping with APA style, discussions of prior research, descriptions of procedure, or statements of results, should be written in the past tense. For example:

Literature review: Leo's study found (not finds)
Procedure: The research subjects were (not are)
Results: Standard deviation scores were (not are)

There are times when you can use the present tense if the subject you're writing about continues to be applicable in the present. For example:

Definition: Soprano (2006) defines "the Mob" as a society of wise guys.
Theory: Macho (2003) says that one of the problems with studying men is the ever present impact of Freud, who believes that men confuse their wives and lovers with their mothers.
Hypothesis: Men who have working mothers are emotionally healthier than men who have stay-at-home mothers.
Results: Jackson demonstrates that clients with anger problems seldom improve with the use of anger management techniques.
References to tables or figures: Table 3 shows that academics over the age of 65 are at their creative peak.

Correct Person and Voice

There is a good deal of criticism from writing specialists about human service professionals writing in the passive voice. The active voice suggests action ("The dog ate the steak and enjoyed every bite"). The passive voice indicates something is happening to the actor ("Every bite of the steak was eaten and enjoyed by the dog"). In the passive voice, the steak is more important than the dog. Scientific papers are often written in the third person and use the passive voice. For example, "The focus group was attended by the researcher" when a better way to write this would be, "I sat in on the focus group." The passive voice and writing in the third person often result in detached writing. The purpose is to remove the researcher or writer from the events and to make the report sound more scientific. It is always better to write in the active voice, that is, "The dog walked through the maze in an amazing 15 seconds" rather than, "It was determined that the dog took 15 seconds to walk through the maze."

Agreement of Subject and Verb

In a sentence, something or someone (the subject) is acted on (the verb). In the active voice, "The ball hit John in the face." "The client wore a tennis outfit." "Our cat Oliver is sick today." An incorrect agreement would be something like this: "I am (present tense) watching the sun set over Morro Bay. It was (past tense) a wonderful experience." The word *am* means you're doing something now. The correct way to write these two sentences is to stay in the present tense and write, "I **am** watching the sun set over Morro Bay. It **is** a wonderful experience."

Correct Use of Singular and Plural Forms

Many of us get confused over the correct singular and plural forms of commonly used words in the human services. For example:

Singular	*Plural*
criterion	criteria
phenomenon	phenomena
apparatus	apparatus or apparatuses
stimulus	stimuli
analysis	analyses
datum	data
appendix	appendixes or appendices
crisis	crises
hypothesis	hypotheses

Avoid Language That Stereotypes or Is Demeaning

We've had an epiphany in the human services about not using language that assumes everyone is a man. We used to say, "Man has developed slowly over the years," when what we meant to say was that human beings have developed slowly over the years. The words "men" and "man" no longer speak for everyone. Gender and racial stereotyping are also not used because they diminish people. "Jews are a special group because they come from homes that are highly cohesive." Ah, were that only true, but it isn't. "Men are all abusers in their hearts." Now that one really hurts. It's not true, and it's pejorative to say something that includes all men. "Women are better with people than men." Another stereotype you often hear that isn't true. Some women may be better with people, but not all women.

On the other hand, the attempt to keep language as homogenized and completely inoffensive as possible sometimes moves us to use politically correct speech that becomes meaningless. For example, "follicly challenged" or "lacking a full set of hair" for bald or "height challenged" for short. These are silly ways of writing. One can always use other words without offending. Here are a few rules on the use of words that are still appropriate and inoffensive without being politically correct:

- Don't use the words "girls" or "boys" unless you are speaking specifically about children; use "women" and "men" instead. It's demeaning to call an adult man, boy, or an adult woman, girl.

- Substitute "person" for "man" and "people" for "men" unless you are talking specifically about males.
- Use current job titles instead of those that demean or are sexist. Examples of appropriate titles include: police officer (not cop); flight attendant (not stewardess); secretary (not office girl); clinician (instead of shrink); server or waitress (instead of bar maid).

Style

Avoid long convoluted sentences. Short, direct sentences are easy to read and follow. Try to avoid highly emotional or dramatic words such as "astonished," "desperate," or "drastic" unless the word is appropriate. "I was astonished when the client told me about his incestuous relationship with his mother" would be more professionally apt if it read, "I was surprised to hear of the client's incestuous relationship with his mother because he'd given no indication in prior sessions that this was the case." On the other hand, the following would be correct: "Three badly malnourished children were removed from the home and immediately hospitalized in the intensive care unit because of the desperate state of their health."

Provide Evidence

When making statements, it's best not to make generalizations that seem to apply to everyone, but really don't. "All Americans support the President on the issue of aid to Iraq" may be true of some forms of aid and some Americans, but it's not true of all Americans. It's also important to give proper documentation that demonstrates you've done your research and lends authority to your work. For example:

Based on a sample of 30,000 graduate social workers spanning a 30-year period, Foster (2007) found that the best predictor of success in graduate school was the grade point average (GPA) attained as an undergraduate. The higher the GPA as an undergraduate, the higher the GPA in graduate school. However, there was no indication that GPA in graduate school was an indication of success in the profession. In follow-up studies of 30,000 graduates of MSW programs, the best indicator of success in the profession was the application letter students wrote to be admitted to graduate school indicating why they wanted to be social workers. The more client-oriented the application letter (I want to help others because . . .), the more likely the applicants would succeed as professionals. The more applicant-oriented the letter (I've always wanted to be a social worker because it makes me feel good about myself), the less likely they were to be successful as professionals.

Be Aware of How Something Sounds

We often focus on the content of our writing and forget to actually read it carefully. For that reason we need to read what we write with care and with awareness of the mistakes we all make.

For sale: Antique dresser for woman with thick legs and large drawers.

That wouldn't do the job at all, would it? The same thing can be said accurately by writing:

For sale: Woman's antique dresser with thick legs and large drawers.

Metaphors

Harris defines a metaphor as "a nonliteral phrase that makes writing more vivid and interesting" (p. 154). Haley (1986) says that metaphors are communications that have multiple meanings. We use metaphors all the time. We might say, "I studied hard and kept my nose to the grindstone." We didn't actually keep our noses to the grindstone, but used it as a metaphor for hard work. Or we might tell someone, "I went to the car dealer because of noise in the engine but they wouldn't fix it, so I complained to the manufacturer and, sure enough, the squeaky wheel gets the grease." We all know that this metaphor means that by being assertive, we often get what we want. I think metaphors are very important in the clinical work we do. I'm going to give you an example from a piece I wrote on metaphors in clinical work with men (Glicken, 2005, pp. 133–136).

According to Hendrix (1992), therapeutic metaphors help clients see similarities in situations and connect events in their lives that may seem disconnected, but are not. Zuniga (1992) says that metaphors help clients overcome perceptions of events that inhibit dealing successfully with a problem. Martin, Cummings, and Hallberg (1992) argue that metaphors may encourage new learning and help clients provide new meaning to important events in their lives. Heston and Kottman (1997) write that, "The parallels between the client's situation, relationships, self-perception, and those of the protagonist of the metaphor must be clear enough so that the client can make the bridge of personal connection" (p. 93).

Therapeutic metaphors can be very helpful with clients since language often fails to adequately allow clients to express inner feelings and cultures have traditionally invented ways to transmit shared, highly personal feelings through music, art, and literature using metaphors to suggest implicit meaning. Even though metaphors connect incompatible subjects, most people understand their implicit meaning. When metaphors are conveyed through humor, stories, poetry, literature, proverbs, and music, they have a power to influence clients who might not otherwise understand connections between incompatible or misunderstood subjects. Penn (2001) believes that people in difficulty are surrounded by negative metaphors that suggest, "dependence, poor genes, repressed personalities, weak constitutions" (p. 33). Our task in treatment is to replace negative metaphors with positive ones. People often think of metaphors as being spoken or written, but Barker (1985) includes a number of additional ways in which metaphors are used and classifies therapeutic metaphors as:

1) Major stories that address complex clinical problems; 2) anecdotes or short stories focused on specific or limited goals; 3) analogies, similes or brief figurative statements or phrases that underscore specific points; 4) relationship metaphors, which can use one relationship as a metaphor for another; 5) tasks with metaphorical meanings that can be undertaken by clients between sessions; 6) artistic metaphors which can be paintings, drawings, clay models or creations which symbolize something else. (Zuniga, 1992, p. 57)

Humor as Metaphorical

The use of self-deprecation and gallows humor often strikes clinicians as dysfunctional, but generations of immigrant people, particularly Jewish immigrants, have learned to laugh at problems and to make fun of themselves as a way of coping with difficult life issues. Clinicians can use humor since it is a familiar way for clients to convey subtle emotional messages. The humor used, however, must be constructive and insightful. It's purpose is to help people laugh at their behavior and to recognize that as bad as things are, there is still an opportunity to see the funny side of any situation, and to feel a sense of shared identity with others having similar experiences. Humor can serve to solidify a feeling of collective purpose and a common bond.

An example of a joke with metaphorical meaning was used with a client who was losing his temper at the noise made by his next-door neighbors. Unable to just go over and talk to them, he was obsessing about the situation to the point of being continually upset. To help him better deal with the situation, the worker told him the following joke:

A writer is sitting at his computer trying to write, when his parrot starts calling him names. "You're so stupid, you're lazy, you don't feed me enough, I hate you," the parrot screeches. The writer tries to calm the parrot down, but to no avail. Starting to do a slow burn, the writer threatens the parrot.

"If you don't stop that noise, and I mean stop it now," the writer yells, "I'm putting you in the freezer, and I mean it."

The parrot doesn't take the warning seriously and keeps up a steady flow of criticism. "You're a pet-hater, you have a thing against birds, my beak is bigger than yours," and so on until, in a rage, the writer puts the parrot in the freezer.

Twenty minutes later, the writer takes the parrot out. Shivering and full of frost, the parrot apologizes. "I'll never do that again," he says. "I've learned my lesson. I know what I did wrong and I'll never interrupt you again while you're writing. But tell me," the parrot asks, "I'm curious. Just what did the chicken do?"

This joke, about going too far with anger and the fact that the person punished gets the last laugh, helped the client see how troubled his behavior had become. After listening to the joke and talking to the worker about its meaning, he was willing to go to his neighbors and talk to them in a calm and reasonable way. And if the noise level didn't decline, or if the neighbor was unwilling to comply, the client understood that there were legal options. However, the alternatives turned out to be unnecessary. When asked to lower the noise level, the neighbor readily agreed, apologizing in the process. The joke had held special metaphorical meaning for the client since it was the way his parents often spoke to him, preferring to tell stories or jokes about important issues rather than using direct statements with clear meaning.

Rosen (2003) describes his immigrant father's use of black humor to explain the immigrant Jewish way of making bad luck and misery seem somehow funny.

The humor and the odd link to more conventional elements of Jewish tradition (the Messiah, for example, has been about to not come for a long time now) somehow saved these utterances from seeming like embodiments of despair. They were, in a complicated way, an answer to despair. Or at least they captured an aspect of Jewish tradition that has always fascinated me—a wise pessimism that emphasizes the perpetuation of tradition rather than individual salvation. As Kafka memorably said, "There's plenty of hope in the world—just not for us." (p. 87)

Using Meaningless Words

A common problem in human service writing that often forces the reader to guess what a writer means, is the use of words such as *normal*, *appropriate*, and *average*. These words have no absolute meaning unless the writer behaviorally explains what normal and average mean. "The client was appropriately dressed" tells us nothing, since we don't know the writer's standard for appropriate dress. A better way to write this would be, "The client came directly from his job as a roofer. He wore bib overalls, working boots, and a T-shirt stained with tar and soot." Ordinarily, one would find the client's clothing curious, but the fact that he just came from work makes it perfectly appropriate. It's much better to describe the client's clothing and any circumstances related to the clothing. Let the reader decide whether it's appropriate or not. "The client came to treatment wearing high heels and a bikini style swimsuit in the middle of winter" might give us pause about the client's idea of what one should wear to treatment and whether something is really quite wrong with the client. Again, the writer needs to give us any additional information to suggest a reason for the clothing worn. "When the worker noted her dress and wondered if she wasn't cold, the client replied, 'Oh, this old thing? It's what I was wearing when my ex and I broke up. I thought that wearing it would get me back in the mood to talk about the old SOB, but all it's done is to freeze my a_ _ off.'" Well, borderline appropriate, but now we know.

The use of words like "normal" and "average" are generally incorrectly applied or have no basis in fact. I've just come from the Pasadena Humane Society. Dogs are evaluated for their behavioral skills using a behaviorally oriented scale. A pretty cocker spaniel we liked was given a "C" for behavioral skills by the staff when he was first brought into the shelter. We couldn't understand why. In the kennel, he came to the gate and seemed very interested in us. Once he was taken to an area where he could freely roam and we could interact with him, not once in 20 minutes did he come to us. We were told that most dogs take a few minutes to check out their surroundings, but that having been given a "C" by the staff and now viewing how distracted he was, we could expect him to be aloof and distracted at home. It was good to have a behavioral evaluation that agreed with what we saw. It also gave us an anchor by which we could evaluate other dogs in the shelter. Try not to use vague words in your writing since they only leave the reader guessing.

Using Initials

When using initials, each letter stands for a word. Many common initials are so familiar that we don't need to write them out for the reader to know what they mean. FBI, HMO, HBO are examples. The general rule for less obvious initials is to write the full name of an organization or diagnosis and, thereafter, use the initials.

The client went to Jewish Family Service (JFS) for help with his obesity. After losing 100 pounds, he took the JFS staff out for dinner.

The client suffered from Restless Leg Syndrome (RLS) and had trouble sitting still. Once he was relaxed, however, his RLS seemed under control and his leg stopped jerking.

Irrational Statements

An irrational statement is one that defies logic:

The client spoke in a strange dialect, but oddly enough, I understood everything he said.

Oddly enough, for sure. Is the writer making this statement because he or she is reading body language, or do they have the ability to empathize to such an extent that language isn't necessary? A more logical way to say this would be:

> The client's facial expressions and body language conveyed a strong degree of sadness. Every few minutes he would look at a picture in his billfold, slump over, and begin to sob. Although he spoke in a language I didn't understand, it appeared to me that he was grieving over some person or event in his life.

SUMMARY

This chapter discusses common punctuation and rules of grammar. Examples of each are given. The chapter also discusses the use of metaphors as well as illogical words and phrases that have no meaning unless the writer provides behavioral explanations. Words such as *average, appropriate,* and *normal* are examples of meaningless words when behavioral guidelines are absent. Singular and plural words used commonly in professional writing are also included in the chapter.

FIND THE MISTAKES

1. Glicken, the author of this book is also a great tennis player! His tennis playing is so legendary, that he has become interested in Zen Tennis, a new approach to therapy which holds promise for not one—but two types of cures—obesity and substance abuse.
2. Where are all the great therapists. It seems that nobody is left after the great ones died except maybe OPUS, the wise Doonesbury Penguin.
3. Forrest Gump was paraphrasing the strengths perspective when he said life is just a bowl of cherries. The obvious question for therapists is whether they are natural or sugar-coated cherries.
4. Freuds use of dreams and his concept of the unconscious had a powerful affect on American psychotherapy.
5. When the cartoon character said, we have met the enemy and he is us he was saying that the problems we are experiencing are of our own making which begs the question it seems to me of how others effect our lives.

REFERENCES

Alkon, A. (2003). All you need to know about men. *Boise Weekly,* 16(5), 17.
Ambien. (2007). Fictitious source.
Barker, P. (1985). *Using metaphors in psychotherapy.* New York: Psychology Press.

Foster. (2007). Fictitious source.

Glicken, M. D. (2005a). *Working with troubled men: A contemporary practitioner's guide.* Mahwah, NJ: Lawrence E. Erlbaum Associates.

Glicken, M. D. (2005b). *Ending the sex wars.* Omaha, NE: iuniverse.

Goldfarb. (2004). Fictitious source.

Haley, J. (1986). *Uncommon therapy: The psychiatric techniques of Milton H. Friedman, M.D.* New York: Norton

Harris, R. W. (2003). *When good people write bad sentences: 12 steps to better writing habits.* New York: St. Martin's Press.

Hendrix, D. H. (1992). Metaphors as nudges toward understanding in mental health counseling. *Journal of Mental Health Counseling, 14,* 234–242.

Heston, M. L., & Kottman, S. (1997, Dec.). Movies as metaphors: A counseling intervention. *Journal of Humanistic Education and Development, 36*(2), 92–100.

Jackson. (2007). Fictitious source.

Macho. (2003). Fictitious source.

Martin, J., Cummings, A. L., & Hallberg, E. T. (1992). Therapists' intentional use of metaphor: Memorability, clinical impact, and possible epistemic/motivational functions. *Journal of Counseling and Clinical Psychology, 60*(1), 143–145.

Penn, P. (2001). Chronic illness: Trauma, language, and writing: Breaking the silence. *Family Process, 40,* 33–52.

Rosen, J. (2003). My Kafka problem. *American Scholar, 72*(3), 85–91.

Soprano. (2006). Fictitious source.

Updike, J. (2006a). 90% hateful. *New Yorker,* LXXXII(14), 76–80.

Updike, J. (2006b). *Terrorist.* New York: Knopf.

Zuniga, M. E. (1992). Using metaphors in therapy: Dichos and Latino clients. *Social Work, 37*(1), 55–60.

4

Using the Correct Word

CHOOSING THE RIGHT WORD AND
SPELLING IT CORRECTLY

In this era of word processing spellcheckers on your computer, it's difficult to imagine that spelling is a problem. Unfortunately, it is. The spellchecker isn't a mind reader. It provides you with a choice of words to choose from when you've misspelled a word. Obviously, you must know the correct spelling and meaning of each choice it gives you or you may choose the wrong word. Once you've used the spellchecker, you'll need to go through your paper to see if you've chosen the wrong word. Apparently the word *practitioner*, if misspelled, looks enough like *parishioner* for a spellchecker to assume you mean *parishioner*. Imagine how I felt getting a letter back from a psychology journal telling me that it did not publish religiously oriented articles. I hadn't reread my article after using my spellchecker and submitted my article with the word *practitioner* replaced throughout the article by the word *parishioner*. This happened 47 times in the article.

Instructors and others reading your work always know when it's been written at the last minute because there are spelling errors and incorrectly used words. This chapter includes many of the words that are frequently misused. I'm sure there are many other words that confuse readers and require a close relationship with dictionaries. Read the chapter carefully, learn to apply words correctly, and use a dictionary if you're unclear about the meaning of a word or phrase. All the computer software in the world won't be able to assure good writing if you haven't edited your work carefully.

Some word processing programs include suggestions about grammar. They are often incorrect and misleading. If you use those suggestions, you may have a paper with an inordinate number of errors. For that reason alone, edit your work. Read it several times or more, and make the necessary corrections.

CHOOSING THE RIGHT WORD:
SOME COMMON MISTAKES

Here are some words that are commonly misused. Thanks to Perfesser Cumber (2006) for the use of his website. In using his work, I'm quoting from his website:

> A short list of Perfesser Cumber's pet peeves is presented alphabetically below. The perfesser will no doubt be adding to it from time to time. We feel that this material is far too valuable to sell, so we are giving it away—you may download this page with our blessing and do anything you want with it (apart from claiming that you wrote it yourself—the perfesser is almost as ill tempered as Bert when he doesn't get credit). If you should choose to take issue with any of Perfesser Cumber's pronouncements, you can write him at qcumber@acebo.com.

Perfesser Cumber's Pet Peeves

Term	Perfesser Cumber's Comments
also	Except under *extreme* provocation, do not start sentences with "Also, . . .".
assure vs. *ensure*	Unplug the toaster to *ensure* against electrocution. *Assure* the user that he will not be electrocuted.
as well as	If you mean *and*, say so.
authored (as a verb) vs. *write*	Mark Twain never *authored* anything, but he *wrote* quite a bit. If *writing* was good enough for Twain, it should be good enough for most of the rest of us.
desire	*Desire* is not a polite way to say *want*. If you mean *want*, say *want*.
desirous of	Don't even *think* of using this expression unless you are *desirous of* becoming a laughing stock.
empower	Don't just *empower* someone; *empower* someone to DO something: *The new legislation* empowers *parking enforcement officers to use lethal force.*
hanged vs. *hung*	When *hang* means, as it generally does, "to suspend," then *hung* is the correct past-tense and past participial form of the verb: "Yesterday, I *hung* a picture on the wall"; "I have *hung* many pictures on many walls." When *hang* means "to put to death by hanging," however, *hanged* is the correct past tense and

	past participal form: "We *hanged* the horse-thieving varmint yesterday"; "We've *hanged* nigh unto forty horse thieves this year."
insure vs. ensure	*Insure* your car or your life. *Ensure* your safety by not stepping in front of an uninsured truck.
it's vs. its	*It's* is a contraction of *it* and *is. Its* is a possessive pronoun. "*It's* not that I don't like *its* location; *it's* just that *its* price is too high."
make use of	*Use* means the same thing, is two words shorter, and doesn't make you sound like a pompous ninny.
may vs. can	*May* is not a polite way to say *can.* If you mean *can,* say *can.*
may vs. might	*Might* is the past tense of *may.* In the sense of granting permission, *might* is genuinely past tense and is seldom used in modern American English: "Mother said I *might.*" (Most Americans would say, "Mother said I *could,*" while the rest of us would say, "Mom said it was OK.") In the sense of expressing probability, *may* is stronger than *might.* That is, something that *may* happen is more likely than something that *might* happen. If there's a good chance that making a given mistake will erase the hard disk, use *may.*
may have vs. might have	"My father may have been killed when his ship was torpedoed" means *either* that I don't know whether or not he's dead, *or* that I know he's dead, but I'm not sure whether or not the torpedoing of his ship had anything to do with it. In either case, I am in some current doubt as to the outcome. "My father might have been killed when his ship was torpedoed" means that his ship *was* torpedoed, and there was, at the time, a real probability of his death, but he did, in fact, survive.
mission statement	Most intelligible missions can be expressed in less than a sentence. If your mission isn't something on the order of "sell more widgets" or "improving student reading scores by 10%," mission statements become meaningless.
myself	Use *me* when you are the object of some action, even if you have one or more accomplices. It is perfectly OK to say, "They gave Frank and me the boot." "They gave Frank and *I* the boot" is just plain wrong, while "They gave Frank and *myself* the boot" is nearly as wrong and sounds unbearably pompous. One trick is to read the sentence without Frank present. "They gave *I* the boot" is obviously incorrect, while "they gave me the boot" is correct.

(continued)

none	*None,* is generally considered to be a singular verb: "*None* of the horse thieves *was* (not *were*) hanged." There are constructions in which it becomes difficult to treat *none* as singular: "*None* of my friends *like* each other." Just *try* to keep *none* singular.
on vs. upon	Whenever you are tempted to use *upon,* stop and consider carefully whether *on* would not do just as well.
people vs. persons	In all situations but one, *people* is acceptable as the plural of *person.* The one exception arises when *person* is used to refer to someone's body or clothing: "The smugglers secreted the drugs on their *persons.*" In all other known contexts, when the number of human beings under discussion is small and specific, you can use either *people* or *persons.* When the number of beings in question is very large or is unknown, or when you are stating a generalization, *people* is mandatory: "Over eight million *people* (not *persons*) have the good fortune to live in New York City."
presently vs. currently	*Presently* means pretty soon. Use *currently* or "at present" when you mean right now.
proactive	There's no such word. For those of you who don't want to take the Perfesser's word for anything, consider this: For the adjective *proactive* to exist, the verb *proact* would first have to exist. I trust that you are with me in maintaining that there is no verb *proact.* But why not? you may ask. For the good and sufficient reason that, if there were such a verb, it would mean exactly the same thing as *act* and would thus be entirely redundant.
put/place in/into	You can *put* it *in.* You can *put* it *into.* You can *place* it *in.* Please don't *place* it *into.* In general, prefer *put* to *place* in most contexts.
regarding	See "with respect to" below. Nuke it.
series comma	Humor me and use the series comma, even if your favorite style guide says you don't have to: ". . . this, that, and the other" not ". . . this, that and the other." **Author's Note**: I agree completely with Perfesser Cumber on this. You'll note that I use series commas throughout this book.
serve vs. service	*Serve* a customer. *Serve* the educational community. *Service* a car (but only if you're a qualified mechanic).
something of vs. somewhat of	Short version: "Something of," as in, "He's *something of* a traditionalist," is correct. "Somewhat of," as in, "He's *somewhat of* a snot," is incorrect.

that vs. which	*Which* is not a polite or high-class way of saying *that;* the words mean two different things. Use *which* in nonrestrictive clauses only: "This widget, which cost me an arm and a leg, works fine." (Note the commas.) Use *that* in restrictive clauses: "The widget *that* works cost me an arm and a leg. The other one was free." (No commas.)
their and they're	"When people lose *their* tempers, *they're* usually sorry about it later" is fine. "When a person loses *their* temper, *they're* usually sorry about it later" is incorrect. So, what do you do when you need to refer to a single person whose gender is unknown? "His or her" may be awkward, but it is acceptable as are variants such as "his/her," "her or his," "her/his," etc.
use vs. utilize	There may be some legitimate excuse for the existence of the word *utilize*, but I have yet to encounter it. Use *use.*
who vs. whom	There is no good excuse for using *whom* where *who* is the correct choice. The person who says, *"Whom* shall I say is calling?" would be more correct to say "Who is calling, please."
wish	*Wish* is not a polite way of saying *want.* If you mean *want,* say *want.*
with respect to	There's no excuse for this construction. Figure out the precise nature of the relationship you're trying to describe, and then describe it. Rather than, "In respect to Mr. Jones and his need for counseling service," you would be more grammatically correct to write, "I am writing to refer Mr. Alfred Jones for counseling."

MORE INCORRECT WORDS

Here are some additional words that we often use incorrectly. Many thanks to Brandon Royal (2004) for some of these words found in his excellent book *The Little Red Writing Book* (2004, pp. 119–125).

A

- *Accept* **and** *except*: **Accept** is an action, often meaning to take something (to accept a present). **Except** means "excluding" (Everyone can come except the therapist).
- *Affect* **and** *effect*: **Affect** means "to influence" (The client affects my view of life). **Effect** can be a result (The effect of the study was to change our policy) or it can mean "to bring about" (He wants to effect change). The second usage doesn't occur very often. The use of the term *client affect* (his or her emotional state as noted in nonverbal behavior and

body language) would be more precise if we described exactly what we are seeing. Rather than saying that the client's affect was depressed, we would be better off telling the reader exactly what we saw. For example: "The client cried often, bent forward, and sometimes gripped his chair as if he might fall over."

- *All together* and *altogether*: **All together** means "being together" or "united" (We were all together for Thanksgiving). **Altogether** means "completely" or "entirely" (You are altogether wrong).
- *All ready* and *already*: **All ready** means you are prepared (I am all ready to take the trip). **Already** refers to time (Is it time to go already?).
- *Allusion* and *illusion*: An **allusion** is an indirect reference (Did you hear his allusion to my article?), while **illusion** is a misconception (His work gave the illusion of using the cognitive approach but he certainly knows nothing about cognitive therapy).
- *Alternately* and *alternatively*: **Alternately** means "one after the other" (We alternately spun the wheel in the game). **Alternatively** means "on the other hand" or "one or the other" (You can choose a large bookcase or, alternatively, you can buy two small ones).
- An *antidote* is a treatment for a disease whereas an *anecdote* is an account of something that happened.

B
- *Bare* and *bear*: **Bare** means naked while **bear** refers to the animal (the Grizzly bear) or the ability to hold up or cope with something (as in being able to bear the pain).
- *Beside* and *besides*: **Beside** means "next to," as in, "Stand here beside me." **Besides** means "also," as in, "Besides, I need to tell you about a new approach to treatment."
- *Between* and *among*: Use **between** when referring to only two things or parties (There is strong disagreement between my wife and my mother), use **among** when referring to three or more things or parties (There was strong disagreement among members of the group).
- *Bimonthly* and *semimonthly*: **Bimonthly** means "every two months," **semimonthly** means "twice a month."

C
- *Capital* and *capitol*: **Capital** refers to a city while **capitol** refers to a building where lawmakers meet. **Capital** also refers to wealth or resources. (The **capitol** has undergone extensive renovations. The residents of the state **capital** protested the development plans).
- *Cite* and *site*: **Cite** means "refer to an authority or example" (I cited Freud in my paper). It also means "formally recognize" (The social

work profession has cited Freud for his contribution to the field). It can also mean "summon before a court of law" (Last year the company was cited for pollution violations). **Site** means "location" (They chose a new site for the school very close to my home).

- *Climactic* and *climatic*: **Climactic** refers to a climax or the point of greatest intensity in an event. **Climatic** refers to weather conditions.
- *Complement* and *compliment*: **Complement** means something that completes or makes up a whole: "The red sweater is a perfect complement to the outfit." **Compliment** means "to praise."
- *Concurrent* and *consecutive*: **Concurrent** means that something is happening at the same time as something else. **Consecutive** means successive or following one after the other: "The union called three consecutive strikes in one year."
- *Connote* and *denote*: **Connote** means "imply" or "suggest" (The word "counseling" connotes life changes). **Denote** means "indicate" or "refer to specifically" (The "r" in statistics denotes correlation).
- *Conscience* and *conscious*: **Conscience** refers to your moral or ethical beliefs, and **conscious** means that you're aware of something or awake.

D
- *Discreet* and *discrete*: **Discreet** means being careful or modest. **Discrete** means "separate" or "distinctive" (Each department in the agency operates as a discrete entity).
- *Disinterested* and *uninterested*: **Disinterested** means "unbiased" or "impartial" (The disinterested marriage mediator helped facilitate our divorce). **Uninterested** means "not interested" or "indifferent" (The lawyer seemed uninterested in the mediator's work).

E
- *Each other* and *one another*: **Each other** refers to two things (My wife and I love each other), while **one another** refers to three or more things (In our family, we have a great deal of love for one another).
- *Emigrate from* and *immigrate to*: **Emigrate** means to leave one country to settle in another: In 1923, my father *emigrated* from Russia. **Immigrate** means to enter another country and reside there: Many Russians *immigrated* to the United States to avoid communism.

F
- *Farther* and *further*: **Farther** refers to physical distance (The town is farther on), while **further** refers to extent or degree (We can discuss this example further after class).

- *Fewer* and *less*: **Fewer** indicates that something can be counted, as in the number of clients or the amount of money; while **less** indicates that something can't be counted, as in ego.
- *Figuratively* and *literally*: **Figuratively** means metaphorical or symbolic: "I was so happy to see my wife that I figuratively jumped out of my shoes." **Literally** means "actually" (I'm not exaggerating when I say I literally jumped out of my shoes when I saw my wife). **Literally** also means the exact meaning of the words: "I translated the Latin passage literally."
- *Flaunt* and *flout*: **Flaunt** means to show off: "Eager to flaunt her knowledge of psychotherapy, Helen dreamed of being the star student in her social work practice class." **Flout** means to show contempt: "Jason so disliked Helen's behavior in class that he took every opportunity to flout the class rule against put downs of other students."
- *Foreword* and *forward*: **Foreword** means an introductory note or preface: "In the foreword of my book I explained why writing was easy." **Forward** means toward the front: "Helen sat in the forward section of the class." **Forward** also means to send something: " I forwarded my new book to a former student."

I
- *i.e.* and *e.g.*: The abbreviation *e.g.* means for example: "Her talents were many and varied (e.g., magic tricks, sewing, softball and race car driving)." The abbreviation *i.e.* means *in other words*: "The joys of my existence, i.e., writing and playing tennis, give my life special meaning."
- *Indicted* and *inducted*: When a person is **indicted**, he's charged with a crime. When a person is **inducted**, he's been given a new job or honor, as in being inducted into the Psychotherapy Hall of Fame.
- *Infer* or *imply*: **Infer** means to draw a conclusion (I infer from the client's statements that he is anxious), while **imply** means to suggest something (are you implying that your client is anxious?).

L
- *Lay* and *lie*: **Lay** refers to putting an object down. **Lie** means that you lie down to sleep or relax.
- *Lend* and *loan*: **Lend** and **loan** are both acceptable when it comes to the literal meaning of each word as in: "Can you lend (or loan) me a dollar?" the word **lend** should be used in a figurative sense as in "Will you lend me a hand?"

M
- *Maybe* and *may be*: Maybe means perhaps (maybe you can go to see the film). **May be** means possibly (it may be necessary to do the assignment over).

N

- *Nonplussed* and *calm*: **Nonplussed** means perplexed, agitated, or bewildered. It is often thought to mean calm or unfazed. It doesn't. **Calm** means unruffled.

P

- *Passed* and *past*. **Passed** means you've completed or moved by someone (I passed the motorist in my car. I passed the exam). **Past** refers to time (I always consider the past when I work with clients in therapy).
- *Precede* and *proceed*: **Precede** means to come before. **Proceed** means to move ahead or forward: "He preceded me into the program but once I caught up with him, I proceeded to become a much better therapist."
- *Principle* and *principal*: **Principle** refers to a rule or standard; if you're a person with principles, you follow a set of standards about what you believe is right or wrong. **Principal** refers to the main or most important thing (The principal reason for this book is to help human service professionals write clearly. The chief investigator is the principal investigator). The person who runs the school is the principal. When in doubt remember what my third grade spelling teacher told me as a way to remember the spelling of a school principal: "The principal of Belmont School is our pal." This is the guy who told my father I'd flunked every spelling test in the third grade. Some pal.

S

- *Stationary* and *stationery*: **Stationary** refers to being still and **stationery** refers to the paper you write on.

T

- *Than* and *then*: **Than** is used in comparing things (John is taller than Jack). **Then** refers to time (Back then, people were a lot smaller) or consequence (If the school is closed, then you'll have to work at home).
- *Too*, *to*, and *two*: **Too** means "also" or "very." **To** means going somewhere, as in "going to the movies." **Two** is the number 2.

REDUNDANT AND UNNECESSARY WORDS

We have a tendency to use words in a redundant or unnecessary way. Below is a short list of a few redundant words, thanks to Harris (2003, pp. 80–81).

Redundant Phrase	Better Equivalent
absolutely necessary	necessary
close scrutiny	scrutiny

final outcome	outcome
future plans	plans
past history	history
sudden impulse	impulse
totally unanimous	unanimous

Incorrect	**Correct**
suppose to	supposed to
use to	used to
towards	toward
anyways	anyway
could care less	couldn't care less
feel badly	feel bad

FOREIGN PHRASES

I hate it when people use foreign phrases when an English phrase is available, but it's *de rigueur* to use them, *n'est-ce pas*? Ugh! So here are some foreign phrases and their English equivalents. Thanks for some of these to Harris (2003, pp. 64–65). Don't use foreign phrases if your audience hasn't a clue about their meaning unless it's vital to the writing, as in,

> It was difficult to get my newly immigrated Mexican American client to understand the concept of therapy until I used the term, *de corazón a corazón* (talking heart to heart).

In Mexico, this concept of a close personal relationship in which true feelings can be communicated has various levels of meaning. It is sometimes associated with the process called *el desague de las penas* (unburdening oneself), or what North American therapists might call venting. You can understand how, in this case, the foreign phrase had great meaning to the client and was appropriately used.

Foreign Phrase	**English Equivalent**
alta cocker	old fool
au naturel	naked
bon mot	witticism
capice?	understand?
de rigueur	customary
en masse	as a group
fait accompli	done deed
l'chaim	to life

mas cerveza	more beer
mishugah	mentally unstable
Je ne sais quoi	special something
n'est-ce pas?	isn't it so?
schmuck	jerk
vis-à-vis	in relation to

SLANG

It's amazing to me how often students use slang when there are perfectly good and appropriate professional words to use. Words like *dude* ("My client is a righteous dude." Honestly, a student wrote this in a paper); *cool* ("His wife is really a cool babe." Yup, same surfer dude); *booze* ("He's into booze real bad"); *retard* ("My client is sort of a retard"); *Jewed down* (cheated, and we Jews smack anyone who uses that term, including students); *pissed off* ("My client was really pissed off at me"); *ballistic* ("He went ballistic during the session); *bonkers* ("The client went bonkers"); down in the dumps; couldn't get it up; limp; frigid; whore; bogus; suck up; gross; nifty; super; awesome; and a host of other words. None of these words has a place in a professional's vocabulary unless you are correctly quoting a client.

PSYCHOBABBLE

Psychobabble is a term used to describe *jargon* (commonly used words) from the human services that is either meaningless or incorrectly used. Psychobabble occurs when a legitimate term from the humans services is incorrectly applied or, it might have a meaning that is so vague and non-specific that no one really knows what it means. Psychobabble uses words that have vague or even incorrect meanings but have entered the popular culture to describe common behaviors. The following is a list of words that are often incorrectly used in popular culture to describe emotional events, but which need specific definable meaning when used by professionals. Most of these words were found in an article on psychobabble in Wikipedia (2006). Some common words might include:

- authentic
- blocked
- breakthrough
- closure
- co-dependent

Chapter 4

- congruence
- empowerment
- envision
- getting it
- grounded
- holistic
- integration
- new paradigm
- meaningful relationship
- metamodel
- resonate—as in "I really resonate with your ideas," meaning "I support what you just said."
- self-actualization
- spaced out—as in "I'm feeling a little spaced out today," meaning "I'm not really at my best."
- stressed out
- stuff—as in "My stuff" gets in the way of . . . ," meaning "I experience inappropriately strong emotions around some subject which stops me from thinking clearly."
- synergy
- transformation
- validation
- well-being
- win-win

An example of psychobabble might be the following:

My client was in the midst of *healing* from a divorce. She told me that therapy had been a *transforming* experience for her when she began having marital difficulties, and how she needed a therapist who was *authentic* and would provide her with a sense of *well-being*. She is looking for a *breakthrough* in her understanding of self so that she can gain *closure* on her *co-dependent* approach to relationships and become a *grounded* and *empowered* woman.

Huh? What does this mean? I think it means that the client is still having problems related to a divorce and wants a therapist who can help her. But what does grounded mean? I often see this word in the professional literature. Does it mean emotionally stable? What does closure mean? Does it mean getting over something or ending something with the belief that it won't ever bother us again? You can see that these words are vague and undefined. They are nice words, and they sound good, but what the heck do they mean? When we begin to use vague words that are meaningless because they have a popular, but not a scientific meaning, we develop a jargon that is indecipherable to everyone.

BUREAUSPEAK

Bureauspeak is the language of the bureaucracy. It is so vague, convoluted, and devoid of beauty that it becomes almost meaningless. The whole point of bureauspeak is to say something in a way that leaves the reader confused and unclear about its meaning. Consider the following beautiful verse from Ecclesiastes 9:11 (Holy Bible, p. 620) and how it sounds when put into bureauspeak, slang, and psychobabble:

> **The original:** I returned and saw under the sun, that the race is not to the swift, nor the battle to the strong, neither yet bread to the wise, nor yet riches to men of understanding, nor yet favor to men of skill; but time and chance happeneth to them all.
> **Bureauspeak:** "Objective consideration of contemporary phenomena compels the conclusion that success or failure in competitive activities exhibits no tendency to be commensurate with innate capacity, but that a considerable element of the unpredictable must invariably be taken into account." (Poynter, 2006, p. 1)
> **Slang:** If you can keep your cool, better stuff will happen because your head will be on straight.
> **Psychobabble:** The wise person understands that well-being is a function of enriched self-awareness. By not accepting other-directed behavior, the synergy of life will provide each of us with a new and more positive paradigm to guide our lives.

Compared to the original, each attempt to put the verse from Ecclesiastes into more modern language fails miserably. Psychobabble, slang, and bureauspeak have no place in the human services. We are objective, empirically oriented professionals whose practice is based on best evidence and research. Using words that are meaningless and written in the flat, unemotional language of the bureaucrat is not what we're about. If you use words like *spiritual, grounded,* or *authentic,* you will need to define them in an objective way or, like their use in the popular culture, they not only become meaningless, they begin to suggest that you're practicing a new aged, unscientific, self-centered therapy we associate with the worst sort of self-indulgence.

SUMMARY

This chapter on the correct use of words considers some common words that are often incorrectly used. *Ensure* and *insure* would be examples of words that are commonly confused. Thanks to Perfesser Cumber for his contribution. The chapter also discusses words that are used in a redundant (unnecessary) way. *Future plans* versus *plans* is a good example. Plans, unless they've been acted upon (past plans) are always in the future. The chapter discusses the use of slang and why it has no role in professional writing and two of the more heinous and grievous problems in human service writing: psychobabble and bureauspeak. Finally, the chapter considers the use of foreign phrases. I strongly caution against foreign phrases, but if you must, *bubbeleh*, you should use them in good health and with *mazel*.

FIND THE MISTAKES

1. I'm so tired I feel like laying down and sleeping till noon and then getting up and playing some tennis; maybe I'll go to the central park or maybe to the health club: it's pretty close to the house.
2. When I see a client I always assure them that they will never need therapy again and if they do, I insure that they'll get it.
3. The focus of therapy will be on client empowerment and a decrease in blocked emotional responses which inhibit authenticity.
4. I saw the client several years ago. Than he was suffering from depression but more then ever, he seems to have slipped into a flat state of synergistic apathy and existential vagueness.
5. It is absolutely necessary that we maintain close scrutiny of the client or the final outcome may be a sudden impulse to resist closure.

REFERENCES

Cumber, P. (2006). Perfesser cumber's pearls of wisdom. Retrieved May 25, 2006, from www.acebo.com/cumber.htm

Harris, R. W. (2004). *When good people write bad sentences: 12 steps to better writing habits.* New York: St. Martin's Griffin.

Poynter, D. (2006). Newspeak. Retrieved May 25, 2006, from www.dansmind.com/?p=136

Royal, B. (2004). *The little red writing book.* Cincinnati, Ohio: Writer's Digest Books.

Wikipedia. (2006). Psychobabble. Retrieved September 20, 2006, from http://en.wikipedia.org/wki/psychobabble

5

The APA Crib Sheet

The American Psychological Association style is the style of writing used by journals published by the American Psychological Association (APA). APA style is used almost exclusively by journals published in most of the human services and by social work and psychology instructors. The style is documented in the *Publication Manual of the American Psychological Association, 5th Edition* (American Psychological Association, 2001). The APA's style manual began as an article published in the *Psychological Bulletin* in 1929. By 1952, the guidelines were issued as a separate document called the *Publication Manual*. Today the manual is in its fifth edition, and the APA format is a widely recognized standard for scientific writing in psychology, social work, and education.

Some of the more commonly used rules and reference formats from the manual are listed here. However, this summary is no substitute for the 440-page APA manual itself, which should be purchased by any serious student in the human services. Special thanks are given to Russ Dewey, professor emeritus at Georgia Southern University's Department of Psychology, Bill Scott of the College of Wooster, Doc Scribe, and Owen Williams, director of the University of Minnesota, Crookston Library, for providing help and examples for this brief summary.

Let's start with the APA approach to references within the body of the report. After that, we'll consider the way to put references in their proper order and form at the end of the report. Finally, we'll consider some of the more important APA style requirements including punctuation, ethnic, racial and gender issues, abbreviations, and quotations.

APA RULES FOR CITING A REFERENCE IN THE TEXT

- For two-author citations, spell out both authors on all occurrences (Johnson & Johnson, 1987).
- For multiple-author citations (up to five authors) name all authors the first time, then use "et al.", so the first time it is Smith, Jones, Pearson, and Sherwin (1990), but the second time it is (Smith et al.), with a period after "al" but no underlining.
- The first time an "et al." reference is used in a paragraph, give the year; thereafter (if the citation is repeated in the paragraph) omit the year.
- For six or more authors, use "et al." the first time and give the full citation in references. You must provide all authors in the reference section, even if it's many more than six.
- Include a page reference after the year, outside quotation marks. For example: The author stated, "The placebo effect may explain spontaneous remission from mental illness" (Renaud, 1993, p. 311), but the author has doubts and found that "spontaneous remission often occurred in people who were not given medication, psychosocial treatments, or medical care" (p. 311). The sentence quoted begins with a capital letter only if it follows a comma, and is a complete sentence not merged into the flow of the text.
- If two or more multiple-author references shorten to the same "et al." form, making them ambiguous, give as many author names as necessary to make them distinct, before "et al." For example: (Smith, Jones, et al., 1991) to distinguish it from (Smith, Burke, et al., 1991).
- Join names in a multiple-author citation with *and* (in-text) or an ampersand (&) in reference lists and parenthetical comments. For example: As Smith and Sarason (1990) point out, the same argument was made in an earlier study (Smith and Sarason, 1990).
- If a group is readily identified by its initials, spell it out only the first time. For example, "As reported in a government study (National Institute of Mental Health [NIMH], 1991), and thereafter, "The previously cited study (NIMH, 1991) found that . . ."
- If the author is unknown or unspecified, use the first few words of the title—in quotation marks for an article or chapter, in italics for self-contained items, for example: ("Cognitive Dysfunction," 1992) or (*Good Writing*, 2004).
- If citing multiple works by the same author at the same time, arrange dates in order. In general, use letters after years to distinguish multiple publications by the same author in the same year, for example: Several studies (Johnson, 1988, 1990a, 1990b, 2008 in press-a, 2008 in press-

b) showed the same thing. Always go from the earliest to the most recent citations.

- For old works, cite the translation or the original and modern copyright dates if both are known, for example: (Freud, trans. 1931) or (Jung, 1912/1983).
- Always give page numbers for quotations, for example: (Cheek and Buss, 1981, p. 332) or (Shimamura, 1989, chap. 3, p. 5).
- For e-mail and other unrecoverable data use "personal communication," for example: (Randy Savage, personal communication, September 28, 2008). Personal communications, including e-mails, telephone conversations, or interviews do not appear in the reference list.
- For quoting electronic documents without page numbers, cite paragraph numbers if given, indicated by the paragraph symbol or the abbreviation *para.* in the citation (e.g., Smith, 2000, para. 17). If there are no paragraph numbers, cite the nearest preceding section heading and count paragraphs from there (e.g., Smith, 2000, Method section, para. 4).

CITING SOURCES AT THE END OF A CHAPTER OR PAPER: THE REFERENCE SECTION

The APA *Publication Manual* (American Psychological Association, 2001) contains 95 examples of different reference types (pp. 240–281). Here are a few examples of the most commonly used formats. Double space reference items if your paper will be submitted to a publication for editing or review. The following discussion on referencing discussion uses examples from Williams (2005).

Journal Article, One Author

Simon, A. (2000). Perceptual comparisons through the mind's eye. *Memory & Cognition, 23,* 635–647.

Journal Article, Two Authors

Becker, M. B., & Rozek, S. J. (1995). Welcome to the energy crisis. *Journal of Social Issues, 32,* 230–343.

Magazine Article, One author

Garner, H. J. (1997, July). Do babies have a universal song? *Psychology Today, 102,* 70–77.

Newspaper Article, No Author

Study finds free care used more. (1982, April 3). *Wall Street Journal*, pp. A1, A25.

Book, Two Authors

Strunk, W., & White, E. B. (1979). *The elements of style* (3rd ed.). New York: Macmillan.

Edited Book

Letheridge, S., & Cannon, C. R. (Eds.). (1980). *Bilingual education.* New York: Praeger.

ERIC Document

Peterson, K. (2002). *Welfare-to-work programs: Strategies for success* (Report No. EDO-JC-02-04). Washington, DC: Office of Educational Research and Improvement. (ERIC Document Reproduction Service No. ED467985.)

Entry in an Encyclopedia

Imago. (2000). In *World Book Encyclopedia* (Vol. 10, p. 79). Chicago: World Book Encyclopedia.

Report from a Private Organization

Kimberly-Clark. (2002). *Kimberly-Clark (Annual Report).* Dallas, TX: Author.

Dissertation

Olsen, G. W. (1985). Campus child care within the public supported post-secondary educational institutions in the state of Wisconsin (dare care) (Doctoral dissertation, University of Wisconsin-Madison, 1985). *Dissertations Abstract International*, 47/03, 783.

Videotape

Mass, J. B. (Producer), & Gluck, D. H. (Director). (1979). *Deeper into hypnosis.* (Motion picture). Englewood Cliffs, NJ: Prentice Hall.

ELECTRONIC FORMATS

The citation is done as if it were a paper article and then followed by a retrieval statement that identifies the date retrieved and source. Note that web addresses are not followed by a period.

Internet Article Based on Print Source

Sahelian, R. (1999, January). Achoo! *Better Nutrition,* 61, 24. Retrieved September 17, 2001, from Academic Index.

Web Page With Private Organization as Author

Midwest League. (2003). *Pitching, individual records.* Retrieved October 1, 2003, from www.midwestleague.com/indivpitching.html

Chapter or Section in an Internet Document

Thompson, G. (2003). Youth coach handbook. In *Joe soccer.* Retrieved September 17, 2004, from www.joesoccer.com/menu.html

Web Page, Government Author

Wisconsin Department of Natural Resources. (2001). *Glacial habitat restoration areas.* Retrieved September 18, 2001, from www.dnr.state.wi.us/org/land/wildlife/hunt/hra.htm

Company Information from Aggregated Database

Ripon Pickle Company Inc. (company profile). (2003). Retrieved September 18, 2002, from Business and Company Resource Center.
Ingersoll-Rand Company Limited (company profile). (2004). In *Hoovers.* Retrieved April 29, 2004, from Lexis-Nexis.

Personal Communications

Personal communications may include e-mail messages, interviews, speeches, and telephone conversations. Because the information is not retrievable, it should not appear in the reference list. These citations should appear as follows in the text:

P. Fox (personal communication, September 20, 2006) indicated that . . .

In a recent interview (P. Fox, personal communication, September 20, 2006), I learned that . . .

ADDITIONAL APA STYLE RULES

This discussion of some of the remaining rules of APA style comes from Russ Dewey, professor emeritus at Georgia Southern University's Department of Psychology and Bill Scott of the College of Wooster (2006), with thanks.[1]

Abbreviations

- Avoid abbreviations except for long, very familiar terms (MMPI).
- Explain what an abbreviation means the first time it occurs: American Psychological Association (APA).
- If an abbreviation is commonly used as a word, it does not require explanation (IQ, LSD, REM, ESP).
- The following abbreviations should **NOT** be used outside parenthetical comments:

  - **cf.** [use **compare**]
  - **e.g.** [use **for example**]
  - **etc.** [use **and so forth**]
  - **i.e.** [use **that is**]
  - **viz.** [use **namely**]
  - **vs.** [use **versus**]

    Incorrect: "I saw what Glicken calls e.g. northern lights in South America."

    Correct: "Glicken saw many unusual colors in the sky in South America (e.g., northern lights).

- Use periods when making an abbreviation within a reference (Vol. 3, p. 6, 2nd ed.)
- Do not use periods within degree titles and organization titles (PhD, APA).
- Do not use periods within measurements (lb, ft, s) except inches (in.).
- To form plurals of abbreviations, add "s" alone, without apostrophe (PhDs, IQs, vols., Eds.).
- When referring to several pages in a reference or citation, use the abbreviation pp. (with a period after it and a space after the period).
- Do not use the abbreviation "pp." for magazine or journal citations in your reference list; just give the numbers themselves. Do use "pp." for

citations of encyclopedia entries, multipage newspaper articles, chapters or articles in edited books.
- Use two-letter postal codes for U.S. state names (GA).

Avoiding Biased and Pejorative Language

In general, avoid anything that causes offense. The style manual makes the following suggestions:

DO NOT use . . .	when you can use . . .
ethnic labels (e.g., "Hispanic")	geographical labels (e.g., "Mexican Americans" if from Mexico)
"men" (referring to all adults)	"men and women"
"homosexuals"	"gay men and lesbians"
"depressives"	"people with depression"

Correct Use of the Terms "Gender" and "Sex"

The term "gender" should be used when referring to men and women as social groups, as in this example from the *Publication Manual:* "Sexual orientation rather than gender accounted for most of the variance in the results; most gay men and lesbians were for it, most heterosexual men and women were against it" (APA, 2001, p. 63).

The term "sex" refers to biology and should be used when biological distinctions are emphasized, for example, "sex differences in hormone production."

Avoid gender stereotypes. For example, the manual suggests replacing "An American boy's infatuation with football" with "An American child's infatuation with football" (see APA, 2001, p. 66).

Sensitivity to Labels

Be sensitive to labels. A person in a clinical study should be called a "patient," not a "case." Avoid equating people with their conditions. For example, do not say "schizophrenics," say "people diagnosed with schizophrenia." Use the term "sexual orientation," not "sexual preference." The phrase "gay men and lesbians" is currently preferred to the term "homosexuals." To refer to all people who are not heterosexual, the manual suggests "lesbians, gay men, and bisexual women and men" (APA, 2001, p. 67).

In racial references, the manual simply recommends that we respect current usage. Currently both the terms *Black* and *African American* are widely accepted, while *Negro* and *Afro-American* are not. These things change, so use common sense.

Capitalize *Black* and *White* when the words are used to refer to social groups. Do not use color words for other ethnic groups. The manual specifies that hyphens **should not** be used in multiword names such as Asian American or African American.

Labels can be tricky, and the manual has a lot to say about them. For example, "American Indian" and "Native American" are both acceptable usages, but the manual notes that there are nearly 450 Native American groups, including Hawaiians and Samoans, so specific group names are far more informative.

The terms "Hispanic," "Latino," and "Chicano" are preferred by different groups. The safest procedure is use geographical references as in "Cuban American" if referring to Americans from Cuba.

The term "Asian American" is preferable to "Oriental," and again, the manual recommends being specific about country of origin, when this is known (for example, "Chinese" or "Vietnamese").

In general, call people what they want to be called, and do not contrast one group of people with another group called "normal" people, for example: "We compared people with autism to people without autism" and not "we contrasted autistics to normals." Do not use pejorative terms like "stroke victim" or "stroke sufferers." Use a more neutral terminology such as "people who have had a stroke." Avoid the terms "challenged" and "special" unless the population referred to prefers this terminology (for example, Special Olympics). As a rule, use the phrase "people with _____" (for example, "people with AIDS," not "AIDS sufferers").

In referring to age, be specific about age ranges; avoid open-ended definitions like "under 16" or "over 65." Avoid the term "elderly." "Older person" is preferred. "Boy" and "girl" are acceptable when referring to children in high school and younger. For persons 18 and older, use "men" and "women."

Capitalization

- Capitalize formal names of tests (Beck Depression Inventory).
- Capitalize major words and all other words of four letters or more, in headings, titles, and subtitles outside reference lists, for example, "A Study of No-Win Strategies."
- Capitalize names of conditions, groups, effects, and variables only when definite and specific. (Group A was the control group; an Age x Weight interaction showed lower weight with age.)

- Capitalize the first word after a comma or colon if, and only if, it begins a complete sentence. For example, "This is a complete sentence, so it is capitalized." As a counter example, "no capitalization here."
- Capitalize specific course and department titles (CSU Department of Psychology, Psych 150).
- Do not capitalize generic names of tests (Stroop color test). "Stroop" is a name, so it remains capitalized.
- Capitalize nouns before numbers, but not before variables (Trial 2, trial x).
- Do not capitalize names of laws, theories, and hypotheses (the law of effect).
- Do not capitalize when referring to generalities (any department, any introductory course).

Commas

- Do not use commas to separate parts of measurement (9 lbs 5 oz).
- Use commas before "and" in lists, such as, *height, width, and depth.*
- Use commas between groups of three digits, for example: 1,453.
- Use commas to set off a reference in a parenthetical comment (Patrick, 1993).
- Use commas for a series within a paragraph or sentence, for example: "The three choices in this test are (a) true, (b) false, and (c) don't know."
- Use commas in exact dates, for example, April 18, 1992 (but not in April 1992).

Hyphenation

- Do not hyphenate *-ly* and words showing praise (*widely* used test, *best* informed students).
- Do not hyphenate common prefixes (posttest, prewar, multiphase, nonsignificant) **unless** they are needed for clarity (pre-existing).
- Do not hyphenate foreign terms, letters, or numeral terms, for example: a priori hypothesis, Type A behavior, heart rate scores.
- Do not hyphenate if a noun comes first (a therapy was client centered, results of t tests).
- Hyphenate phrases such as role-playing technique, high-anxiety group, two-way analysis.
- Hyphenate two connected descriptive words coming before the name of something (a noun). In the following example a noun would be the words *therapy* and *scores.* One would use a hyphen in the terms *client-centered therapy, cognitive-therapy,* and *t-test scores.* Do not hyphenate

when the noun includes a very positive statement such as, "the best written paper."
- Hyphenate when using an abbreviation such as pre-UND, or pre-FBI.
- Hyphenate if the base word is capitalized or a number (pre-Freudian, post-1960).
- Hyphenate if the words could be misunderstood without a hyphen (co-worker).
- If in doubt, consult a recently published dictionary. Standards change. For example, "data base" is now "database," and "life-style" is now "lifestyle."

Italics (Underlining)

- Do not italicize or underline common foreign words and abbreviations (vice versa, et al., a priori).
- Do not italicize or underline to emphasize a point.
- Italicize or underline the titles of books and articles, species names, introduction of new terms and labels (the first time only), words and phrases used as examples, letters used as statistical symbols, and volume numbers in reference lists.

Colons, Dashes, Parentheses, and Numbering Paragraphs

- Do not use "and/or." Write things out. For example, "Monday, Tuesday, or both" is preferable to "Monday and/or Tuesday."
- Use parentheses to introduce an abbreviation, for example, the galvanic skin response (GSR).
- Use *appendixes* as the plural of *appendix*. Use *datum* as singular, *data* as plural. Use *matrix* as singular, *matrices* as plural. *Phenomenon* is the singular form of the plural *phenomena*. Use *schema* as singular, *schemas* (not schemata) as plural.
- When listing separate paragraphs in a series, use a number and a period, not parentheses, for example: *4.* and not *(4)*. Remember to indent when using numbers, for example:
  1. The first paragraph goes here.
  2. The second paragraph goes here.

Numbers

- Spell out common fractions and common expressions (one-half, Fourth of July).
- Spell out numbers beginning sentences (Thirty days hath September . . .).

- Spell out numbers that are inexact, or below 10 and not grouped with numbers over 10 (one-tailed *t* test, eight items, nine pages, three-way interaction, five trials).
- Use numerals for numbers 10 and above, or lower numbers grouped with numbers 10 and above (for example, from 6 to 12 hours of sleep).
- To make plurals out of numbers, add *s* only, with no apostrophe (the 1950s).
- Use combinations of words and numbers as in (five 4-point scales).
- Use combinations of words and written numbers for large sums (over 3 million people).
- Use numerals for exact statistical references, scores, sample sizes, and sums (multiplied by 3, or 5% of the sample). Here is another example: "We used 30 subjects, all two-year-olds, and they spent an average of 1 hr 20 minutes per day crying."
- Use the percent symbol (%) only with figures (5%) not with written numbers (five percent).

Quotation Marks

- Use quotation marks for an odd or ironic usage the first time but not thereafter, for example, "This is the 'good-outcome' variable, but as it turns out, the good-outcome variable predicts trouble later on . . ."
- Use quotation marks for article and chapter titles cited in the text but not in the reference list. (In Smith's [1992] article, "APA Style and Personal Computers," computers were described as "here to stay" [p. 311].)

Extended Quotations

- If you use italics to add emphasis to part of an extended quotation put [italics added] immediately afterward.
- For quotations over 40 words in length (about 4 lines), indent the whole quoted passage and single space. This is called a block quotation or block indent. APA policy allows quotation of up to 500 words from copyrighted articles in APA journals without obtaining permission.
- Some professors expect single-spaced abstracts, block indents, and references in the final print-out. Others want their students to practice the rules for submitting an article to a publication, in which case double spacing is expected throughout. If in doubt, ask your professor.
- If there are paragraph breaks within an extended quotation, indent the first line after the paragraph break five more spaces (one-half inch, 1.25 cm).

- Always provide author, year, and page citation.
- Expand or clarify words or meanings in a quotation by placing the added material in brackets. For example, "They [the Irish Republican Army] initiated a cease-fire."
- Reproduce a quote exactly. If there are errors, introduce the word *sic* italicized and bracketed—for example [*sic*]—immediately after the error to indicate it was part of the original source.
- Use three dots with a space before, between, and after each dot (ellipsis points) when omitting material. Use four dots, with no space before the first, if the omitted material includes the end of a sentence. Do not use dots at the beginning or end of a quotation unless it is important to indicate the quotation begins or ends in midsentence.

SUMMARY

This summary of APA style is no substitute for the actual *Publication Manual of the APA*, which any serious student and professional should purchase and have readily available. It is true that most instructors in the human services require APA style in papers submitted, but some may require other styles. Students in these classes should make themselves aware of style requirements and use them appropriately.

FIND THE MISTAKES

1. APA style says you can quote 500 words from a journal article so it's not necessary to get permission from the copyright holder if you keep quotes below 500 words.
2. Rood, Surly, and Harry (2006, 2003, 1998) suggest that heart (1978) was correct when he said all men are not created equal, some have more money (p. 98). Or maybe it was Fitzgerald who told Hemingway that the rich are different than the rest of us and Hemingway said, yes they have more money.
3. Why can't we all get along. That's what somebody said after the Los Angeles riots. I think it was Rodney King but I'm not sure.
4. 55 pages is the correct number of pages for a report although sixty-six might be better if you're trying to suck up to a teacher and you need a good grade.
5. Viz a viz the authors name. I think its Johnson.

NOTES

1. *APA Research Style Crib Sheet*, by Russ Dewey, Georgia Southern University Psychology Department [Emeritus]. [This page is a summary of rules for using APA style, originally written by Russ Dewey, revised and updated by Bill Scott of the College of Wooster and Doc Scribe. We have made every effort to keep this document accurate, but readers have occasionally pointed out errors and inconsistencies that required correction. We are grateful to them and invite additional feedback. This document may be reproduced freely if this paragraph is included.]

REFERENCES

American Psychological Association. (2001). *Publication Manual of the American Psychological Association, 5th Edition.* Washington, DC: American Psychological Association.

Williams, O. E. (2005). *American Psychological Association format (5th edition)*, University of Minnesota, Crookston. Retrieved May 18, 2006, from www.crk.umn.edu/library/links/apa5th.htm

Dewey, R. (2002). *APA Research Style Crib Sheet.* Retrieved May 18, 2006, from www.psywww.com/resource/APA%20Research%20Style%20Crib%20Sheet.htm

6

Plagiarism, Proper Credit to Original Sources, and the Role of Human Subjects Protection

This chapter discusses the definitions of plagiarism and provides the reader with some examples. The chapter also discusses the need to protect people from involvement in research studies that might violate their civil rights. Plagiarism is the process of using the words and ideas of others as if you wrote them, while human subject protections require researchers to get approval for any research conducted as a student or employee of an organization, no matter how minor the research or how small the sample size may be.

PLAGIARISM

People occasionally get a little lazy when it comes to using the words of another writer. Sometimes they forget to place quotation marks around a block of words that someone else wrote. Other times they lift whole sections of someone's writing from an article or book and claim that it's theirs. Well, they don't necessarily claim that it's theirs, but they conveniently forget to note that it isn't. Plagiarism is considered cheating and it is an offense punishable by dismissal in many universities. My experience in reading thousands of student papers is that plagiarism is rampant. Students want professors to see how wise they are and it becomes a real temptation to substitute the wisdom and writing ability of a published author for their own efforts.

We now have another threat: Internet companies that sell papers on academic subjects, or tailor a paper for someone's use. It's a terrible temptation and you must, in the words of Nancy Reagan, "Just say no."

Here are the rules. Do your own writing. If you write badly, use the writing centers most universities provide to help students with writing problems. Have them look at your work, and let them help you write more smoothly. Give people credit for what they've written. If you are taking a sentence or two, or even a paragraph from someone's published work, place the material in quotes and provide the source with the name of the author, the date of the publication, and the page number, following the rules of the writing style you are using. Most human service fields use APA style. Chapter 5 should tell you almost everything you need to know about proper quotations but you may want to buy the *APA Publication Manual* (American Psychological Association, 2001) and consult it if you are in doubt. And don't use the Internet term paper mills that some of you may be considering. Professors know the difference between student work and professional work. There are now services that can identify papers written by Internet term paper mills.

> The head librarian at my former university told me an interesting story about plagiarism. A librarian checking graduate research projects was curious about the title of a project because it seemed so similar to one he had just seen. It turned out that the research project was a verbatim copy of a professional monograph. The student had taken it, title and all, and used it in place of his own original work. Let's forget that the professor who approved it must have been asleep at the wheel. The librarian notified the dean of students, who consulted the school attorney, the degree granted to the student was rescinded, and the record was changed to show that the student was expelled for cheating. This meant that the ability of the student to ever apply for state licensure was denied and that any government job application on which one lied about the episode and was hired would result in immediate termination.
>
> Plagiarism has major consequences. If you think professors are always going to miss plagiarism, or that they only scan your paper, or count the number of pages (I used to think that as an undergraduate and I'd write jokes in the middle of a paper until a professor called me in and told me how unfunny he thought it was), some instructor with strong feelings about plagiarism is going to walk into your life and make it miserable. (Glicken, 2003, pp. 83–84)

As another example of the existence of plagiarism, an educator in a graduate program in the human services told me the following story:

> I got an angry call from the mother of a graduate student I'd just taught in a course required to graduate. I don't know why the mother got involved, but the student had written me to ask me what her grade was. I had previously written her (prior to graduation) to tell her there was a "problem" with her final paper. When she wrote me, of course, it was after grades had been sub-mitted and she didn't ask me about her paper, she just wanted to know what her grade was. If she had responded to me prior to submission of grades, and

if she had taken responsibility for what she did, I likely would have given her an incomplete. Instead, I failed her for the assignment, which meant she didn't get a passing grade in the class. After I sent the e-mail telling the student the grade and why she got that grade—her mother called and asked what I meant giving her daughter a failing grade. I indicated that I was sure this was upsetting but that I wouldn't talk to her about her daughter's grade and would be happy to talk to her daughter. The student then called and started out saying that she was "insulted" that I would say that she plagiarized the paper. I calmly (more so than I felt because I thought it was likely that the mother was on an extension) explained that she had cut and pasted from four or five different websites and that I would be happy to show her the evidence of that. She then started crying and said good-bye. The next thing I heard was that she asked another professor to change her final grade in that class, which he wouldn't do. This all meant that she had to take another class to get her grade point average up—one of my colleagues agreed to do an independent study with her over this summer, which I assume she completed. That's it. In another case, it was a midterm paper, an "organizational assessment" which again, the student copied from the organization's website. In this case, the student took responsibility—well, she said she didn't mean to plagiarize and didn't know that she'd done it. She agreed to go to the writing center on campus, redid the paper, and earned a passing grade on it. (Personal communication, August 14, 2006)

I suspect that a good deal of plagiarism is unintentional, and that it occurs when students download material from the Internet and either forget the original source or forget that it was taken from another source altogether. Over the course of many weeks of writing a paper, the memory grows dim. For that reason, make certain that you immediately give credit for any material used in a paper by placing the author's name in the body of your paper as well as in the reference section at the end of your paper. When editing, be suspicious of any writing that doesn't look like yours. If you've paraphrased someone but haven't given them credit, go back to your notes and make certain to give the author credit for the material. These small mistakes often lead to concerns by your instructor that the writing isn't yours.

Rather than even considering plagiarism, you should consult with your instructor or others on your campus who can help you develop your paper and who understand the rules of plagiarism. As Susan Tschabrun, reference librarian at California State University, San Bernardino (2000, p. 1), writes in her paper on plagiarism, "Many term papers available for sale on the web are old and out-of-date." She goes on to add (and now I'm paraphrasing what she said and still giving her credit for the ideas) that instructors can help this process by checking drafts of a student's work as it progresses. They can ask for material and suggest that students bring in source information for any published article, book, or monograph from which they used any portion.

SOME PRACTICAL QUESTIONS AND
ANSWERS ABOUT PLAGIARISM

In this section, we will examine the proper use of citations. This can be a complex issue since book publishers and journals may have different rules when it comes to how much material you can use in a quotation without first asking permission of a book publisher or journal editor. The guiding principle is to ask for permission before using quotes of more than 300 words from any source. Even though APA journals allow you to use quotes of up to 500 words from an APA journal article, it's important to understand that the journal and probably the book publisher hold the rights to the material. They should be queried about permission and not the author, unless he or she holds the copyright. You can discover who holds the copyright by checking the front of the book. Even if I am quoting myself, I need to follow the same rule. If the quote is beyond a certain number of words, I require the permission of the publisher to reprint what I've written because the publisher may hold the copyright (ownership) of my books. Most publishers and journal editors are very generous in giving permission when your work is academic in nature, but not always. The National Association of Social Work charges, at last contact, $135 to reproduce the NASW Code of Ethics. Works of fiction, poetry, and music almost always carry a charge. A former publisher paid a poet $100 for a poem I used in a book. It was a great poem and worth it. Many authors of research instruments charge a fee. When in doubt, query the publisher or the editor of a journal in which the instrument appeared. Now, on to the rules giving credit to original sources, as followed in academic fields.

Rule 1: You must give the author credit in the body of the paper. Acknowledging the author's contribution in the reference section isn't sufficient.

Rule 2: Even though you are paraphrasing or summarizing the words of an author, you must still give the author credit within the body of the paper by providing the author's name and the date of the publication.

Rule 3: Although you have given the author credit before, it's safer to continue giving the author credit in the body of your paper whenever his or her ideas appear. If you are mentioning something that is common knowledge, however, it is not necessary to reference anyone. We all know that overeating leads to an increase in weight or that the use of illegal drugs may be addicting.

Rule 4: If you use the author's exact words, you will need to place quotation marks around the words, or indent and single space passages of more than four lines, for example:

As Soprano (2006) characterized psychotherapy in his novel about the Mob, "Mob member would never go to a psychotherapist. The guys on Second Avenue South in the Bronx know this as a fact. The word on the street is that you don't talk about your disagreements with anyone outside of the family. If you do, you end up sleeping with the fishes" (p. 143).

Rule 5: If you use material from sources that may not be accepted in your field, be sure to give support to those sources by showing that other authors or research studies agree. For example:

Hovanian (1984) believed that much of Freud's psychoanalytic approach was taken from passages and stories found in the Old Testament. Using content analysis, he found that 98% of Freud's concepts and theories can be found in the Old Testament, a finding replicated by David and Goliath (1988) and Samson and Delilah (1998).

MAKING UP DATA OR SOURCES

Of course, making up sources to pad a report is absolutely forbidden. Now mind you, I do it for the sake of examples, but I always alert the reader or make it so obvious that the reader knows I've made up a source. Well that's not quite true. A copy editor asked me to provide sources for a work that I'd written containing such gems as Macho and Mann, Taco and Bell, and Short, Brutish, and Surly. I guess what's obvious to one person isn't to another. It's best to alert readers just in case they think Soprano (2006) and his definition of the Mob are real.

Another type of plagiarism occurs when students and professionals make up data on a research report to support their original hypotheses. There are troubling examples of this practice in medicine and, unfortunately, in the human services. The following example comes from medicine, where a well-known researcher was accused of falsifying data related to the treatment of breast cancer. I'm using quotes sparingly and summarizing the article to keep the writing style consistent. As you read the following report, think about yourself or your loved ones grappling with the most effective form of breast cancer treatment and how you would feel later on, after making a decision about the best treatment, knowing there were serious problems with the research data whose findings helped you make your decision.

Falsifying Research Data: Reporting on the falsification of research data related to breast cancer, Fackelman (2004) describes the fright 32-year-old Jill Lea Sigal felt when she found out the data used to recommend that she have a lumpectomy for breast cancer had been falsified by the researchers. The landmark study found that taking a small amount of tissue from the breast and then using radiation to kill any remaining cancer cells was just as effective as a mastectomy where the entire breast was removed.

Fackleman (2004) reports that "Investigators discovered a number of cases in which key dates had been changed to make a patient appear eligible for a trial. In others, a crucial laboratory test, such as a hormone receptor value, had been altered" (p. 1). The Department of Health and Human Services also found that laboratory results were altered and that dates were changed by the researchers, according to Fackelman (2004).

Ironically, further research on the debate between mastectomies and lumpectomies has found that lumpectomies have significant value as a course of treatment in the early stages of breast cancer. However, because of concerns over the validity of the earlier studies, many women are skeptical about lumpectomies and remain unconvinced about their effectiveness, according to Fackelman (2004).

You should never falsify data. Science isn't about proving something, it's about testing variables until you find those that correlate. If they don't correlate, then you report those results. Unfortunately, falsifying data and plagiarism are ongoing problems in a society that is as "results oriented" as ours. My strong suggestion is that you work very hard at not plagiarizing or falsifying data.

HUMAN SUBJECT PROTECTIONS

Before a project involving human subjects (people) can be approved, even small research projects done for class assignments, the request for approval must be sent to a committee of an organization often called the human subjects committee. In some organizations it may also be called the institutional review board. In either case, its task is to make certain that your research does not violate the rights of subjects, and that the project is within ethical guidelines for the conduct of research. The request should contain the following information:

1. A letter (or letters) from any organization you intend to use to collect information stating that you have the right to conduct the research within the organization. Someone who speaks with authority for the organization must sign the letter.
2. Instruments (questionnaires, psychological tests, measures of social functioning) used in your study created by someone else must have the written approval of the author(s), or you must have evidence that the instrument is free to use and a letter of approval isn't necessary. Free instruments are often said to exist in the *public domain*. Sometimes instruments are created for the use of other researchers and are

free to use, but they may have copyrights, in which case you must have the author's approval in writing. Instruments that have copyrights may also require payment, although a student discount is sometimes offered. You must have evidence of approval for the use of an instrument before you can receive human subjects clearance, and you must include any instrument, developed by you or created by someone else, in the request for approval materials you send along for human subject review.

3. Your methodology must be free of anything that could potentially violate human rights. *Unobtrusive studies* where the subject doesn't know that he or she is being studied might be an example. Using people under the age of 18 without the consent of their parents would be unacceptable. Using incarcerated subjects who have lost certain rights without getting the consent of the organization that holds those rights (prisons, juvenile courts, etc.) would be unacceptable. Using subjects who can't read or understand their rights would be another example of a methodology that would not be acceptable to a human subjects review committee. This is why all material provided to subjects must be written in very simple language, or in the language the subject speaks. If consent and debriefing statements (discussed later in the chapter) are read to a subject, they must be read slowly, providing the subject with an opportunity to ask questions meant to clarify any statement that might be confusing or unclear.

4. You must include two additional documents in your request for human subjects approval. The first is known as an *informed consent* statement. This statement explains the research study and defines the rights of the subject. I've included a sample informed consent statement later in this chapter. The second document is a *debriefing statement*, which is given to subjects when they have completed their part in the study. The debriefing statement explains what the research study was trying to accomplish. It also tells subjects how they can get the final results of the study, and indicates where subjects can go for help if any of the questions asked on the instrument, or if any aspect of the study, caused them emotional pain. An example of a debriefing statement will also be found later in the chapter.

You may wonder why your small pieces of research may cause subjects pain. Occasionally, we ask subjects questions that make research subjects depressed or anxious since the questions remind them of early life experiences that were unpleasant or abusive. Some questions may make subjects feel bad about their current lives or they may prompt them to consider emotionally or physically self-destructive behaviors. Imagine what a job satisfaction survey might do to someone close to committing workplace violence against a co-worker? Remember that an organization is legally liable for any research study. If you've failed to get human subjects' approval from the correct committee, you'll be held liable, particularly if you've been told to get approval first and fail to do so. Never do a study before you have approval, and no matter how small the study may be, you should get guidance from your instructor or agency supervisor regarding the proper approval process before data collection begins.

An example of a study done without approval comes to mind. A student wanted to find out whether children taken from parental homes because of sexual abuse were molested in foster homes—a very important subject. The agency refused to allow the study arguing that the student didn't know the definitions of molestation well enough to make clear judgments. Furthermore, the agency worried that public knowledge of even occasional abuse in foster homes might so sway the courts against taking children from their highly dangerous parental homes where abuse was almost guaranteed to continue, that children would be at greater risk than ever. The agency agreed to allow the student to collect socio-demographic data on abusive biological families in cases where foster home placements were made. The extent of the study was to only collect information about race, ethnicity, income, and the gender of the accused abuser. That was the extent of the approval.

The student, a child victim of incest, as we discovered later, did exactly what the agency and the human subjects review board said she could not do. She used the records of child abuse victims to show high rates of continued abuse in foster care. She then gave the data to the local newspaper and, for months, the agency had to defend itself against charges of child endangerment. The agency sued the student, who was given a failing grade in her research course and was asked to appear before the university disciplinary board. Much as we can commend the student for the importance of the information she provided, to do a study at variance with the limits placed on the study by the human subjects review committee is unethical, and it could result in very serious repercussions.

5. You will need to describe any immediate and/or long-term risks to subjects that may result from the study. Risks may be legal, physical, social, emotional, or economic. Common risks might include side effects from the experimental input, risks from placebos, risks because of normal delays in treatment, questions that remind subjects of prior traumatic events, or risks to subjects as they look critically, and perhaps negatively, at their lives. You should also indicate any precautions you will take to minimize these risks as well as any anticipated benefits to participants and others as a result of the knowledge obtained in the study.

GUIDELINES FOR INFORMED CONSENT

1. The researcher(s) must identify themselves and give their organizational affiliation.
2. The researchers must explain the nature and purpose of the research, the research methodology, the expected length of time it will take for the subject to complete his or her part in the research, a description of the procedures to be followed, and a truthful disclosure of any procedures that might be harmful. You must be completely honest. If it takes most subjects 20 minutes to complete the study, you may not tell subjects on the informed consent form that it takes 10 minutes to complete. Also, you must tell the subject, in very clear and easily understood language, what the study is really about. You may not say it's about one thing in the informed consent and about something else in the debriefing statement.
3. A description of any foreseeable risks or discomfort to the subject must be included. If you have evidence from pretesting the study that the study may cause subjects discomfort, or if prior published research suggests risks to subjects, you must share those risks in your informed consent statement. Not to share them would be unethical even if it may discourage some subjects from taking part in the study.
4. A description of the benefits the research will have for the subjects or others must also be included. These benefits should either come from prior research or should be concluded after careful consideration. It is not fair to tell a subject that they will benefit from involvement in the study or that others will benefit if you have absolutely no plan to use the data in any constructive way. Publishing an article or presenting the findings at a conference might be constructive ways of using the data to benefit subjects.
5. A statement regarding the confidentiality of responses and the safeguards that protect the subject from being identified by his or her responses must be included in the informed consent. This is very important. At a former university, I filled out a questionnaire regarding how I felt about a certain issue and identified myself as a member of the social work faculty. To my amazement, the response was printed verbatim in the report and no one had any trouble identifying me as the source of the comment. The instrument had promised confidentiality but the researchers failed to use common sense in the way that promise was kept. In my view, their behavior was highly questionable since it breeched confidentiality and put me at risk. Similarly, when only a few members of a gender or ethnic group are included in a study, most people can easily identify the respondents when data are presented. Be careful that when you assure subjects of confidentiality, you actually provide it.

6. If injury to the subject is possible (as in the case of medical or physical experiments), an explanation of compensation and the availability of medical care, if injury takes place, must be included. In the social sciences, emotional risk may be present because questions negatively affect the subject by bringing up traumatic experiences from the past that are emotionally upsetting. It may not be enough to suggest avenues of help if this happens. Rather, the organization may be *required* to offer free services for any unintended risk.

7. The name of the person to contact in order to receive answers to pertinent questions about the project, the subject's rights, or research-related injuries or emotional problems brought about by the research should be included on the informed consent statement. This is usually your research instructor thesis chair or agency supervisor. You should not use their names unless they consent to having them used.

8. A statement must be provided in the informed consent that participation in the study is voluntary. Furthermore, the informed consent should make clear that there are no penalties for refusing to participate in the study, and that at any time during the study, the subject may voluntarily discontinue his or her involvement. This is very important. The guarantee of voluntary involvement cannot be too strongly stated. Remember that the word "voluntary" is often a very loosely defined term. By offering failing students added points for involvement in a study, the term "voluntary" takes on a different meaning. If a subject thinks that not taking part in a study might offend a teacher or an employer, the term "voluntary" obviously takes on a different meaning. Voluntary means that direct or subtle pressure to be included in a study cannot be placed on a subject. If it is, involvement in a study is no longer voluntary.

9. Minors under the age of 18 cannot be involved in a research study without the written consent of their guardians. If the child is above the age of 7, the child's consent is also required. Sometimes a waiver of parental approval can be requested if the study involves no risks to the child and isn't about a topic that may be sensitive to the subject. In this case, the organization in which the study is being done would contact the parent and describe the research. The organization would also note that it is giving the researcher permission to conduct the study and explain why but that parents can contact the school in writing to deny their child's involvement in the research study.

An Example of an Informed Consent

The following is an example of an informed consent statement (Glicken, 2003, p. 233). You should be sure that your informed consent statement is similar to the one normally used at your university or organization.

The study in which you may voluntarily participate is a study of stressors related to work on the MSW Degree. The study is being conducted by Dr. Jesse McBain, Dean of the Brower Michigan University School of Applied Social Service in Mt. Pleasant, Michigan. The study has been approved by the Institutional Review Boards of Brower Michigan University and the BMU School of Applied Social Service. The school and the university require that you give your consent before participating in this or any other research study.

In this study, you will fill out a three (3) part survey. The first part asks socio-demographic questions such as age, gender, years of education, etc. The second part contains the Beck Anxiety Measure (the BAM). The third part contains questions related to the reasons (if any) for your level of stress, and whether it directly relates to being in an MSW Program. The instrument you will be given will not have your name on it to ensure complete anonymity of responses. Please note that you are not required to fill out the instrument and you can refuse to take or complete it at any time you wish. Completion of the instrument has taken most of our test respondents about 20 minutes, but it may take you more or less time than that.

Please be assured that findings will be reported in group form only. No identifying information will be used that may identify you. At the conclusion of the study, you may, upon request, receive a copy of the findings.

Questions related to stress as a result of the MSW may cause you emotional discomfort. The debriefing statement, which will be given to you when you have completed your part in the study, has the names and numbers of mental health and family service agencies you may contact to help discuss and resolve any emotional discomfort. You may also contact the counseling center at Brower Michigan University.

If you have any questions about the study, or if you would like a report of the findings, you may contact Dr. Jesse McBain at 012-434-6711. If you have any questions about this research study, your rights as a participant, or potential injuries or negative emotional side effects, please contact the Institutional Review Board of the university at 012-434-6711.

By checking the box provided below and dating this form, you acknowledge that you have been informed and understand the nature of the study and freely consent to participate. You further acknowledge that you are at least 18 years of age.

I Agree to Participate in the Study: _____ (Check if you agree)
Today's Date Is: _____

_____   _____
Participant's Signature   Date

_____   _____
Researcher's Signature   Date

THE DEBRIEFING STATEMENT

The debriefing statement is given to the subject upon completion of his or her role in the study. The debriefing statement is a way of informing the subject about the intent of the study and clarifying how the results will be used. In essence, the debriefing statement tries to answer questions the subject might have after taking part in the study. You should include the following in your debriefing statement:

1. An explanation of what the study is actually about. If methods were used that were somewhat misleading (as in the case of the researcher who asks questions about one topic when the study was actually about something very different), that deception must be explained along with the reason for the deception. An example of a deception is the student who asked therapists to use the diagnostic manual of the American Psychiatric Association (the DSM-IV, American Psychiatric Association, 1994) to diagnose clients with certain emotional problems. Vignettes were created describing the client, but three different versions were given identifying the client as Christian, Jewish, or Muslim. The purpose of the study was to determine if the religion of the subjects somehow affected the diagnosis given by the therapists. The student found that clients in the vignette who were described as Christian had the least serious diagnosis, Jewish subjects were given a more serious diagnosis, while Muslim subjects were given the most serious diagnosis. Had she initially told the subjects what she was doing, she may have received very different results. She explained the research method in her debriefing statement and the reason she used it, but might the research subjects think that they'd been misled? You be the judge.
2. If the subject has an unexpected physical or emotional response to the study, provisions must be included to describe where he or she might get help and who will pay for it. If we're really ethical, treatment for all problems that result from involvement in a study should be paid for by the researcher. Of course, determining if we're actually liable can be difficult. Most researchers don't include the issue of payment in the debriefing statement, believing that subjects will seek unneeded help if they do. Other researchers may contract with an organization to provide free help if a subject requires it. Again, we should be guided by the principle of doing what is right.
3. The subject must be given the name of a person he or she can contact to receive the results of the study. That person must be a member of the organization under whose auspices the research was done. Your research instructor would be a good example.

4. You may want to add a statement asking subjects not to reveal the predicted outcomes of the study to other potential subjects since revealing the outcomes may bias the final results of the study. Although this is a good idea, it is one that may be difficult to enforce. Some researchers deal with potential problems of contagion by adding to the debriefing statement that final results of the study cannot be reported until all data are tabulated. Sharing the predicted results or the purpose of the study with other participants may give misleading information and may unduly upset participants. Subjects who know what a study is about before they participate is always a problem for researchers.

An Example of the Debriefing Statement

This research study was conducted by Dr. Jesse McBain, Professor of Social Work and Dean of The Brower Michigan University School of Applied Social Service in Mt. Pleasant, Michigan. Its purpose is to find out whether the MSW Program you are in has caused you unmanageable levels of stress. The instrument used in the study was the Beck's Anxiety Measurement, an instrument that is frequently used to measure levels of anxiety. The study was approved by the Institutional Review Board at Central Michigan University in Mt. Pleasant, Michigan.

Stress in academic programs is sometimes controllable and the study you participated in will try and determine those aspects of a student's level of stress that can be controlled for by the academic program. Examples might include when courses are offered (time and day of the week), duplication of assignments, when assignments are due, and many other issues the school can and will control for if students report unwanted levels of stress.

If any of the questions asked on the Beck's Anxiety Measurement or any aspect of the research caused you any emotional stress, you can contact your local family service agency. You can find the number of the agency in the yellow pages of your telephone book or by calling 1-800-564-8956.

A brief summary of the findings and conclusions of the study will be available after June 1, 2008 and can be obtained by calling Dr. McBain at 021-434-6711. Thank you for your participation in the study. (Glicken, 2003, p. 236)

SUMMARY

This chapter discusses that troubling aspect of writing known as plagiarism, or using someone else's work and letting the reader assume it is yours. There are serious consequences for plagiarizing, including dismissal from school. The chapter cautions against falsifying data in research reports or making up sources that don't exist to pad reports. Also included in the chapter is information about human subjects approval for research projects and the material needed for approval. Examples of informed consent and debriefing statements are provided in the chapter.

FIND THE MISTAKES

1. It is permissible to use material you've previously written without citing that source if you hold the copyright or, in the case of a course, if you've done the work yourself.
2. It is permissible to use papers written by others as your own work as long as you've paid the author and, somewhere in the paper, give the author credit for the work.
3. Teachers warn students about plagiarism but, in reality, do little to a student once they find that something the student has done is plagiarized. Teachers only care about whether you know the material.
4. Falsifying data is done every day. As long as you write an intelligent paper, there's nothing wrong, ethically or in reality, with making up data and sources. Lots of writers and scientists do it every day.
5. We live in a world where reality and fiction collide with one another. Just read the newspaper or watch TV. You can never really say that what you've read or watched is true since corporations manipulate the news for their own gain. It's no big deal to make things up because made up material is much more entertaining and can often make a stronger impression on the reader.

REFERENCES

American Psychiatric Association. (1994). *Diagnostic and Statistical Manual of Mental Disorders*, 4th ed. New York: American Psychiatric Association.

American Psychological Association. (2001). *Publication Manual of the American Psychological Association*, 5th ed. Washington, DC: American Psychological Association.

David and Goliath. (1988). Fictitious source.

Fackelman, K. A. (2004). Breast cancer research on trial; Congress hears a tale of false data, delays, and doubts. Originally published April 20, 1994, in *Science News*. Retrieved June 9, 2006, from www.findarticles.com/p/articles/mi_m1200/is_n18_v145/ai_15407317/print

Glicken, M. D. (2003). *Social research: A simple guide*. Boston: Allyn and Bacon/Longman.

Hovanian. (1984). Fictitious source.

Samson and Delilah. (1998). Fictitious source.

Soprano. (2006). Fictitious source.

Tschabrun, S. (2000). Plagiarism: Internet style. *John M. Phau Library Newsletter*, 1–2 [online]. Retrieved December 31, 2001, from www.lib.csusb.edu

7

Writing Objective Client Assessments

The issue of objective client assessments is not just one of correct writing; it also involves worker objectivity and knowledge. Before we consider an example of an objective client assessment, perhaps a discussion of the problem of worker objectivity and the approaches we use in assessment might be helpful.

In an attempt to make client assessments more objective, the profession has developed a number of diagnostic tools, including the *Diagnostic and Statistical Manual* (DSM) series. The DSM-IV (American Psychiatric Association, 1994) provides clinicians with easy to follow guidelines that permit a diagnostic category to be chosen that should, if the guidelines are followed accurately, be consistent with the diagnosis other clinicians would give for a particular emotional problem. However, the DSM has been roundly criticized because it fails to provide an individual framework from which to fully understand the environmental and historical factors affecting the client and, as a result, seems to be overly focused on pathology (Saleebey, 1996). The client's uniqueness is seldom represented by a DSM diagnosis, nor are positive client behaviors noted that often determine whether the client will improve. Cloud (2003) has a more fundamental concern about the DSM and writes:

> . . . [C]an even a thousand Ph.D.s gathered at a dozen conferences ever really know the significance of such vague symptoms as "fatigue," "low self-esteem" and "feelings of hopelessness"? (You need only two of those, along with a couple of friends telling the doctor you seem depressed, to be a good candidate for something called dysthymic disorder.) Though it's fashionable these days to think of psychiatry as just another arm of medicine, there is no biological test for any of these disorders. (p. 105)

Cloud has additional concerns about the DSM-IV: diagnostic categories were determined by ad hoc committee decisions that were often contentious and were only resolved by pleas for agreement and consensus, and DSM-IV is just a checklist of symptoms used to justify an emotional condition.

Whaley (2001) believes that Caucasian clinicians often diagnose African American clients with paranoid symptoms that are more fundamentally a cultural distrust of Caucasians because of racism. He believes that the diagnostic process with African American clients tends to discount the negative impact of racism and leads to diagnostic judgments suggesting more pathology than really exists. This tendency to misdiagnose, or to diagnose a more serious condition than may be warranted, is what Whaley calls "pseudo-transference" and has its origins in cultural stereotyping by clinicians who fail to understand the impact of racism, ultimately leading to "more severe diagnoses and restrictive interventions" (p. 558) with African American clients. Whaley's work suggests that clinicians may incorrectly use diagnostic labels with clients they either feel uncomfortable with, or whose cultural differences create some degree of hostility, casting doubt on the accuracy of diagnostic labels with an entire range of clients based on race, ethnicity, gender, religious orientation, and social class.

In describing examples of incorrect diagnoses, "Morey and Ochoa (1989) asked 291 psychiatrists and psychologists to complete a checklist of symptoms for a client whom they had diagnosed with a personality disorder. When the checklists were later correlated with the DSM criteria, nearly three of four clinicians had made mistakes in applying the diagnostic criteria" (McLaughlin, 2002, p. 259). In a sample of 42 psychologists and 17 psychiatrists, Davis, Blashfield, and McElroy (1993) had the sample read and diagnosed case reports containing different symptoms of Narcissistic Personality Disorder (NPS). Ninety-four percent of the sample of clinicians made mistakes applying the diagnostic criteria, while 25% diagnosed NPS when less than half of the DSM criteria were met.

In another example of incorrect diagnosis based on first impressions, Robertson and Fitzgerald (1990) randomly assigned 47 counselors to watch videos of a depressed male portrayed by an actor. The only changes made in the videos were the client's work (professional vs. blue collar) and the client's family or origin (traditional or nontraditional). The researcher found that counselors made more negative diagnostic judgments when the actor portrayed a blue-collar worker and came from a nontraditional family. The signs and symptoms of any specific emotional disorders were secondary to the worker's bias.

In yet another example of a type of bias known as a self-confirmatory bias, or diagnosis based only on the information collected by the clinician that confirms his or her original diagnosis, Haverkamp (1993) had counseling and counseling psychology students watch a video of an initial counseling session and then write down the questions they wanted to ask in a follow-up session with the client. The results were that the majority of students (64%) wanted to ask questions that confirmed their original diagnostic impression of the client. A follow-up study by Pfeiffer, Whelan, and Martin (2000) came to similar conclusions. In a similar type of error, the error of using treatment approaches that confirm one's original diagnosis, Rosenhan (1973) had research associates admitted to a psychiatric hospital after complaining of auditory hallucinations. Even though the researchers stopped complaining about their symptoms once admitted, the treatment staff continued to diagnose their behaviors as symptoms of a serious mental illness when none was present.

REDUCING ERRORS IN DIAGNOSIS

McLaughlin (2002) suggests the following ways of reducing errors in diagnosing:

1. Don't make too much or too little of the evidence at hand.
2. Try to note the biasing effect of your workplace that may routinely diagnose everyone in the same way.
3. Try to disprove a diagnosis.
4. Consistently use all of the DSM diagnostic criteria and keep current about revisions.
5. Be aware of other disorders, or a dual diagnosis, and delay making a diagnosis until you have more data.
6. Use symptom checklists to make certain your diagnosis adheres to DSM categories, and follow a logical protocol to collect and evaluate data about the client before finalizing a diagnosis.
7. If you use psychological instruments in diagnosis, make certain they are valid and reliable with the type of client you are diagnosing (by age, gender, ethnicity, etc.).
8. Be absolutely certain your expectations for the client do not reflect racial, ethnic, gender, or religious bias, or self-fulfilling prophecies about certain diagnostic categories.
9. Remember the importance of social factors in diagnosis and that the DSM may have a built-in bias against certain groups.
10. Consider other diagnostic possibilities and understand that the more time you take to get to know the client, the more likely you are to arrive at a correct diagnosis.
11. Consider the pros and the cons of a diagnosis before formally using it with a client.

12. Use multiple diagnostic instruments to determine a diagnosis, and accept a diagnosis only if those instruments are in agreement with one another.
13. Focus on what may be atypical about a client and follow those leads to help determine a diagnosis.
14. Follow ethical standards.
15. Use training to improve your diagnostic work, particularly with diverse ethnic and cultural groups.

WRITING AN OBJECTIVE CLIENT ASSESSMENT

A client assessment is our best effort to place all of the relevant information we know about a client into a concise statement that permits another professional reader to understand the client and the client's problem(s) as well as we understand them. Assessments should be tightly written without rambling or excessive theorizing about the client that may confuse the issue and the reader. The more factual and objective the writing, the better the assessment. I'm not happy with clinicians who take notes while clients are trying to tell their story since it breaks the flow for the client and makes the client wonder if you're more interested in the client or in the report you intend to write. If you've ever watched clients who are talking to clinicians who write notes, they tend to slow down and wait for the clinician to finish writing. Note-taking also makes clients a little paranoid. Not without reason, they wonder what they said that prompted the clinician to write something down. I try to summarize at the end of the session and then ask the client if I have it right. After the interview is done, I then write my notes for the assessment.

Client assessments differ from DSM-IV diagnostic statements in that they provide brief historical information about the possible causation of the problem. They also try to describe behavior rather than labeling it. It's much more difficult to describe the behavior of a person who appears depressed than to just use the label. The benefit of the description of behavior is that, in the final analysis, you may be describing something very different than depression. You may also miss many of the client's positive attributes that aren't available to the reader when using a label. The word "depression" implies sadness and lack of energy. Your client may have this behavior, but he or she might also show great resilience, positive behavior in work and parenting, a very positive value base, and many other attributes that trump the term "depression."

Learning to describe behavior requires very tight writing skills, the accurate use of language, and refined observational skills. You must see and hear what the client says and does nonverbally at a very high level to accurately

describe behavior. Let's consider a client who appears to be exhibiting depressed behavior and see how this evolves when we describe the behavior
rather than label it.

> Jason Anderson is a 57-year-old unmarried middle school teacher who says that
> his main problem is a chronic, long-lasting depression of more than 5 years'
> duration. Although Mr. Anderson describes bouts of crying and sadness, he is
> always at work on time, never misses work because of his depression, is a lov-
> ing and attentive father to his three adult children, works in the community as
> a volunteer big brother to children whose fathers are absent, and writes pub-
> lished poetry. He says that he seldom drinks alcohol and never uses drugs. He
> indicates that his health is excellent but he has not had a physical examination
> or been to a doctor in more than 10 years.
>
> During the interview, Mr. Anderson used a number of hand and facial
> gestures to emphasize a point he was making. He told several very funny self-
> deprecating stories about himself, which he told while smiling. He noted that
> he loves his work and that working with children gives him great joy. His eyes
> became teary when he spoke about his work. He leaned forward in his chair
> throughout the interview, smiled a great deal, and seemed very comfortable
> and forthcoming. He was able to talk openly about his feelings of depression
> and had charted when he felt depressed and what seemed to trigger the prob-
> lem. He had also done a great deal of reading about depression, and shared
> his confusion with the worker over many articles describing depression in ways
> that were not consistent with how he felt. He shook hands at the end of the
> session. His handshake was firm and his hand was dry. He looked directly at
> me and thanked me for my suggestions and attentiveness. He said he had some
> "stage fright" about the interview in the beginning, but he felt comfortable with
> the process very quickly. He said he was optimistic about the suggestions I had
> made.
>
> He has never thought that his feelings of sadness might have a biological
> origin. At my suggestion, he had a physical that found a hypothyroid condi-
> tion, which often results in feelings of depression. A month after beginning a
> regimen of medication to raise his thyroid level to acceptable levels, he no
> longer experiences feelings of depression. He has asked to continue seeing
> me concerning problems he has experienced in finding suitable people to
> date.

As you can see, it would have been easy to label the client as depressed,
since that is how he saw himself, but the evidence seemed to indicate that
he wasn't depressed in a traditional way. He works, he volunteers, he has
a loving relationship with his children, and he wants to improve his social
life. He seemed very positive and animated in the interview. These are not
necessarily the behaviors of a depressed person, and the worker correctly
suggested a physical cause. It turns out the worker was right, and what could
have been a long drawn out process to treat his depression became a very
different and much more helpful process.

Although psychosocial assessments are problem focused, they also provide an evaluation of the client's strengths. The following case study is done using a strengths perspective approach to assessment as described in the following statement by Van Wormer (1999):

> At the heart of the strengths perspective is a belief in the basic goodness of humankind, a faith that individuals, however unfortunate their plight, can discover strengths in themselves that they never knew existed. No matter how little or how much may be expressed at one time, people often have a potential that is not commonly realized. The first step in promoting the client's well-being is through assessing the client's strengths. A belief in human potential is tied to the notion that people have untapped resources—physically, emotionally, socially, and spiritually—that they can mobilize in times of need. This is where professional helping comes into play—in tapping into the possibilities, into what can be, not what is. (p. 51)

AN EXAMPLE OF AN OBJECTIVE ASSESSMENT: MR. SOLOMON

This case study first appeared in modified form in Glicken (2005, pp. 92–105). It is used to demonstrate how one might write an objective client evaluation. The outline used is for illustrative purposes only. Under each heading there is a description of the information one might include. The important thing to remember is that the assessment provides information to other professionals. It necessarily needs to include all of the information relevant to the case.

Section I

Brief Description of the Client and the Problem: In this section of a client assessment, the worker should include the client's age, marital status, family composition, what the client was wearing, the client's level of verbal and nonverbal communication, the client's affect, and anything of interest that happened in the interview. You should also include the defined problem(s) as stated by the client. Interpretations are normally not made here and only relevant factual information is included. Section I might be written as follows:

> Hal Solomon is a 32-year-old entrepreneur whose presenting problem is a sense of unworthiness over earning more than a million dollars each year in the past 10 years of his work career. He says that the amount of money he has earned is considerably out of keeping with the degree of energy used, and that compared to people who do "real work," it seems completely wrong for him to earn so much money.

Mr. Solomon came to the interview on time, wore dress slacks and a polo shirt, is deeply tanned, and says that he is 6'1" and weighs 165 pounds. He runs 5 miles a day and works out in the gym at least an hour every day. He wore no rings or other jewelry, but he did have on a gold Rolex watch. Initially, he moved around a great deal in his chair and his fingers continually tapped on the arm of his chair. After 5 minutes, he slumped back in his chair and, from time to time, wiped tears from his eyes as he discussed the impact his career has had on his former marriage, family life, and on issues of intimacy. He comes to treatment for help in resolving problems of continued feelings of unworthiness, depression, and guilt that have lasted a duration of more than 2 years and which began with his divorce several years ago.

Section II

Historical Issues: This section includes any past issues of importance in understanding the client's current problems. Continuing on with Mr. Solomon, these might be the salient points to include in the historical section of our report:

Mr. Solomon became an entrepreneur in the computer field after his sophomore year at Stanford University. He has not returned to finish his degree and says that his lack of formal education makes him feel insecure about his intellectual abilities. However, he reads a great deal and has tried to make up for his lack of formal education by reading books recommended by people he respects. Mr. Solomon has an older brother (3 years older) and a younger sister (4 years younger). His parents, both deceased, were very opposed to his decision to become a businessman. In his strict Orthodox Jewish family, this seemed to his parents to be a career that would take him away from the moral, religious, and spiritual beliefs of his Orthodox Jewish background. His father frequently told him that businessmen were the very people who most condoned anti-Semitism in Nazi Germany, and who often do whatever is situationally necessary to make money. His parents wanted Mr. Solomon to enter a service field, and had hoped that he would become a scholar or a physician.

Both parents were Holocaust survivors. The client describes them as serious, hyper-vigilant, continually fearful, and unaffectionate. When they died, he was not speaking to them because of their opposition to his career and because he had married a non-Jewish woman. He has only a superficial relationship with his siblings, seldom seeing or calling them. He has no other contact with a small extended family consisting of an aunt and uncle and several cousins on his father's side of the family, all of whom live more than a thousand miles away. Almost all of his extended family perished in Europe during the Holocaust.

Mr. Solomon and his ex-wife had serious problems because his business career required him to be away from the home a great deal. The couple often fought and, on several occasions, hit one another. Mr. Solomon believes that his wife was trying to make him jealous. In time, he discovered that she was having an affair with one of her co-workers. As a result, the marriage ended in a bitter divorce two years ago following five years of marriage. There were no children.

Mr. Solomon has felt depressed since the divorce. The negative feelings about his career and the money he has made began about the time of the divorce and with the death of both parents shortly after the divorce. He feels angry that they had stopped talking to him because of his marriage, and said that he had a great deal of "unfinished business" with them when they both died within a year of his divorce. The most important piece of unfinished business was that his parents performed the ancient Jewish ritual of saying *Kaddish* over him (the prayer for the dead), because his wife was non-Jewish, which effectively removed him from the family. They never tried to contact him after he became divorced. He said that in his most important hour of need his parents were not there for him.

He is proud to be Jewish but thinks it is a religion that often causes friction because it can be so demanding, and because it tends to isolate Jews from non-Jewish people. To help him deal with his ambivalent feelings about his religion, Mr. Solomon attends discussion groups, reads a great deal about Jewish history and traditions, and has tried to understand and resolve his confused relationship with Judaism. It is an attempt that isn't always successful, but he continues to try.

He describes an early life full of success and accomplishments because of his ability with computers. His relationships with people, however, have always been difficult, and he describes himself as being shy, introverted and unable to trust others. He has few friends in the business world and feels very much alone because he is the only Jewish businessman in his area in a business dominated by non-Jewish people. He has experienced a great deal of anti-Semitism in his work and says that the people he is in competition with can be very cruel in their continuing efforts to try and "psych" him out by making rude and bigoted remarks about Jews in his presence.

He reports just one other episode of depression or anxiety in his life, which occurred about the time he decided to marry. He believes the cause of the depression was the conflict with his parents over the marriage. He says that he is healthy, although he sometimes feels easily fatigued. He has no sleeping problems and has kept his weight fairly stable. He is not currently in a relationship and feels that his trust level for relationships is very low. He was on a tranquilizer several years ago because of anxiety and depression during the divorce but cannot remember the name of the medication. He says that it made him sleepy and that he discontinued its use because it interfered with his work.

Section III

Diagnostic Statement: The diagnostic statement is a brief overview of the most relevant problems experienced by the client, and includes their potential causation. In the diagnostic statement, we combine material from the prior two sections and summarize the most relevant information in a brief statement. The conclusions we draw must be logical and need to follow the information we've noted in prior sections. Continuing with Mr. Solomon, this is an example of the diagnostic statement:

> Mr. Solomon is a 32-year-old divorced Jewish entrepreneur who seeks help for feelings of guilt and depression over the large amount of money he has made in a career that he describes as "frivolous." He describes ongoing feelings of isolation and loneliness and is concerned over his inability to trust others. The onset of these feelings seems to have coincided with the death of his parents and the divorce from his wife as a result of her infidelity. All three events took place within months of one another.
>
> Further issues that need exploration include his relationship with his deceased parents; his difficulty in handling the anti-Semitic behavior of his colleagues; problems in relating to people, particularly women; the degree to which an increasingly troublesome depression is interfering with his life; and feelings of guilt over his choice of a career that has earned him a large amount of money in a field of work he considers frivolous.
>
> Mr. Solomon has many positive behaviors that should be particularly helpful in his treatment. He is successful at work; he has a very strong value system; he is introspective and feels concern over his current emotional state; and he has some insight into the origins of his problems with his parents, siblings, and former wife. He appears to be highly motivated to change. Although he suffers from a steady degree of depression, he is still able to work at a successful level. He longs for more intimacy and wants to form the types of caring relationships that have been so elusive in his life. He values education and has made a conscious effort to improve his general level of knowledge in an attempt to make up for an early withdrawal from college. He also seeks more information about his religion and seems genuinely interested in finding out more about the history and the traditions of Judaism—information he resisted earlier in his life.
>
> Currently, a beginning diagnostic impression is that his depression and feelings of unworthiness may be related to his parents' opinion of his career. Their death before he could resolve serious problems with them and his divorce about the time his parents died have reinforced a belief that he is being punished for a career at odds with his parents' notion of the serious and high-minded work they envisioned for him—work that might serve to be a repayment for the fact that his parents both lived through the Holocaust while others, more worthy perhaps, perished. His depression may stem from a belief that a frivolous career has somehow made him a frivolous person, and that work has destroyed his primary relationships.
>
> There is no evidence at this point of severe emotional problems that might result in further depression or suicide. He appears to think rationally, is highly motivated to change, is articulate and bright, speaks about his problems openly and without anxiety, and relates easily. He has never been in therapy. Although he is fearful of the process, he is optimistic that it will help him. While he complains of depression and fatigue, he continues to do well in his

work, exercises daily, and has wisely invested his large income for the future. He is an avid reader and has tried to use available literature to understand and resolve many of his problems, sometimes effectively. The prognosis for improvement is very positive at this initial stage of treatment.

Section IV

The Treatment Plan: The treatment plan describes the goals of treatment during a specific period of time and comes from the agreement made between the worker and client in the contractual phase of treatment. In this example, I am using 12 sessions over a 3-month period. The treatment plan for Mr. Solomon might be written as follows:

> The goals of treatment the client and the worker have mutually agreed on during the initial three-month contract are as follows:
>
> (1) To help Mr. Solomon understand important connections between his current feelings of depression and guilt, the consequences of his choice of careers, the conflict with his parents, and an unsuccessful relationship with his ex-wife; (2) to help him develop new relationships and to discuss issues of intimacy; (3) to continue to evaluate his depression and to refer him for a psychiatric consult to consider medication for relief of lingering symptoms of depression; (4) to evaluate the issue of anti-Semitism in his business dealings, and to help him develop better ways of coping with that problem; (5) to help him explore the possibility of continuing his education; (6) to help him understand his ambivalent feelings about Judaism; (7) to help him develop a relationship with his siblings and extended family; (8) through the therapeutic relationship, help him to "defrost, to open up, to experience and to accept himself. This becomes possible for the patient only in a warm, mutually trusting relationship in which, often for the first time in his life, he feels truly accepted as he is, accepted with those aspects of himself which early in life he had felt compelled to reject or repress" (Weiss, 1961, p. 474). In this way, Mr. Solomon will ". . . begin to reveal surprising aliveness and depth, passionate longings, and strong feelings of loss." (Weiss, 1961, p. 475)

Section V

Contract: This is the agreement between the worker and the client. It determines the problems to be worked on in treatment, the number of sessions agreed to, and other relevant rules related to time, payment, and cancellation policies. Many workers put these rules in written form, with the client and the worker signing the contract. A contract with Mr. Solomon might read as follows:

> Mr. Solomon has agreed to 12 one-hour sessions to be held over the next 3 months. However, he understands that more therapy might be necessary. The

treatment plan, outlining the areas of work during the next 3 months, was developed jointly with Mr. Solomon and all the areas of treatment have his approval. We have agreed to evaluate the effectiveness of our work together after each session. After 12 sessions, we will evaluate the cumulative impact of treatment to date and renegotiate additional sessions, if required. He has signed the contractual agreement that spells out the other issues of the contract, including time, payment, and the cancellation policy.

DISCUSSION OF THE CASE

Although this is a book about writing, it is also a book that is meant to help you understand the issues we write about. When I work with clients, I read the literature to better understand the client and the issues about which I may know very little. I went to the literature on Holocaust survivors and their children to better understand Mr. Solomon's family life. It's difficult to overstate the harmful consequences to normal family functioning that such an experience might have. With the children of survivors of genocide, one often finds hypervigilance, lack of trust, an inability to form relationships, very superficial notions of intimacy, confusion about identity, deep feelings of despair over what happened to their parents, and the child's impossible job of empathizing with the parents' early life traumas when parents are sometimes emotionally distant, critical, or have very high expectations (Hass, 1991, p. 97).

Children of survivors often sense fragility in parents who sometimes suffer from serious physical and emotional problems because of their experiences. Survivors may have nightmares about the death camps, or they may have obsessive thoughts about real or imagined dangers that are transmitted to their children. They may see their homes as a fortress and not permit anyone but a few trusted people inside. They may suffer from deep-seated and long-lasting depressions. Their worldview may be cynical and pessimistic, and they may use their children to help protect them against the potential danger they always anticipate. In this type of environment, there is a strong sense that children must obey their parents. If they don't, horrible things might happen to the family. Stories are shared that reinforce the terror parents experienced in the camps, stories that often make their children frightened and distrustful (Baron, Eisman, Scuello, Veyzer, and Lieberman, 1996).

The attempts by Mr. Solomon's parents to stress obedience probably come from a deep reservoir of fear that what happened to them in the death camps of Europe could also happen to their children. Many survivors of genocide have problems with intimacy. For Jewish survivors of genocide, the people who are seen as threats to their continued safety and survival are non-Jews. For Mr. Solomon's parents, the act of marrying a non-Jewish woman could have been seen as an act of betrayal, and not just betrayal, but a threat to the very beliefs that kept them functioning from the time of their incarceration in the death camps to their own deaths. This feeling of betrayal by their son, although harsh for many of us, is a strongly felt belief among some Jewish survivors of the Holocaust and, if Bosnia and Cambodia can be used as a comparison, among many other victims of genocide.

Survivors of genocide sometimes feel overwhelming guilt that they lived while others, more worthy perhaps, did not. Consequently, professions for children to follow are sometimes those with high social worth: the human services, teaching, medicine, law, perhaps, but certainly not something as base and materialistic as business. Is this always the case? No. There are many survivors who see the accumulation of wealth as an ultimate form of self-protection. But for Mr. Solomon's parents, business was not a profession with dignity because it would probably not please their God.

This may sound very rigid and irrational to people unfamiliar with those who lived through the Holocaust, but it is an understandable rigidity when seen in the light of what happened to his parents. Mr. Solomon's parents believed that people who once did them harm could harm them again. Only through vigilance and self-protection would their family survive.

In Mr. Solomon, we have an example of a survivor's child trying to gain his own identity and then being criticized and punished for that effort by his parents. The resulting impact on Mr. Solomon is guilt at having tried to establish his own life, and parental rejection for his efforts. The end result, not surprisingly, is Mr. Solomon's depression and sense of unworthiness. Is it a mild depression or does it have potential to be more serious? One can only speculate that any depression has potential for serious consequences.

The dilemma for children of survivors who grow up in an environment with very limited intimacy could result in what Weiss (1961) calls an "existential crisis." An existential crisis is one without any apparent reason for its onset. It usually does not progress into a prolonged clinical depression. Instead, existentially depressed people lose a desire for newness in life. They may be cynical about relationships and prone to isolation and withdrawal. Their goals in life may be limited by a sense of futility in even caring or trying. They may view the world as a place full of suffering and torment, and obsess about the negative events in the world around them. As Weiss (1961) notes, in paraphrasing Karen Horney, ". . . it [an existential crisis] is a remoteness of the client in crisis from his own feelings, wishes, beliefs and energies. It is a loss of feeling of being an active, determining force in his own life [and results in] an alienation from the real self" (p. 464).

The treatment approach in this case is to utilize the many positive attributes of the client. He may be confused and unclear about the early life events that shaped him, but he has great potential for change. As a child, Mr. Solomon had to establish his own identity in a family where autonomy issues became confused with pleasing and protecting his parents. Mr. Solomon chose to become independent and to put his considerable talents and abilities into the process of becoming successful. Most families would applaud Mr. Solomon for his efforts. His parents' rejection of his independence and success confuses Mr. Solomon. He thinks that what he did was healthy and necessary for his own survival.

Mr. Solomon doesn't understand that many of the coping skills he has developed that helped make him successful at business also make relationships difficult. The parental attempt to give children the ability to succeed and survive, but to deny them the ability to love and achieve intimacy, is a common problem in families who experience genocide. To survive, one must be single-minded and tough. Security always overshadows personal happiness. Perhaps Mr. Solomon's parent's never actually modeled examples of happiness or intimacy and, instead, replaced messages of intimacy with those related to hard work, determination, persistence, and religious observance. Mr. Solomon could admire his parent's will to survive while failing to recognize that he had all too little preparation for intimacy. This recognition now comes in adulthood as the financially successful client realizes how unhappy he is. Perhaps he has even come to believe that his parents were right about his choice of careers.

USING A POSITIVE APPROACH WITH MR. SOLOMON

Again, although this is a book about writing well, I think it's important to know why I chose the strengths approach to help this client. Writing a psychosocial assessment includes a treatment plan. While mine is problem-focused, my underlying belief is that Mr. Solomon will respond to an approach that emphasizes his strengths. Most of Mr. Solomon's values, behaviors, and beliefs are very positive. His determination, persistence, financial success, and introspection bode well for treatment. But successful treatment of Mr. Solomon's problems requires, in Saleebey's (2000) words, an approach to treatment that "obligates us to understand . . . to believe that everyone (no exceptions here) has external and internal assets, competencies and resources" (p. 128).

Having worked with victims of the Holocaust and their children, I've found the strengths approach compatible with the dynamics related to resilience and survival. You may have another interpretation of the case and the best treatment approach to apply. Just as we need to be objective in our assessment of clients, it is also important that we use the research literature and our own successful experience to objectify treatment. When assessment and treatment are both objective, that's when we may have a real revolution in the effectiveness of our work.

SUMMARY

In summary, the psychosocial assessment is a way of describing areas of client difficulties and strength. It is important that we approach assessments in an objective and unbiased way. Used objectively, the assessment can provide the practitioner with an understanding of the connecting elements that have lead to the current crisis in a client's life. This chapter includes a psychosocial assessment and an explanation of the diagnostic and treatment decisions made in the case.

FIND THE MISTAKES

1. Mr. G. comes from an average American home and describes a normal early family life.
2. While Mr. H. has a background in economics, like so many African-American men, he seems undecided whether he wants to be a professional or hang out in the hood.
3. Miss J. has a typical female approach to life. She expects little in the way of happiness and is never surprised when her life choices are incorrect and become problematic.
4. Mrs. F's fundamentalist early life triggers a great deal of guilt about sex and is likely causing her frigidity.
5. Because she is an Orthodox Jew, Mrs. L. only enjoys intimate relations with her husband if the purpose is to have another child.

REFERENCES

American Psychiatric Association. (1994). *Diagnostic and Statistical Manual of Mental Disorders,* 4th ed. New York: American Psychiatric Association.

Baron, L., Eisman, H., Scuello, M., Veyzer, A., and Lieberman, M. (1996). Stress resilience, locus of control, and religion in children of Holocaust victims. *Journal of Psychology,* 130(5).

Cloud, J. (2003). How we get labeled. *Time,* 161(3), 102–106.

Davis, R. T., Blashfield, R. K., & McElroy, R. A. (1993). Weighting criteria in the diagnosis of a personality disorder: A demonstration. *Journal of Abnormal Psychology,* 102, 319–322.

Glicken, M. D. (2005). *Improving the effectiveness of the helping professions: An evidence based approach to practice.* Thousand Oaks, CA: Sage.

Hass, A. (1991). *In the shadow of the holocaust: The second generation.* London: I. B. Tauris & Co.

Haverkamp, B. (1993). Confirmatory bias in hypothesis testing for client-identified and counselor self-generated hypotheses. *Journal of Consulting Psychology,* 40, 305–315.

McLaughlin, J. E. (2002). Reducing diagnostic bias. *Journal of Mental Health Counseling, 24*(3), 256–270.

Morey, L. C., & Ochoa, E. S. (1989). An investigation of adherence to diagnostic criteria: Clinical diagnosis of the DSM-III personality disorders. *Journal of Personality Disorders, 3,* 180–192.

Pfeiffer, A. M., Whelan, J. P., & Martin, J. L. (2000). Decision-making in psychotherapy: Effects of hypothesis source and accountability. *Journal of Counseling Psychology, 47,* 429–436.

Robertson, J., & Fitzgerald, L. F. (1990). The (mis)treatment of men: Effects of client gender role and life-style on diagnosis and attribution of pathology. *Journal of Counseling Psychology, 37,* 3–9.

Rosenhan, D. L. (1973). On being sane in insane places. *Science, 179,* 250–258.

Saleebey, D. (1996). The strengths perspective in social work practice: Extensions and cautions. *Social Work, 41*(3), 296–305.

Saleebey, D. (2000). Power to the people; strength and hope. *Advancements in Social Work, 1*(2), 127–136.

Van Wormer, K. (1999). The strengths perspective: a paradigm for correctional counseling. *Federal Probation, 63*(1).

Weiss, F. M. (1961). Self-alienation: Dynamics and therapy. In E. Josephson and M. Josephson (Eds.), *Man alone: Alienation in modern society* (pp. 463–479). New York: Laurel.

Whaley, A. L. (2001). Cultural mistrust: An important psychological construct for diagnosis and treatment of African Americans. *Professional Psychology: Research and Practice, 32,* 555–562.

8

Business Letters, Referrals, Complaints, Committee Minutes, and Reference Letters

Professionals write business letters, complaints, reference letters, and referrals almost everyday. Until we are comfortable with the format and wording of this type of writing, we often obsess over wording, tone, and length. This chapter discusses the not-always-fun necessity of doing formal writing for an audience that isn't always friendly or understanding.

THE BUSINESS LETTER

In the following discussion I've summarized the suggestions that Beare (2006) makes for word choices when writing a business letter:

1. **The Start**
   a) *Dear Dr. Adler.* It's always preferable to use the person's name, if you know it, rather than using a vague title like "director."
   b) *Dear Sir or Madam,* but only if you don't know the person's name. Be certain that you have the gender right when using sir and madam.
   c) *Dear Mr., Mrs., Miss* or *Ms.* Use Ms. if you are uncertain if the woman is married, or if you know that this is her preference.
   d) *Dear Oscar.* If the person is a close business contact or friend, it's fine to use his or her first name. Be certain that the other person feels that you are both on a first-name basis.
2. **The Reason for the Letter**
   a) I'm writing in response to the job advertisement in *NASW News,* October 12, 2007.

   b) I'm writing in response to your phone call today.
   c) I'm writing in response to your letter of March 5, 2007, to inquire
      about . . . , to apologize . . . , or, to confirm.
3. **Requesting**
   a) I would appreciate receiving.
4. **Agreeing to Requests**
   a) I would be pleased . . . , delighted . . . , happy to speak at your
      agency.
5. **Giving Bad News**
   a) Unfortunately . . . , I am afraid that . . . , It is with regret that I in-
      form you.
6. **Enclosing Documents**
   a) I am enclosing the following documents.
   b) Please find the following documents enclosed with this letter.
   c) Enclosed with this letter are the following documents.
7. **Closing Remarks**
   a) Thank you for your help.
   b) Please contact us again if we can help in any way . . . , if there are
      any problems . . . , if you have any questions. You could also say,
      "Please feel free to call me if you have any questions."
8. **Reference to Future Contact**
   a) I look forward to hearing from you in the near future . . . , to meet-
      ing you next Tuesday . . . , to seeing you next week.
9. **The Finish**
   a) Yours truly (if you don't know the name of the person you are writ-
      ing to). Sincerely yours or Very truly yours (if you know the name
      of the person you're writing to). Best wishes, Best regards, or Warm
      regards (if the person is a close business contact or friend).

SAMPLE BUSINESS LETTERS

Letter 1: Denial of Counseling Services

                    The Health Maintenance Organization of Dakota County
                                     1515 So. Forks Ave.
                                   Little Rock, Kansas 66104

June 14, 2008

Mr. Jack Olson
1245 West 16th St.
Sumner, Kansas 66105

Re: Denial of additional counseling sessions

Dear Mr. Olson:

I regret to inform you that your health care policy no longer provides for counseling sessions during the current calendar year. As your handbook of coverage shows on page 23, you are entitled to 20 sessions of counseling in a calendar year if you are referred by your primary doctor. You may also be provided additional sessions in a calendar year if requested by your counselor. You requested additional sessions through your counselor, Ms. Jeffries. She informed you that she could not support the request and wrote in her opinion regarding the request that, "Mr. Olson has made significant progress this year. He came to counseling with problems related to anxiety and the inability to sleep. He no longer suffers from either problem and, in my view additional counseling would not be advised. I have encouraged Mr. Olson to join a group for anxiety sufferers in the community, which would be free and would, I think, provide the supportive care he needs."

We trust that this letter explains our policy. Should you think the policy is misinterpreted or not fair in your case, we urge you to read the complaint section of your handbook on page 16 and follow the guidelines noted.

Sincerely yours,

Jeffrey Fetig, PhD
Director, Department of Mental Health

This is the type of letter many of us receive from our health care providers. In response, Mr. Olson wrote the following rebuttal:

Letter 2: Response to the Denial of Mental Health Services From the Client

June 23, 2008

The Health Maintenance Organization of Dakota County
1515 So. Forks Ave.
Little Rock, Kansas 66104

Att. Dr. Jeffrey Fetig

Dear Dr. Fetig:

I am responding to your letter of June 14, 2008, denying me additional sessions for my anxiety and sleeping problems.

While I respect Ms. Jeffries, my counselor at HMODC, I must respectfully disagree with her conclusion that I no longer need professional counseling. The fact is that I have not made much progress and still suffer daily anxiety attacks and panic attacks and sleep less than three hours a night. I have chronic anxiety disorder and, noting the DSM-IV and other research articles I've read, specifically Larson and Copland (2005), and Johnson and Edgar (2006), anxiety is one of the most difficult problems to deal with. Medication seldom works and clients often need supportive help for a long period of time. Larson and Copland said the typical client with anxiety requires at least 15 months of treatment. Johnson and Edgar, who studied over 10,000 clients with anxiety problems, said that, on average, clients require 27 months of treatment to reduce anxiety levels to those of non-anxiety-afflicted people.

It seems pretty clear to me that 20 sessions are not enough and that my current problems require much more help. According to page 17 of the handbook, I have a right to request an independent arbitrator, someone in the counseling field, to determine if my request is reasonable. I request an independent arbitrator and will, as the policy states, accept his or her conclusions regarding my need for additional treatment.

Sincerely,

Jack Olson
1245 West 16th St.
Sumner, Kansas 66105
Phone: 817-234-7658
SS#: 562-99-9087
Policy #: 654A768B

In response, Dr. Fetig agreed to bring in an independent arbitrator who met with Mr. Olson for 2 hours. The following response to that meeting was written by Dr. Fetig to Mr. Olson.

Letter 3: The Outcome

The Health Maintenance Organization of Dakota County
1515 So. Forks Ave.
Little Rock, Kansas 66104

July 12, 2008

Mr. Jack Olson
1245 West 16th St.
Sumner, Kansas 66105

Dear Mr. Olson:

I am writing to provide feedback from your meeting with Dr. Clive Barkley, Clinical Psychologist. As Dr. Barkley told you, it is his professional judgment that your anxiety and sleep problems require additional attention. Because you and Dr. Barkley seem to have developed good rapport in your meeting, I am pleased to inform you that HMODC will provide 20 additional sessions this calendar period and more if Dr. Barkley recommends them. We are pleased that you took the initiative to contact us with your request and wish you the best of luck in your future work with Dr. Barkley. Please contact Dr. Barkley's office at your earliest convenience to set up your next appointment. His number is 817-643-9091.

Sincerely yours,

Jeffrey Fetig, PhD
Director of Department of Mental Health

In the next section in this chapter on writing complaints you will discover how Mr. Olson fared in his additional treatment with Dr. Barkley.

GUIDELINES FOR WRITING COMPLAINTS

We write complaints for a number of reasons, but our dissatisfaction is the primary one. In professional writing it is very important that you keep written complaints to a minimum since most professionals would prefer to have concerns worked out on a personal level. Written complaints have ramifications since they tend to put the person you're complaining about on the hot seat. If you must write a complaint, I've summarized the major points suggested by Muyesseroglu (2002). They are as follows:

1. Write the letter while it is still fresh in your mind, but read it over four or five times before you send it. I usually let it sit a few days to calm myself down and to get clarity about the event.
2. Have someone else who knows nothing about the problem read it for feedback.
3. Explain the problem clearly, briefly, and fairly. In the first and last lines of the letter, state your expectations of the other party. Chapman (2005) suggests that a good beginning is to state: "I'd really appreciate your help with" (p. 1) then go on to explain the problem.
4. Try to limit the letter to one problem. If there are several problems, choose the problems that require immediate attention. Briefly list these problems and indicate how you expect them to be resolved. Chapman

(2005) suggests that "If the situation and solution is complex, state also that you'll be as flexible as you can to come to an agreed way forward" (p. 1).

5. Focus on how the problem can be solved. Avoid unimportant details, stick to the facts, and avoid emotional language. Chapman (2005) suggests complimenting people who have given you good service in the past or products you've been pleased with and adding that "you've no wish to go elsewhere and hope that a solution can be found" (p. 1).

6. Make the tone of the letter positive and try to use polite language that doesn't blame or threaten to sue. The purpose of the letter is to solve the problem.

7. Include dates and other important aspects of the problem. Indicate how you can be reached. If the problem requires it, attach copies of receipts but be sure to keep your letter and the originals of everything you're including in the letter for your files.

8. End your letter by indicating that you are confident the problem will be satisfactorily resolved. Chapman (2005) suggests saying "that you look forward to hearing from them soon and that you appreciate their help" (p. 1).

9. End the letter with your signature but below it type your name, title, and position.

10. If copies of the letter are going to other parties, put ccs below your name with the names and the organizations to whom you are sending copies.

11. Below the ccs place enc. This describes the enclosures in your letter such as bills, other correspondence, etc.

EXAMPLES OF COMPLAINT LETTERS

Letter 1: Mr. Olson Complains About His Lack of Treatment

September 25, 2008

The Health Maintenance Organization of Dakota County
1515 So. Forks Ave.
Little Rock, Kansas 66104

Att. Dr. Jeffrey Fetig

Dear Dr. Fetig:

As you suggested in your letter of July 12, 2008, I contacted Dr. Barkley and arranged to meet with him to work on my anxiety and sleep problems. We had very productive meetings for six sessions. On September 25, 2008, Dr. Barkley informed me that HMODC had not paid him for his work with me and, although he had contacted the agency repeatedly, he was given, in his words, "the run-around" by your staff. He said that until he had been paid he was unable to continue working with me and implied that because of the problems he had in getting paid he might not be able to work with me at all.

I think it's highly unethical of HMODC to send me to a private practitioner for help and then not pay for his services. In effect, it seems to me that you are denying me the very help you told me I was entitled to receive. I sincerely hope you can resolve this issue with Dr. Barkley and allow me to continue receiving the fine help he is providing.

Jack Olson

Letter 2: Response From Dr. Fetig

The Health Maintenance Organization of Dakota County
1515 So. Forks Ave.
Little Rock, Kansas 66104

October 4, 2008

Mr. Jack Olson
1245 West 16th St.
Sumner, Kansas 66105

Dear Mr. Olson:

I am very sorry Dr. Barkley ran into difficulties receiving payment for the services he provided that had been approved by HMODC. I can assure you that Dr. Barkley will be paid. He apparently did not know, nor did our staff inform him, that all services billed required a special form (65870) submitted to our billing department and approved by me. He also apparently did not know that we pay for services quarterly and that it usually takes up to a month for payments to be made. I can see how, in Dr. Barkley's view, we were not paying for his services. We have processed his bill and I have personally contacted him to ask if he will continue seeing you. He has agreed and you are encouraged to call him at your earliest convenience to make an appointment.

Sincerely yours,

Jack Fetig. PhD
Director, Department of Mental Health

Letter 3: Further Concerns From Mr. Olson

October 25, 2008

The Health Maintenance Organization of Dakota County
1515 So. Forks Ave.
Little Rock, Kansas 66104

Att. Dr. Jeffrey Fetig

Dear Dr. Fetig:

In this continuing saga of my treatment with Dr. Barkley, after meeting with me for two additional sessions, Dr. Barkley informed me that HMODC had paid him at only a third of his normal fee and that he would be unable to continue working with me. He said that in your initial discussions your agency had agreed to pay him his normal fee and that HMODC knew about this arrangement and had approved it. He also said that he had received a letter with his first check covering eight sessions, indicating that only the chief administrator could approve such an arrangement and that you did not have the authority to promise that he would receive his normal fee.

I am bitterly disappointed and concerned that someone suffering from anxiety disorder would be put through this type of treatment by your agency. I have decided to proceed with a complaint to the state insurance commission.

Jack Olson

Letter 4: Apology and Resolution

The Health Maintenance Organization of Dakota County
1515 So. Forks Ave.
Little Rock, Kansas 66104

November 4, 2008

Mr. Jack Olson
1245 West 16th St.
Sumner, Kansas 66105

Dear Mr. Olson

Please accept my sincerest apologies. I am new in my job and did not realize that arrangements with Dr. Barkley were to be made only by the chief administrator. I have since spoken to her and we are approving all of Dr. Barkley's prior sessions at his normal rate and eight additional sessions at his normal rate for the current calendar year. Because we are obligated to keep our expenses at a minimum by maintaining low premiums, we cannot pay for additional services with Dr. Barkley for the coming calendar year. You are certainly welcome to continue working with Ms. Jefferies, your prior counselor, or you may choose to see anyone on staff, including our clinical psychologist, Dr. Weber. We have also approved a full year of services (52 sessions) in the coming year and encourage you to seek additional help from a number of excellent groups in the community composed and run by people with ongoing anxiety problems.

Again, please accept my sincere apologies for any discomfort or confusion you may have experienced over the past several months.

Sincerely yours,

Jack Fetig. PhD
Director, Department of Mental Health

Did these series of letters help Mr. Olson reach some resolution of the problems he was having with the HMO? Mr. Olson told his therapist, "It was very frustrating dealing with HMODC, but it's a big organization and a part of me was very sympathetic to Dr. Fetig's problems as a new employee. He's a caring professional and I received, and continue to receive, excellent care. I pay a co-pay of $10 per session. A private practitioner like Dr. Barkley charges $150 for a 50-minute session, so I can see how costly it would be for the HMO to pay for Dr. Barkley, and I can't complain about the help I'm getting. The medical care I get at HMODC is pretty terrific and given how little hassle it entails, it's a great medical plan. At a personal level, I learned that dealing with issues when they arise actually lowers my level of anxiety so, in a way, I learned a lot about helping myself. I also learned that I have a lot more power than I thought I did, and that's also helped lower my level of anxiety. Anxiety is about the feeling that you're not in control and that outside forces control your life. I learned a lot about controlling my life through writing these complaints. I tried to make them very businesslike and not too angry-sounding. You can see that it worked pretty well."

THE REFERRAL

Professionals refer clients to other professionals almost every day. Using the prior client assessment (chapter 7) as a starter, the client in our assessment is being referred to a psychiatrist for an evaluation. The reader might recall that this was one of the goals of treatment in the assessment and it is reasonable given the client's current problem with depression. The competent professional refers clients to other professionals when problems exist beyond their own area of expertise. An evaluation of the need for anti-depressives is clearly a medical decision. Asking for additional help in evaluating a client's potential for continued depression may help in the client's treatment and may prevent liability issues in the future.

Example 1

Dear Dr. Jones:

I am referring Mr. Ira Solomon for a psychiatric evaluation. Mr. Solomon's psychosocial assessment is attached for your added information.

Specifically, I would like to have some feedback on Mr. Solomon's prior use of anti-depressants and whether he might benefit from any of the current medications. I would also appreciate any information you might provide on his overall physical condition and whether there might be medical reasons for his current bout of depression. Finally, any information you might provide to determine his long-range likelihood of experiencing additional problems with depression and his risk for suicide would be very much appreciated.

Please contact me should you have any additional questions. I have enclosed a signed release of information form accompanying the assessment. Mr. Solomon will contact you next week to set up an appointment time.

Thank you.

Example 2

Dear Rabbi Brown:

Mr. Ira Solomon is a client of mine who is experiencing problems in his professional life with anti-Semitism. I would be grateful if you could meet with Mr. Solomon to discuss the problems he is experiencing and to possibly include him in one of the groups at your synagogue that help people cope with anti-Semitism.

Mr. Solomon is also confused about his Jewish heritage and could benefit from some help in this regard. He is also lonely and perhaps the social groups at the synagogue might be of some help to him.

I look forward to discussing Mr. Solomon with you and to our continued conversations.

Thank you.

COMMITTEE MINUTES

One of the more unpleasant but obviously necessary professional writing responsibilities is that of writing committee minutes. In some organizations this may be done by a staff member rather than a professional but, as many of us have discovered, staff members are often not informed about many of the matters discussed at a meeting and may not report them correctly. Instead, that responsibility may be turned over to professionals chosen on a rotating basis. The following guidelines and examples may help you write acceptable minutes. Remember that minutes have legal and policy implications. Minutes need to be approved by the committee and few things are as painful as having your minutes torn to shreds because your reporting is inaccurate or shoddy.

GUIDELINES FOR WRITING MINUTES

The Purpose of Minutes: (1) They remind participants about the actions taken at the last meeting. (2) They inform people who were not at the meeting about the results of the meeting, including votes taken, policy changes, and problems dealt with. (3) They provide a basis for the agenda of the next meeting. (4) They are an organization's permanent record of the results of the meeting.

Types of Minutes: There are two types of documentation, *verbatim minutes*, where every word is recorded (for example, legal matters, or matters dealt with by a legislature) and *action minutes*, where only the decisions are recorded. The type of minutes you write depends on the purpose of the meeting and the type of agency you work for. Minutes may be read as part of a legal proceedings where policies were discussed by the board or the staff and may help describe the organization's history.

The Agenda: The agenda forms the schedule for a meeting and includes all relevant business. This might be a typical agenda:

1. **Apologies for absences at a prior meeting:** The roll call is taken at every meeting to make certain a quorum (usually half or two-thirds of the membership) exists and that votes taken have the required number of members present. Without a quorum, policy issues cannot be voted on or approved.
2. **Acceptance of the previous minutes:** Minutes are sent to all committee members as soon as they are done so that any corrections to the minutes can be noted and discussed at a future meeting.
3. **Any unfinished business:** Outstanding issues from the last meeting, as noted in the minutes, are addressed.
4. **New business:** The recording secretary should include new agenda items indicated from the last meeting. It's considered appropriate to also ask for new items before the final agenda is set.
5. **Date, time, and place of the next meeting**
6. **Motion to adjourn**

Examples of Committee Minutes

The following is a suggested way to write minutes with examples:

1. Make certain you are familiar with each item on the agenda. If not, ask the prior recording secretary to explain anything that is unclear or that may present itself as a problem in the meeting in which you are writing the minutes.
2. Write notes on the agenda during the meeting.
3. As soon after the meeting as possible, write the minutes from your notes. Run the minutes by several people you respect to make certain they are accurate before passing them out for the next meeting. It is always a good idea to pass the minutes out as soon as possible so that people's memories of the meeting are fresh and any corrections can be made before the next meeting when the minutes are approved. In your note to committee members with the draft of the minutes, you should ask for feedback and corrections but give a deadline for changes to be made of no more than three to five days or people will forget about the minutes completely. Having done this hopefully prevents a contentious discussion of the minutes at the next meeting.

Using the prior agenda, the following is an example of how to write minutes of a meeting:

Minutes of the Professional Staff Meeting: The Olympic Family Service Agency

12-17-2008

1. **Apologies for Absences:** John Jacobs was unable to attend the last meeting (11-23-08) because he was ill.
2. **Acceptance of previous minutes:** Because there were no changes to the minutes of the last meeting, the chair confirmed that the minutes of the last meeting (11-23-08) were accepted without change.
3. **Unfinished business from the last meeting:** Only one piece of unfinished business was discussed: the question of whether we should have a permanent recording secretary. The discussion that followed was largely opposed to changing the current system of rotating secretaries. Jim Johnson moved and Oscar Peterson seconded that we keep the current system. The motion carried by a unanimous vote.
4. **New business:** Two pieces of new business were discussed and voted on. The first motion was made by Jack Bradley and read: "Out of respect for the diverse populations we serve, the agency should not display anything symbolizing Christmas." The motion did not receive a second and was defeated. Jim Nelson offered an alternative motion: "Displays of the holi-

day season were good for the agency and most people appreciated them. Out of fairness to diverse populations, the displays should include those consistent with the world's major religions and, to make that possible, the agency will consult with religious leaders in the community and try to come up with suggestions for next year's holiday season to be discussed and approved by the committee." Jill Fargo seconded the motion. After a lively discussion, the vote was called for and the motion passed with a simple majority of 15-7.

5. **Items to be discussed at the next meeting:** (1) The professional development budget and a clear policy on the determination of funding for conferences, workshops, and other professional activities; (2) concerns about workloads and whether workload limits can be developed; (3) staff turnover and why the agency has lost a third of its professional staff members this year.

6. **Date, time, and place of the next meeting:** The next meeting will be held January 21, 2009, from 2–5 PM in the agency conference room. Dr. Swenson, the agency's CEO has been invited to attend.

7. **Motion to adjourn:** Andy Weber moved and Jay Johns seconded that the meeting be adjourned. The motion carried unanimously.

THE REFERENCE LETTER

Everyone has his or her approach to writing reference letters. My approach is not to write one unless I can enthusiastically support a candidate. I prefer to be enthusiastic since nothing negates a person's chances for a job more than an innocuous or neutral reference letter. The example of a reference letter given here provides strong support for the applicant. It shows my relationship to the applicant, and it gives my judgment of her work in a personal way. Personalizing reference letters is the best way, in my view, to make certain the applicant gets the job. I suggest that reference letters contain the following information:

1. Name, title, and address of the person being sent the reference letter.
2. Date.
3. Salutation. It's preferable to use the person's name, as in "Dear Mr. Smith." If you don't know the person's name, then "Dear Sir or Madam" and "To whom it may concern" are always acceptable.
4. Refer to the length of time you have known someone so that it's clear you know him or her well enough to evaluate his or her performance and responsibilities.
5. Do not include confidential information such as salary and benefits unless it has been asked for and the worker permits it.
6. Indicate the person's qualifications, strengths, responsibilities, and attitudes toward his or her work.

7. Indicate whether his or her performance was always satisfactory and whether it exceeded expectations.
8. Do not add more than is absolutely called for.
9. Always show the letter to the person you're writing about and have the person sign a copy indicating that they've read it and approve. You don't want that person threatening a lawsuit because the reference caused them to lose the job.

Example of a Reference Letter

To Whom It May Concern: November 23, 2008

I am pleased to write this recommendation for Ms. June Anderson.

Ms. Anderson was the benefits officer and worker's compensation administrator at California State University, Santa Barbara (CSUSB), when I came to know her in 1988. Like most of us on faculty, I'm a dunce when it comes to understanding our benefits package. June helped me in many ways to access the plans and to become a better consumer. I know that many of us on faculty felt such loyalty to her that we continued to bombard her with questions, even when she held a position at another university. Good, gentle, and decent person that she is, she gave freely of her time even though it was no longer her responsibility.

But that's June. I think everyone you talk to will reinforce my perception of her as an extremely competent and loyal person who really knows and understands our retirement system and our health benefits. She is dedicated, available, always pleasant, upbeat, optimistic, very creative, and hardworking. More than anything, she is just a very nice person who gives everything she has to the job and to the people for whom she has responsibility.

As a social worker and former social agency administrator, I'm keenly aware of how important people skills can be in any position of authority. June's people skills are really quite exceptional.

Finally, June has asked me to do several workshops for potential retirees at CSUSB. They were always well organized, well attended, and very useful to anyone interested in retirement planning. Feedback from participants was always positive. On several occasions I stayed and listened to presentations when my session was completed. June had some very high level folks from Social Security, the California Public Retirement System, and several of the voluntary pension plans. I was impressed and I know the participants were equally impressed. People still tell me that attendance at one of the sessions she organized was a turning point in their retirement planning.

In summary, it is my pleasure to recommend Ms. June Anderson to you. She is a warm, highly competent, talented, and creative woman with unlimited potential to do very high level work. I think everyone you talk to will concur that she is a particularly capable woman with exceptional people skills.

Sincerely,

Dr. Morley D. Glicken, Professor
Department of Social Work
California State University, Santa Barbara

SUMMARY

This chapter discusses the business letter and the common professional letters we write, including complaint letters, referrals, and reference letters. Examples of each type of letter are given along with guidelines.

FIND THE MISTAKES

1. **Business Letter:** "Dear Fred. How are you doing? It was nice to see you and Julia last week at the mall. We always enjoy getting together. The thing we talked about at the mall is good to go. We'll look forward to working with you on it. Best, Jake."
2. **Recommendation:** "To Whom it May Concern: Oscar Wilde is a promising young man with a brilliant future ahead. I strongly recommend him for the job and would be happy to discuss him with you by phone. Jack Spratt, Director of Corporate Public Relations, The Center for the Study of Individual Rights and Privacy."
3. **Referral:** "Dear Alice: Bill Faulkner is a client of mine suffering from writer's block. In 12 sessions I have not been able to help him over the hump. I'm thinking that hypnotism might be right for him. Could you see him and tell me what you think. Thanks, Jonathan."
4. **Complaint:** "Dear Dr. Edwards: I have been in therapy with you for 6 months. During that time my condition has gone from awful to terrible. I've had two suicide attempts and a psychotic breakdown, but all you do is sit in your chair, rub your beard, and go "um-hm." What kind of therapist are you anyway to be so aloof to someone's pain and to the poor work you've been doing with me? Jason Hawke."
5. **Response to a Complaint:** "Dear Jason: I can certainly understand why you would feel that therapy is failing you given the tough period you've gone through. But if you think about it, after six months you're doing well enough to write me a critical letter. I think that's very empowering, don't you? And rather than thinking that all I do is listen, I think you'll realize, upon reflection, that I have given you a great deal of direct advice and support. I trust you will come in and discuss these matters with me in person, but thank you for providing this feedback. All therapists want to know how they're doing even if

the client doesn't always think they're doing as well as we do. Sincere regards, Dr. Jonathan Edwards."

REFERENCES

Beare, K. (2006). Guide to basic business letters. Retrieved September 12, 2006, from http://esl.about.com/cs/onthejobenglish/a/a_basbletter.htm

Chapman, A. (1995–2005). Complaint letters. Retrieved September 16, 2006, from www.businessballs.com/complaintsletters.htm

Chapman, A. (2006). Writing reference letters. Retrieved September 5, 2006, from www.businessballs.com/referenceletterssamples.htm

Muyesseroglu, J. (2002). Retrieved September 12, 2006, from http://depts.gallaudet.edu/englishworks/writing/letter/complaints.html

9

Resumes and Cover Letters

There is probably more misinformation written about resumes and cover letters than almost any other form of writing. That is because both are so important in landing the right jobs that it prompts many people to offer advice and folk wisdom rather than concrete information. I can tell you from hiring many people and from my own job-seeking experience that there are certain pieces of information that almost always influence bosses. Trivial information doesn't. Grammatical and spelling errors will almost always get your resume thrown in the trash.

TIPS ON RESUME WRITING

Some of the following suggestions for effective resume writing come from Ms. Yana Parker, who can be found on the Internet at (www.damngood .com). Normally, I wouldn't give you the Internet source until the end of the chapter but Ms. Parker says that if anyone uses her material they must give her name and website. I have paraphrased her suggestions.

1. A resume is a self-promotional document that presents you in the best possible light, for the purpose of getting invited to a job interview.
2. A resume is about you and what you've accomplished in your life. A good resume predicts how you might perform in a desired future job.
3. Put your life in chronological order from present to past. Be sure to include higher education, advanced degrees, and new skills attained.
4. If you lack experience for a job, it's best to get additional experience through volunteer work or education.

5. Don't leave time gaps in your resume. If there is a two-year period when you've traveled around Europe, for example, put down on your resume that you traveled extensively through Europe and that, as a result, you've improved your language skills and cultural understanding of a number of foreign countries. Knowing a foreign language can significantly benefit you in a job search.

6. If you are applying for different types of jobs, change the emphasis of the resume to meet the needs of that particular job.

7. If you have the type of scrambled work experience that most of us have, combine jobs, as in this example:
   2003–2005: Summer Construction and Food Service: Jones Construction, Starbucks, Coffee Bean, Westwood Market, all in Los Angeles, CA.

8. Impress an employer with examples of what you did that helped an organization. For instance, "I was made student manager of the book store at Grand Forks College in my senior year. Sales rose 30%, a new ordering system was initiated, theft was down 60%, and profits increased 40% allowing us to lower the price of books to students."

9. If a job title doesn't reflect your actual responsibility, briefly explain. **Job Title:** Student Manager of the Grand Forks College Book Store (with overall administrative responsibility to manage sales, purchases, and order books and supplies).

10. Avoid age discrimination problems by noting recent or relevant experience without using dates. Do the same with your educational experiences, and again, don't use dates. Is this important? You bet it is! Employers sometimes have an irrational age barrier believing that people over 50 and under 25 are suspect. At 50, some employers may believe that you're too old and worn out, and that if you are under 25, that you are too inexperienced and immature. Neither is true, of course, but that's the way age may be dealt with by an employer.

11. If you have never had a job or done volunteer work, you can emphasize your field practicum experiences in school. It is wise, however, to have actual hands-on experience.

12. You should go far enough back in your work history for employers to know your relevant work history. Having been a cook or waiter, or having worked construction can be lumped together. What an employer wants to know is whether you can do the job and whether there is any evidence of your work competence from past employment.

13. If you haven't quite graduated yet, put down the expected date of graduation and the degree you will receive as well as your major and minor.

14. If you worked for one employer for a long time, be sure to list your various work assignments and responsibilities to demonstrate how you've progressively worked your way up the ladder.

15. List awards and affiliations such as honorary societies or professional organizations.

16. Don't reveal your religious preference. It's no one's business unless you are applying for a job with a religiously sponsored agency. If that's the case, show your involvement in youth organizations and your affiliation, perhaps even noting the church, mosque, or synagogue you attend.

17. If you have a name that can be taken as male or female (Pat, Lee, Sam, etc.), use Ms., Mr. or Mrs., or spell out your full name (Patricia instead of Pat; Lester instead of Lee). I'm a believer in not letting people know that you are married. In the case of women, it might raise the concern that you may become pregnant or move if your husband has a job transfer. For men, marriage gives the false impression that your life is stable. While it may give you an edge, you may be no more stable than anyone else. When the employer finds that out, he or she may react negatively.

18. If you received a degree in a foreign country, next to the degree, indicate its U.S. equivalent and the organization that made that decision. This is very important for jobs requiring licensure and completion of a certain level of education. You need an MSW from an accredited school to apply for your clinical license, for example, and many employers will specify the need for the clinical license since they can bill third parties (insurance and government) for the services you provide.

19. Toot your own horn, but not too loudly. Put down your accomplishments, awards, and achievements, but not in an arrogant way. Being on the dean's list, graduating cum laude (or better), or being in a professional honorary society are all perfectly fine to add, and certainly strengthen your resume.

20. Don't make the resume more than two to three pages long. Do it in a neat and orderly way, and don't use embellishments such as fancy paper or paper with pictures or drawings. The people hiring you are serious. They want you to project who you are, what you've accomplished, and what you can do for the organization in two to three pages.

A BRIEF RESUME

This is an actual resume that led to a job offer.

Amy J. Larson
3643 N. 14th Street
Gerard, Arizona 85716
Phone 820.320.7734
E-Mail: amylarson@msn.com

Education
Master's of Public Health Candidate, Expected graduation date: 6/06
University of Arizona College of Public Health, Tucson, Arizona
- Community Health Practice concentration with coursework in program planning, evaluation, community assessment, biostatics, nonprofit management, etc.

Bachelor of Arts Degree 5/00
Grinnell College, Grinnell, Iowa
- Sociology Major, focus on Gender and Women's Studies and Public Policy

Awards & Scholarships
Helen and Raymond Sarocco Scholarship, University of Arizona College of Public Health
Trustee Scholarship, National Merit Scholarship, Grinnell College
Valedictorian, National Merit Finalist, Dalzell Memorial Scholarship, Dubuque Senior High School

Professional Experience
Graduate Assistant & Intern 1/05–Present
University of Arizona National Center of Excellence in Women's Health, Tucson, Arizona
- Developed and pilot tested the Women's Health Registry, a program designed to increase the participation of women in research studies at the University of Arizona
- Submitted and awarded $10,000 mini grant from the Arizona Department of Health Services
- Chair, Conference Organizing Committee, First Interdisciplinary Women's Health Research Conference at the University of Arizona

Research Assistant Fall Semester 04
Institute for Children, Youth & Families, Tucson, Arizona
- Assisted with program evaluation, including survey collection and Excel data entry

Rural Coordinator 8/01–8/04
Volunteer Lawyers Program, Tucson, Arizona
- Coordinated 125 volunteer attorneys in eight rural counties across Arizona, increasing participation by 100% through volunteer recruitment efforts
- Increased number of clients served by 400% in rural counties
- Organized clinics and referrals for direct legal representation of low income clients in a variety of civil cases, including consumer, probate, housing, and family law
- Attended county bar association meetings, organized recognition and appreciation events, coordinated Continuing Legal Education seminars, wrote press releases, assisted with grant reports, and forged coalitions with community organizations

Clinic Assistant 7/00–7/01
Planned Parenthood of Greater Iowa, Iowa City, Iowa
- Educated and counseled patients regarding their reproductive health decisions based on extensive training related to health issues, including reproductive rights, contraception, sexually transmitted infections, and pregnancy options

Intern Spring Semester 00
Iowa Commission on the Status of Women, Des Moines, Iowa
- Developed a resource guide of girl-serving programs across Iowa
- Assisted with the planning and running of statewide annual events
- Acquired a deeper understanding for public policy issues and governmental processes regarding women's equality in the political, economic, and social spheres

Student Manager 8/99–5/00

Salesperson 2/97–8/99
Grinnell College Bookstore, Grinnell, Iowa

Youth Care Worker in Residential Treatment Center for Adolescent Girls Summer 98
Children and Families of Iowa, Newton, Iowa

Math Tutor for Calculus I-II 8/97–5/98
Grinnell College Math Department, Grinnell, Iowa

Intern Summer 97
Dubuque County Attorney's Office Victim/Witness Program, Dubuque, Iowa

Graphic Design & Technical Experience
Website Development 8/04–Present
- Developed and manage two websites: www.plazma.org & www.persons .com

Graphic Design 8/04–Present
- Provide contract graphic design work for the Volunteer Lawyers Program, including brochures, newsletters, posters, t-shirts, letterhead, business cards, PowerPoint's, etc.

Technical Skills
- Extensive work with Word, WordPerfect, the Internet, Publisher, Adobe Illustrator, FrontPage, Access, and PowerPoint

Professional Training
Mediation Training, Tucson, Arizona 3/01
- Completed 40-hour training on mediation and conflict resolution

Cemanahuac Language Institute, Cuernavaca, Mexico Summer 93/94
- Immersion in Mexican culture at a language-intensive institute

Volunteer Experience
Tutor 9/01–5/04
Lawyers for Literacy

Disc Jockey 1/98–12/98
Grinnell College Radio Station
- Served as a DJ for two radio shows, *Phenomenal Women* and *Living in Heartbeats*

Student Adviser 8/97–5/98
Grinnell College Student Staff
- Counseled and advised floor members on individual problems, roommate conflicts, inter-floor issues, etc.

Sexual Assault Working Group 8/97–5/98
- Helped revise college Sexual Assault Policy and organized campus-wide events

AN ALTERNATIVE RESUME

I use a somewhat different style. I like a more open style. Even if it's a bit longer, it's often easier to read.

GENERAL INFORMATION
Name: Dr. Morley D. Glicken
Address: 1925 Willow Lane
Boise, Idaho 83700
Telephone: (208) 342-0476 (H)
                (208) 283-9799 (Cell)
E-Mail: mglicken@201.com

EDUCATION
- Doctor of Social Work Degree: University of Utah, Graduate School of Social Work, Salt Lake City. Dissertation title: A Regional Study of the Job Satisfaction of Social Workers. Major emphasis: practice, research, administration.
- Master of Public Administration Degree: University of Utah, Department of Political Science, Salt Lake City, Utah.
- Master of Social Work Degree: University of Washington, Graduate School of Social Work, Seattle, Washington.
- Bachelor of Philosophy Degree: University of North Dakota, Grand Forks. Major in social welfare, minors in psychology and social science.

ACADEMIC AND PRACTICE APPOINTMENTS
- Present: Writer/Consultant/Part-time Instructor: Boise State University (Domestic Violence, Community Practice, International Social Work); California State University, San Bernardino (Licensure Workshops); California State University, San Marcos (Licensure Workshops).
- Interim Professor of Social Work, Central Michigan University, Mt. Pleasant, Michigan (teaching, administrative functions, and BSW Accreditation).
- Interim Dean and Professor, Worden School of Social Service, Our Lady of the Lake University, San Antonio, Texas (administration, admissions, reorganization of the curriculum, and grants until full-time dean was found).
- Professor (tenured), Department of Social Work, California State University, San Bernardino, San Bernardino, California (practice, research, crisis intervention, child abuse and neglect, issues of gender and ethnicity, supervision).
- Professor and Original Director of the Department of Social Work, California State University, San Bernardino, California (develop and direct a new graduate department of social work).
- Executive Director, Jewish Family Service of Greater Tucson. Responsibilities included all phases of administering a $700,000, 30 employee nonprofit agency with special emphasis on budgeting, public relations, personnel management and fund raising.
- Various academic jobs including the University of Kansas (Associate Professor with Tenure), Arizona State University, and Wifrid Laurier University.

MOST RECENT JOURNAL ARTICLES (Total of 50)
- Ino, S. M. & Glicken, M. D. (2002). Understanding and treating the ethnically Asian client: A collectivist approach. *Journal of Health and Social Policy*, *14*(4), 37–48.
- Ino, S. M. & Glicken, M. D. (1999, June). Treating Asian American clients in crisis: A collectivist approach. *Smith College Studies in Social Work, 69*(3), 525–540.

MOST RECENT BOOKS (Total of 10)
- Glicken, M. D. (2006, Summer). *Social work in the 21st century.* Thousand Oaks, CA: Sage Publications.
- Glicken, M. D. (2006, Spring). *Learning from resilient people.* Thousand Oaks, CA: Sage Publications.
- Glicken, M. D. (2005, Winter). *Working with troubled men: A contemporary practioner's guide.* Mahwah, NJ: Lawrence Erlbaum Publications.

SELECTED PROFESSIONAL AFFILIATIONS AND ACTIVITIES
- Good Samaritan Center Child Care Agency, San Antonio, Texas (Board Member)
- Board Member, Arrowhead Health Care Systems, San Bernardino, California.
- Board Member, San Bernardino Community Hospital Foundation, San Bernardino, California.

THE COVER LETTER

The following suggestions for writing cover letters are paraphrased from material on a website I highly recommend entitled Jobwerx Career Center (2007). Cover letters accompany the resume. They are short business letters (a page to a page and a half), written in brief paragraphs. You should avoid single line spacing and use a standard, professional-looking font set at a legible size (12 is a good size to use). Cover letters briefly describe your abilities and experience and help the employer to get a better sense of your experience and skills than might be possible just from the resume. There are two types of cover letters: specific and general.

The specific cover letter is sent to a specific company, person, or concerns a specific job. It responds to the potential employer's needs and might be a response to a job ad. It also sends a positive message that you are genuinely interested in the job because you have taken the time to write a cover letter.

A general cover letter is addressed to: Dear Employer, Dear Hiring Manager, or Dear Recruiter, and highlights your qualifications. This type of letter is often sent if the applicant is inquiring about available jobs in the future. The letter should be directed at the agency and its needs. Good managers keep interesting letters. I certainly do. If you get a response saying that nothing is available now but that a position might be available in the future and you'll be contacted, that's often a good sign. It is perfectly permissible to occasionally write the person who responded to your letter and ask if the position is available.

Many employers now allow you to apply online. Although this is certainly useful and efficient, it increases the possibilities of mistakes. I normally write a small note on the e-mail and attach the resume and cover letter as separate documents, which I have carefully proofed and spell checked. Here's a real cover letter I received online from a student applying for a graduate assistantship. See how many errors you can find.

Dear Dr. Glikin:
   I am Shirley Olson, a graduate student in Social Work and I am applying for the graduate assistant job you told us about in class; it's my favorite class, so I was real excited, and I could sure use the money. I'm a real good student and I got good grades in high school and college and so far, I have a B average in Grad school. I could do better but money is short and I have to work 40 hours a week at Kroegers so this job will help a lot so I hope I can get it real soon and thanks a lot Dr. Glicken, you're my favorite teacher."

Give you a clue. It's more than 10. Guess who didn't get the graduate assistantship?

Use direct and uncomplicated language.. Be formal, but not dull, and don't use clichés such as, "I've always dreamed of being a social worker. This job will help me fulfill that dream." Why shouldn't you say this? It's a cliché because so many people say the same thing and, fulfilling your dream isn't anyone's concern in the workplace—it's hiring someone who will do a good job with clients.

In your cover letter, be positive, be polite, be confident, but quickly get to the point. Most important, don't sound as if you're desperate for the job. "Please, please, please give me a job, your majesty, or I fear I will starve to death" may have great pathos, but "Dear Sir: I am writing to apply for the job of assistant to the director of case management at the Pico Avenue Child Guidance Center, a position for which I feel very qualified" is probably the better way to start a cover letter.

Explain why you would like to work for the agency. Be genuine about it. An example might be, "The Fosters Agency has a wonderful reputation for providing excellent clinical supervision. Just having graduated with my MFT degree, I am very interested in working toward my clinical licensure. I think I have good client skills, and that I would be an asset to the agency while I learn and grow as a professional."

If you send a similar letter to a number of different agencies, be sure that you carefully proof each letter, and make certain that you sign it. I've sent out dozens of the same letter to many different organizations at the same time. How embarrassing it is to get a response that says, "Dear Dr. Glicken: Thank you for your application to the Sawtell Family Service agency in Los Angeles. It's a great agency. Unfortunately, you've applied to Memphis Family Service in Memphis, Tennessee."

Make sure you tell the potential employer how and where to reach you. Use a phone number and e-mail address that you frequently check, and return calls immediately. Don't call back from noisy places or from areas where the cell phone signal is weak, and don't call an employer while you are driving since it's difficult to be fully engaged in a conversation while driving.

Be very positive. End the cover letter with something like, "I'm looking forward to hearing from you," or, "I'm looking forward to future communications," or, "Please let me know if I can send additional information." Be sure to keep copies of all letters sent for future reference or you will have the experience I had of applying for a job, not remembering the job or the letter, and trying to figure out why I sent an application for a job in Nome, Alaska, to work on a whaling ship with deserters from the Russian army. All kidding aside, keep letters and have them handy. Most interested employers call to offer you an interview when you are least prepared for the call. I keep my letters on the computer in a file I've named "job applications" with the agency I've applied to and the title of the position as in "Fargo M H, Exec

V P." I also keep the ad under the same file name. That tells me everything I need to know quickly

An Example of a Successful Cover Letter

This actual cover letter, written by someone about to graduate, led to a job offer.

June 12, 2008

Jane Bacon
Executive Director
New Ways
2590 N. Algernon Way
Gerard, AZ 85789

Dear Ms. Bacon,

I am writing to express my interest in the Development Assistant position with New Ways for Women and Children. The possibility of working at New Ways is very exciting for me! It is my greatest hope to work with a nonprofit organization that serves women in need, such as New Ways.

Since August of 2004, I have been a graduate student attending the College of Public Health at the University of Arizona. As a member of the Community Health Practice Concentration, I have focused my studies on women's health issues whenever possible. In addition to having concentrated my career and course work around women's issues, I have a background in recruiting volunteers; organizing trainings, seminars, and conferences; and writing publications such as newsletters. I consider myself to be very detail-oriented. Through the public health program and my graduate assistantship, I have also honed my skills in the areas of grant writing, program planning, and evaluation, as evidenced by receiving a $10,000 mini grant from the Arizona Department of Health Services to fund my internship.

From 2001 to 2004, I served as the Rural Coordinator for the Volunteer Lawyers Program (VLP), which involved coordinating volunteer attorneys in eight rural counties in Southern Arizona. As the Rural Coordinator, I matched volunteer lawyers with clients who would otherwise not have access to the legal system. The clients we served through a grant for victims of domestic violence were primarily low-income women and families. In addition, I organized recognition events, designed brochures, assisted with statewide volunteer recruitment campaigns, sponsored training seminars, wrote press releases, and designed and created the VLP website at www.VLPArizona.org.

The Development Assistant position would be a wonderful fit for me, as I am deeply committed to the mission of New Ways, as well as to issues of program growth and sustainability.

Thank you for your time and consideration!

Best regards,

An Alternative Cover Letter for More Experienced Workers

June 8, 2008

Professor August Johannsen
Graduate School of Celestial Services
Cathedral City College
12789 Heavenly Valley Lane
Cathedral City, CA. 90087

Dear Professor Johannsen

I am writing to apply for the director position in social work at the Cathedral City College. You will note on my vitae that I have had a successful career as a social work educator, program director, agency director, and dean.

In my prior academic administrative positions, I assumed responsibility for every aspect of the programs I managed including public relations, budgeting, accreditation, hiring new faculty, program development, and working with community agencies and boards.

I have written extensively on the workplace in professional journals and in the *Wall Street Journal* publication, *National Business Employment Weekly,* and recently published 10 books.

Regarding my administrative experience, I was the original director of the MSW Program at California State University, San Bernardino. In that position I created all of the courses, the admissions process, hired eight new faculty, did all of the public relations and marketing, and had full responsibility for accreditation. In our first 2 years, every student attending the MSW Program had financial assistance provided through the school or through paid placements. The program was accredited before our first class graduated. Our first classes had significant diversity and very high quality.

I also helped a school in Iowa develop its MSW program. I am very familiar with the new accreditation standards. You will also note that I was interim Dean of the Worden School of Social Service in San Antonio several years ago.

I've worked extensively with students of color and have mentored two students through California state programs that helped each student achieve doctoral educations. Both are currently working in academia and represent two of the three references included.

With over 30 years of experience as an academic, and because of my familiarity with all aspects of academic life, particularly accreditation and program development, I think I have a great deal to offer a developing program.

Thank you for this opportunity to apply for a position that can make such a difference to the people in the area served by the Cathedral City College.

Sincerely,

SUMMARY

This chapter discusses one of the most important writing projects any of us will ever do in our lives: writing resumes and cover letters to obtain a job. Suggestions are made on how best to prepare resumes and cover letters. Brevity and clarity are both highly desirable aspects of resumes and cover letters. Examples of resumes and cover letters are provided.

FIND THE MISTAKES

1. The longer a resume, the more impressive it is.
2. I'm still young and I don't have much experience. How am I going to get a job with the lame resume I have? I really should make up some jobs. They'll never check them out since they're only looking for the big picture.
3. The best way I know of to get a job is to know someone at an agency I'm applying to. That way I can refer to that person who will then give me a great reference.
4. If a job requires three references it's best to double that amount. The more references you have, the better your application will look.
5. My teacher said that she'd write a reference for me but when I asked to see it before she sent it out, she became very upset and wondered if I didn't trust her. I was worried and assured her I trusted her and told her to send the reference out without my having seen it.

REFERENCES

Jobwerx Career Center. (2007). Resume help. Retrieved Feb. 17, 2007, at www .jobwerx.com/resources/ResumeHelp.html

10

Locating Relevant Information for Reports and Research Proposals

The search for data and other useful material to use in reports and research proposals must be done with a certain strategy in mind, or you will find the process frustrating, time-consuming, and unproductive. Titles may be misleading and abstracts are often unrelated to content. The article that starts out with such promise may provide little that is new or useful. As you get further into a research report you may find questionable methodologies that make the findings all but useless. To help you find relevant information, this chapter offers suggestions to assist you in doing a sophisticated search and to save time and effort in the process.

USEFUL AND NOT SO USEFUL SOURCES

In a search for data and opinions, sources have an order of quality. For additional discussion of this subject, the reader may want to read my book on social work research (Glicken, 2003), where the subject is discussed in more detail. I have found the following rank order to be most productive in locating high-quality material:

1. **Refereed Academic Journals:** Information from refereed scholarly journals is of the highest order when considering quality of findings in a literature search. A refereed scholarly journal informs the reader that other professional readers and an editorial board have reviewed and approved the article before publication. The review process may involve asking the author to do extensive revisions of the article and to include more detail to explain the methodology used. Universities

136   *Chapter 10*

sometimes publish academic journals. They might also be the flagship journals for professional organizations such as the National Association of Social Workers, the American Sociological Association, the American Psychiatric Association, or the American Psychological Association.

Some professions have annual reviews that publish summary articles on important topics. The *Annual Review of Psychology* comes to mind. One of the very useful articles for a book I wrote on evidence-based practice came from that publication: "Individual Psychotherapy Outcome and Process Research: Challenges Leading to Greater Turmoil or a Positive Transition?" by Kopta, Lueger, Saunders, and Howard (1999). Another example from the *Annual Review of Psychology* is "Empirically Supported Psychological Interventions: Controversies and Evidence" by Chambless and Ollendick (2001). Both articles are excellent examples of very objective, clearly written, and highly useful pieces of scholarship.

The purpose of research is to share information with a broad audience. If you can't understand the language in an article, the author is either hiding something, the review panel is overly impressed with abstract language, or the material really is too technical to fully understand, and perhaps you should ask for help in deciphering it. Asking for help is essential to becoming an informed consumer of research. All universities and many human service agencies have people who can read and explain statistics and the arcane language sometimes used in very technical writing.

2. **Professional Journals:** These journals are also refereed and have an editorial board, but the articles published in professional journals may be less empirical (scientific) and may include articles that summarize existing research or offer practice wisdom. Professional journals are often practitioner-oriented and are sometimes thought to be somewhat less rigorous than academic journals.

3. **Publishers' Journals:** Journals published by for-profit publishers are written to attract practitioners, and are often more practical than scientific. Publisher journals may focus on specific topics such as family violence, and may be limited to a publication cycle of four to eight editions, or they may devote an entire edition to one topic. Publishers' journals also have a review process and an editorial board, but they are sometimes less stringent than the previous two types of journals. Consistent with other types of journals, the lag time between having a journal article accepted and published may be as much as two years. Many journals provide this information at the end of the article. The wise reader will understand that a two-year lag time in this era of rapid development in social and psychological research may result in

articles that are already outdated and sometimes obsolete by the time they reach the public.

4. **Scholarly Books:** Books are usually contracted out to authors after submission and acceptance of a book proposal and sample chapters. Book publishers have a fairly stringent review process that includes sending the proposal to other academics in the author's field for critical review. Once reviews have been received and the publisher is satisfied that the author will make changes suggested by the reviewers, the author is sent a contract that only obligates the publisher to agree to consider the book for publication when it is done. The book can still be rejected if the publisher believes that it lacks sufficient quality. Once the book is submitted by the author and accepted by the publisher, the usual lag time is 9 months before the book reaches the public. While some books contain original research, many books in the clinical field are summaries of other research on a specific topic. This certainly makes it easier for you to review current research in one place without a fairly lengthy search. But this assumes that the author is compiling all the current research, or that the author's reporting of the research is accurate. For this reason, books should not be used as the sole method of reviewing research or finding best evidence—with the exception of my books, of course. Just kidding.

Books come in two or more types: scholarly and popular. Scholarly books are written for a limited readership composed of students and professionals in the human services, for example. Popular books are written for a mass market. Although they may be very good, there is always the concern that the author has written the book for mass consumption by popularizing (or trivializing) complex and sometimes contradictory material. One can think of any number of books written about co-dependence as examples.

5. **Highly Regarded Magazines and Newspapers:** Highly regarded newspapers and magazines sometimes suffer from quality problems because mental health-related stories are often written by nonprofessionals and articles can be superficial and misleading. Going to the original source for the information is a much better idea and not very difficult with the use of the Internet. However, many professionals are initially informed about interesting topics by first reading the *New Yorker* or the *New York Times*, as several examples. An article in the *New Yorker* (Gladwell, 2002) on the Chicago heat wave and the over 700 elderly or disabled people who died as a result of the heat wave made many of us more aware that a similar problem could affect most cities in America and elsewhere. The more than 15,000 deaths of elderly and disabled people during a heat wave in France in the summer of 2003 was a confirmation that the Chicago experience had widespread

implications. There may have been professional articles written about the subject, but professionals often have their first recognition of the problem in a well-regarded mass media periodical. The ability to get information to the public in a relatively short period of time when compared to professional journals and books is another advantage of reading well-regarded newspapers and magazines. If you find a mass media article of interest you should read more scholarly articles on subjects of interest to confirm or reject stories in mass media periodicals and magazines.

6. **The Popular Press:** Hometown newspapers are generally less reliable sources of information because they often sensationalize or provide misleading information. How many of us have read about new cures for AIDS or radical new treatments for any number of emotional problems only to find out that the promising studies reported are in very early stages of development and, when completed, generally result in unusable treatments? For that reason alone, you should go to the original source for more complete information. Internet searches, to be discussed later in this chapter, can easily provide original data.

EVALUATING THE QUALITY OF REVIEWED ARTICLES

When I review an article, I know almost immediately that it will be of high or low value by looking at the number of articles cited in the reference section, the abstract (short summary) found at the beginning of an article, and the conclusions and implications sections found near the end of the article. The abstract tells me if the title is misleading. Authors sometimes use a title that doesn't accurately describe what the article is about, and journals will sometimes use a misleading title because there is an absence of information on the subject and they want to grab the reader's attention.

Once having read the abstract, I quickly scan the article to see if it has anything new to say. I look carefully to see if it has included other research I've found on similar subjects. I read the conclusions, decide if they are warranted, and look for a section that uses falsification (a way of trying to disprove the results of a study) to show the reader possible problems with the research. Researchers who provide this information get high marks, in my book. I also look for inclusion of literature from other fields and professions. I find the lack of material in many mental health articles from professions other than that of the author to be very disheartening. Articles on positive psychology frequently exclude material from what, in social work, is called the strengths perspective—a very similar approach. This tells me that the author has a narrow focus, hasn't looked very hard for other material, has disdain for other professions, or is only using information from sources with which he or she is familiar. Whatever the reason, it amounts to poor scholarship.

I try to gauge the mood of the article. Many of the articles I read for a book I wrote on violent children under the age of 12 (Glicken, 2004) were so negative and pessimistic that I found it difficult to accept their conclusions. Similarly, highly optimistic articles make me wonder whether the author is being Pollyanna-ish. Research articles should have a neutral feel to them. The language should be controlled and objective while still being clear and precise. Having read many articles about the treatment of various emotional states, I find myself leaning toward conclusions that are logical, well presented, and supported by the weight of a number of other research studies. A sudden breakthrough, or an opinion so divergent from that of most other researchers makes me wonder if the author is really justified in making these claims. If someone has something very new to say, and if it leads to a very different approach to treatment, I applaud the researcher while still being cautious about using the information generated by the study. Very divergent findings from the majority of articles in the literature are usually explained by methodological differences. Looking carefully at the methodology of a study tells me quickly if the findings will be useful. A study using a homogeneous group of clients will always differ from a study using a diverse group. Articles assuming that all clients experience depression in the same way make me nervous. Depression in older adults is very different from depression in young adults. When looking at two studies using different age groups, I want to be careful not to overly generalize the findings to everyone suffering from depression. Definitions can be misleading. What does the term "older adult" mean? Anyone over 50, over 60, or over 70? The researcher must tell us. You can see that being precise is a fundamental requirement of all research efforts.

When I read research, I'm curious about the author's purpose in conducting the study. Has the researcher made a career of studying depression? Is the article on depression the only one the author has written? Familiarity with a subject usually assures me that certain content will be included. Is the study funded by a government source, by private foundation money, by a company? Every funding source puts pressure on the researcher to write articles with a certain emphasis. As an example, I'm astonished at the differences of opinion about the impact of medications for depression. I'm not sure that I can say with certainty that a funding sources had anything to do with it, but I'm really not sure that antidepressives work in reducing the symptoms of depression. I should know, but after reading a number of studies, I'm uncertain. If I'm uncertain, imagine the despair of the client who tries to find out if antidepressives work and gets very divergent opinions?

Finally, there are authors who are very reliable and use scholarly approaches. I tend to look for research articles and books published by those authors and read them first. It saves time and the outcome is usually more beneficial than going on a fishing expedition (searching for sources without any idea of what you'll find in advance). Speaking of fishing expeditions, they're a waste of time. You can narrow your search to such specific parameters on an Internet search that you can be fairly certain you'll find exactly what you're looking for with a minimum of wasted effort.

Hunt and McKibbon (1997, p. 535) provide some additional guidelines for assessing the quality of articles:

1. Before we can apply findings to our patient we must assess the validity of all research at every step of the process.
2. Did the research remain true to its initial problem formulation and follow that problem throughout the article in a logical way?
3. Were important studies missed in the literature reviews of articles we're evaluating? Hunt and McKibbon (1997) believe that "Our confidence in the results of a review is greater when we are certain that no relevant and high-quality studies, either published or unpublished, were missed" (p. 535).
4. Were the standards we used to judge an article in the literature review appropriate?
5. If we did the study again (replicate it) would the findings be the same? You can always tell if this will be the case by reading the methodology section of research articles and determining whether we could reproduce the conditions under which the research was done. For example, a study of children with Autism may include high functioning children whose diagnosis may be in doubt. Or the parents of the children in our study may be very affluent. Finding other parents who are equally as affluent may be difficult if we try to replicate the original study.
6. In our review of research articles were the findings similar in most articles read? "If studies have different findings, pooling results may lead to meaningless or even misleading results" (Hunt and McKibbon (1997, p. 535).
7. How precise are the findings? Is there a great deal of waffling in the articles we've read or is there a sense of assurance that the findings are accurate?
8. "Will the results help in caring for patients? Determining this involves asking several questions: can I apply the results to my patients? Did the studies consider all the clinically important outcomes? Are the benefits worth any associated risks or costs?" (Hunt and McKibbon, 1997, p. 535).

LOCATING RELEVANT INFORMATION

1. **Virtual Libraries:** In this era of the Internet and high-speed computers, much of what you need to know can be located by accessing suitable Internet sites. Universities and colleges throughout the country
have virtual libraries online that allow you to find the most current
clinical research articles directly from your home computer. You'll
need to be a student or have an affiliation with the university, but
it is such an easy way to do a significant literature search that you
may want to contact your local college or university and arrange for
whatever fees it may take to have computer access from your home
or job. Some universities give alumni and associate or clinical faculty
this privilege, and remember that you don't need to be in the same
community as the university to access a virtual library. As an emeritus
faculty member (a retired faculty member who has achieved a position of prominence at a university), I have library privileges at my
former university wherever I live. Articles in the virtual library tend to
be current, and older articles (more than 5 to 10 years old) may not
be available. Articles are often in PDF format, which requires Adobe
Reader (usually downloaded free from the Adobe website).

   Another exciting virtual library development is that some universities
   can now send you an entire book by e-mail. You can check the book
   out by e-mail and it is sent to you as a large attachment to be used for
   the allotted time and then returned by e-mail. Copyright laws apply to
   Internet materials in the same way they apply to printed material.

   Care should be taken when using the Internet to make certain that
   the quality of articles accessed is as high as those in first-tier scholarly
   journals. In a survey of Internet sources located to research the subject
   of depression, Griffiths (2000) wrote:

   > In our review of 21 popular web sites containing information about
   > treating depression, we found that the quality of this information was
   > poor. This finding reinforces concerns raised by other studies which
   > have found inadequate quality or poor coverage of important health is-
   > sues on the web. There is a need to improve the accuracy and coverage
   > of information about depression on the web with regard to the relative
   > effectiveness of different treatments, the main indications for particular
   > treatments, important management issues such as duration of treatment,
   > reviewing and changing treatments, and the relevance of professional
   > expertise and patient preferences. (p. 1514)

   A Warning: As someone who spends 4 to 6 hours a day on the Internet some days, I need to say a word about computer viruses. They're

real and they can ruin your computer and trash your valuable work and research. Keep up to date with the patches available online from Microsoft and other software companies to protect yourself against viruses. Don't open junk mail and *do* get a virus program and firewall that screens your e-mail. If the virus detection program shows a virus in an attachment, trash the e-mail and alert the sender if they are known to you. Your computer will warn you that the attachment may contain a virus. Take that warning seriously, trash the entire message, and tell the sender that it's likely their computer has been infected by a virus.

2. **Libraries:** Many people think that libraries are obsolete because of the advances in online searches. They're not. A number of very important sources not found on the Internet may be available in the resource room of the library or through interlibrary loan. Librarians can show you how to do a very sophisticated literature search online and they can help you locate suitable material held in the library. And remember, while the virtual library can send you books on clinical subjects, this is a new development and most libraries have only a very small number of books available online.

   Another reason to use libraries is that some articles found on the Internet lack statistical tables or correct citations. You may find that Internet articles make it difficult to locate correct names of authors, or the exact references cited at the end of an article. Many academic Internet servers such as EpscoHost have articles dating back only 3 to 5 years. To obtain older articles, you still need to contact the library and ask if they have the article in their collection and, if not, whether they can get the article for you from another library. You can find out if the article is available by checking the library's catalog through their website. Many government documents are not available online, or a government website may only contain very recent documents. You will need to contact your library to see if the document is available at your library or if it has to be ordered from a government agency. Many libraries have journals available only on microfilm. You will need to go to the library to read those articles. You can order back issues of a journal or the specific article from the publisher, but this can be expensive and time consuming. Many journals are no longer published, but some libraries around the country may have what you need in their collection. When in doubt, contact a reference librarian. They really are excellent resources.

3. **Nonlibrary Servers:** Nonacademic search engines including Yahoo, Netscape, Lycos, Infoseek, and Google can also be used for literature searches, but much of what they provide is nonacademic and unreliable, since anyone can create a website and the content of those websites may be completely inaccurate.

4. **Research Abstracts:** Paying to subscribe to research abstracts in clinical practice areas can be an excellent way of accessing important research. Most helping professions have research abstracts that contain short versions covering the major points in an article. You can then find the article and delve more deeply into it. Don't be surprised if the abstract is just as informative as the complete article, and don't get discouraged. Finding good information takes time, patience, and perseverance.

USEFUL WEBSITES FOR THE HUMAN SERVICES

The following list of sources for locating articles and research data on issues of importance to the human services is taken from Glanville and Haines (1998) and the Netting Resource page (2002). While some of these Internet sources are medical in nature, there are often reviews of clinical trials in a number of fields of interest to the human services, including substance abuse, psychotropic medications, comparisons between the effectiveness of medication and psychotherapy, short-term counseling in emergency rooms for substance abuse, mental health factors in physical illness, and the use of adjunct mental health services in illness, death and dying, disabilities, and a host of related issues. Some website addresses change from time to time. If that's the case, a new address is usually given when accessing the original website. Some of the websites are free but some require a nominal subscription fee.

Internet Sources for the Human Services

1. **The Cochrane Library:** Contains a collection of databases including the full text of the Cochrane Database of Systematic Reviews, critical commentaries on selected systematic reviews that have been assessed for quality, and brief details of more than 170,000 randomized controlled trials. Available at www3.interscience.wiley.com/cgi-bin/mrwhome/106568753/HOME
2. **Cochrane Database of Systematic Reviews:** Contains systematic reviews of the effects of health care using randomized controlled trials. Evidence is included or excluded on the basis of explicit quality criteria to minimize bias. Data are often combined statistically, with meta-analysis (a way of summarizing a large number of studies), to increase the power of the findings of numerous studies that are each too small to produce reliable results individually. Although the Cochrane Database of Systematic Reviews is available by subscription only, the Abstracts of Cochrane Reviews are available without charge and

can be browsed or searched. www.cochrane.org/cochrane/revabstr/mainindex.htm

3. **Best Evidence:** Contains summaries of articles from the major medical journals. Details of subscriptions are found at the British Medical Journal site, http://ebm.bmj.com/

4. **Clinical Evidence:** Contains hundreds of clinical questions covering the effects of treatments and interventions based on the best available research. Answers are the result of thorough research commissioned by the prestigious BMJ Publishing Group (British Medical Journal), employing premier medical resources including the Cochrane Library, MEDLINE, EMBASE, ACP Journal Club. www.clinicalevidence.com/ceweb/index.jsp

5. **ClinicalTrials.gov:** The U.S. National Institutes of Health, through its National Library of Medicine, has developed ClinicalTrials.gov to provide patients, family members, and members of the public current information about clinical research studies. http://clinicaltrials.gov/

6. **Database of Abstracts of Reviews of Effectiveness (DARE):** Contains a database of high quality systematic research reviews of the effectiveness of health-care interventions. www.york.ac.uk/inst/crd/crddatabases.htm

7. **Evidence-Based Health Care—Latest Articles:** The latest articles on evidence-based health care provided by the Evidence Based Resource Center in New York. www.ebmny.org/pubs.html

8. **Evidence-Based Medicine Reviews:** Fully searchable database with links to MEDLINE and Ovid full-text journals produced by expert reviewers and information staff of the National Health Service's Center for Reviews and Dissemination (NHS CRD). www.ovid.com/products/clinical/ebmr.cfm

9. **Health Technology Advisory Committee Evaluation Reports:** Reports and issue briefs from the Health Technology Advisory Committee, a Minnesota organization. www.health.state.mn.us/htac/techrpts.htm

10. **Health Technology Assessment (HTA) Database:** Contains health-related abstracts. www.york.ac.uk/inst/crd/crddatabases.htm

11. **InfoPOEMS:** Searchable database of POEMS (Patient-Oriented Evidence that Matters). www.infopoems.com

12. **National Library of Medicine's Health Services/Technology Assessment Text (HSTAT):** Contains guidelines and technology assessments and reviews. http://hstat.nlm.nih.gov

13. **National Research Register:** Ongoing and recently completed research projects funded by, or of interest to, the United Kingdom's National Health Service. www.update-software.com/National/

14. **NHS Economic Evaluation Database (NHS EED):** Contains structured abstracts of economic evaluations of health care interventions. www.york.ac.uk/inst/crd/crddatabases.htm

15. **Primary Care Clinical Practice Guidelines:** Contains research protocols, primary articles, integrative studies, meta-analysis, critically appraised topics, and review articles. http://medicine.ucsf.edu/resources/guidelines/

16. **RehabTrials.org:** Site promotes, encourages, and supports clinical trials in medical rehabilitation. www.rehabtrials.org

17. **SUMSearch:** This site provides references to answer clinical questions around diagnosis, etiology, prognosis, and therapy (plus physical findings, adverse treatment effects, and screening/prevention). http://sumsearch.uthscsa.edu/

18. **Clinical Guidelines from the U.S. Agency for Health Care Policy and Research:** Provides clinical guidelines based on thorough reviews of research evidence. Available at www.ahrq.gov/clinic/cpgsix.htm

19. **Effective Health Care Bulletins:** Reports of systematic reviews presented in a readable and accessible format. www.york.ac.uk/inst/crd

20. *Guide to Clinical Preventive Services*, **2nd Ed.** Evidence-based recommendations on preventive services. Available at http://text.nlm.nih.gov/

21. *Bandolier:* Newsletter alerting readers to key evidence about the effectiveness of health-care treatments and practices. This site has very good evidence-based practice (EBP) material for helping professionals. Available at www.jr2.ox.ac.uk/Bandolier

22. **Effectiveness Matters:** Summaries of published research on a single topic that provide clear messages on effectiveness. www.york.ac.uk/inst/crd

23. **Core Library for Evidence-Based Practice:** This site contains a number of links of direct relevance for helping professionals. Some of the articles are free but others require a fee and a subscription. www.shef.ac.uk/~scharr/ir/core.html

24. **Find Articles:** a website search engine and archive where you can search and retrieve articles. The following web address will get you into articles on psychotherapy, but if you vary the subject (cognitive therapy, research on psychotherapy, the therapeutic relationship) you may find a wealth of downloadable and relevant articles. www.findarticles.com/cf_0/PI/search.jhtml?magR=all+magazines&key=psychotherapy

25. **American Journal of Psychiatry Collections:** Allows very specific searches for material relevant to helping professionals. http://ajp.psychiatryonline.org/collections/

ADDITIONAL SOURCES

Government Documents: If you know the title of a document and you think it may have been distributed as part of a Federal Depository Library Program (FDLP), you would use the monthly catalog on the web, which carries documents as far back as 1994, by entering the title into the search field of the Catalog of U.S. Government Publications at http://catalog .gpo.gov/F. This website is maintained by the U.S. Government Printing Office. Earlier years are available in paper form from any depository library. A depository library is one that has been designated as such by the U.S. government.

If you believe that the source you're looking for may be a technical report and you know the name of the government agency that sponsored the report, you might want to look at that agency's website. (For instance, the Department of Energy has an excellent report finder.)

Full-Text Social Science Databases

Social Sciences:

Britannica Online
EbscoHost
I.D.E.A.L
JSTOR
Lexis/Nexis Universe
Project MUSE
Wilson Web Social Science Index

Citations and Abstracts

General:
EbscoHost (Selected Full-Text)
Wilson OmniFile (Selected Full-Text)
Carl Uncover (Citations)

Specialized:
Social Work Abstracts (citations and abstracts in social work)
PsychInfo (citations and abstracts in psychology)
Sociological Abstracts (citations and abstracts in sociology)
Criminal Justice Abstracts (citations and abstracts in criminal justice)
Lexis/Nexis (full-text law reviews)

Social Work Resources

1. **Institute for the Advancement of Social Work Research** (www
   .iaswresearch.org/).
   The goal of this website is to enhance opportunities for social work
   research, including providing information on resources for funding
   technical assistance and career development in social work research.
2. **National Association of Social Workers** (www.naswdc.org)
   This website includes a catalog of publications, the NASW Code of
   Ethics, accreditation information, links to job resources, and current
   issues in social work.
3. **Social Work and Social Service Website** (http://gwbweb.wustl.edu/
   websites.html)
   From the George Warren Brown School of Social Work, this site is
   broken down into 99 areas of interest.
4. **World Wide Web Resources for Social Workers** (www.nyu.edu/
   socialwork/ip/)
   This site organizes a huge number of links according to subject.

Academic Writing Resources

1. **Academic Writing: Reviews of Literature**—University of Wisconsin, Madison. (www.wisc.edu/writing/Handbook/ReviewofLiterature.
   html)
2. **Writing a Psychology Literature Review**—University of Washington.
   (http://depts.washington.edu/psywc/handouts/pdf/litrev.pdf)
3. **Writing a Literature Review**—Graduate Writing Center, Teachers College, Columbia University. (www.tc.edu/centers/writingcenter/)
4. **Checklist of Sources for a Social Work Literature Review**—
   California State University, Stanislaus. (http://wwwlibrary.csustan.
   edu/lboyer/socwork/sw_checklist.htm)
5. **Resources for Graduate Student Writers**—University of Michigan
   (www.lsa.umich.edu/swc/resources/)

SUMMARY

This chapter discusses the best ways of conducting a search for research data.
Suggestions are made regarding the best sources to use in a literature search
and some guidelines are offered to help readers rank the quality of sources.
The use of the Internet in literature searches is also noted, and a number of
websites of special interest to helping professionals are provided.

REFERENCES

Chambless, D. L., & Ollendick, T. H. (2001). Empirically supported psychological interventions: Controversies and evidence. *Annual Review of Psychology, 52,* 685–716.

Gladwell, M. (2002). Political heat. *New Yorker,* 76–80.

Glanville, J., & Haines, M. (1998). Finding information on clinical effectiveness. *British Medical Journal, 317,* 200–203.

Glicken, M. D. (2003). *A simple guide to social research.* Boston: Allyn and Bacon/ Longman.

Glicken, M. D. (2004). *Violent young children.* Boston: Allyn and Bacon/Longman.

Griffiths, K. M. (2000). Quality of Web-based information on treatment of depression: Cross sectional survey. *British Medical Journal, 321,* 1511–1515.

Kopta, M. S., Lueger, R. J., Saunders, S. M., & Howard, K. I. (1999). Individual psychotherapy outcome and process research: Challenges leading to greater turmoil or a positive transition? *Annual Review of Psychology,* retrieved Aug. 7, 2003, from www.findarticles.com/cf_0/m0961/1999_Annual/54442307/print.jhtml

Hunt, D. L., & McKibbon, K. A. (1997). Locating and appraising systematic reviews. *Annals of Internal Medicine, 126,* 532–538.

Netting Resource page (2002). *Netting the evidence.* Retrieved July 17, 2003, from www.sheffield.ac.uk/~scharr/ir/netting/

11

Writing the Research Report

The research report is the format used to indicate the results of your independent research study. The research report usually consists of five parts: (a) the introduction/problem formulation; (b) the literature review; (c) a discussion of the research methods; (d) your findings; and, (e) a discussion section explaining the meaning of your findings. Some reports might also include an additional section discussing the implications of the study for a specific population of people or for a specific situation. The suggested page lengths for each section are arbitrary. You should follow your instructor's guidelines.

The following is an outline I use for graduate research projects. A master's degree thesis or a senior research paper might be longer and, of course, a doctoral dissertation is normally much longer. While the outline here might suffice for a dissertation, the length of a dissertation could be as long as 300 pages or more plus appendices.

THE RESEARCH REPORT OUTLINE

1. **Introduction and Problem Statement:** In the problem statement, you introduce the reader to the problem you are studying, give evidence of the importance of studying the problem, describe your methodology, and briefly describe the hypothesis, research questions, or research objectives that guide the study. A longer discussion of your methodology comes in the methodology section.

2. **Literature Review:** In the literature review, you summarize the relevant research articles you have read and show how they relate to the

problem you have studied. It is a good idea to briefly describe the sources you consulted during the literature review and, at the end of the review, to summarize the major findings. If you are testing a hypothesis (your belief in what the outcome of the study will be), your literature review should support your hypothesis, although you must also include research that may disagree. The bulk of the research should support your hypothesis or there may be questions about why you did the study in light of the overwhelming evidence that your hypothesis is incorrect. A good length for a literature review is 10 to 15 pages.

3. **Research Design and Methods:** This section should describe what you actually did to collect your data. The sampling process should be explained as well as the data collection procedures. Instruments used should be described, including issues of validity, reliability, and cultural sensitivity. The instrument itself should be placed in the appendix. It is important that you write this section very clearly. Students and professionals who are unsure about their methodology often tend to overwrite this section using unclear language. Your instructor or journal reviewers will see through this immediately and will know that you are unsure of yourself. This section usually takes five to seven pages to write.

4. **Findings:** The findings section presents the relevant data you have uncovered. At a minimum, this section should include measures of central tendency (mean, median mode, range, standard deviation), and any meaningful chi-squares or correlations comparing the independent variables of the sample (age, ethnicity, gender, etc.), with questions asked on your instrument that represent your dependent variables. You will need to explain what statistics were run and why. If you are uncertain about what to do in this section, you should ask someone who knows, but be sure that *you* understand the statistics before you write your paper. When poorly done, this is a section that will raise red flags for your instructor or journal reviewer who might doubt that you did the analysis yourself. More important, they will have questions about whether you really understand what you have written. Many students don't understand the meaning of the data they've run. They've been taught to use SPSS (Statistical Package for the Social Sciences), and they can easily run their data, but once the data are run, the results seem to have very little meaning to them. Statistics can be confusing, so don't feel badly if you need help in understanding the data you've generated and the statistical tests used. Most universities and some agencies have statistical consultants who are often very patient and can help you understand and run the appropriate statistics.

At the beginning of a research report, the researchers should provide a hypothesis, which is an objective prediction of what the study will find based on what similar studies have found in the past. You cannot change the hypothesis based on the findings of your study but must provide your prediction, noting in the findings section if your study proved or disproved your hypotheses. If enough research isn't available to state a hypothesis, researchers may ask a *research question* or they may provide *research objectives* to the study. A hypothesis can be stated in a neutral direction (also called a null hypothesis) or in alternative directions. Most researchers use a neutral hypothesis to show objectivity and to tell readers that the outcome of the study is in doubt. Here is an example from a study that examines how men over 50 disclose heart conditions to family members, comparing men who have been traditionally and nontraditionally socialized. Traditional men have been socialized to think of themselves as providers and protectors with responsibilities to family and community that are strongly felt.

a) **Null (neutral) Hypothesis:** "The disclosure rates of heart problems to family members by traditional men over 50 will be no different than that of nontraditional men."

b) **Alternative Hypothesis:** "The disclosure rates of heart problems to family members by traditional men over 50 will be lower than that of nontraditional men."

c) **Alternative Hypothesis:** "The disclosure rates of heart problems to family members by traditional men over 50 will be higher than that of nontraditional men."

d) **Alternative Hypothesis (a relationship, but no indication of whether it will be positive or negative):** "The disclosure rates of heart problems by traditional men over 50 to family members will be significant."

e) **Research Question:** "What is the disclosure rate of heart problems to family members among traditional men over 50?"

f) **Research Objective:** "The purpose of this study is to determine the disclosure rate of heart problems by traditional men over 50 to family members."

Enough data should be given to justify the findings. Tables, figures, and illustrations should be used to clarify the findings, although some tables can be placed in the appendix and can be referred to by writing, "Additional data are found in appendix" (give the letter assigned to the appendix where one would find that material). When reporting data, do not display all of the raw data or computer print-outs, just the data that are central and have meaning. This section of the report should only present relevant findings. It should not include the interpretations of findings. That comes after the findings are presented to allow the reader to be free of any outside influences, and is done as a courtesy to the consumer of social research. This section usually takes 8 to 10 pages.

5. **Discussion of Findings:** In this section, you will briefly state the significant results of your study and whether your findings support or fail to support your research hypothesis(es) or questions. You might also note whether your results match the results of other similar studies found in your literature review. In this section, interpretations or speculation about your findings are acceptable, even expected. It's perfectly acceptable to speculate, in the discussion section, about methodological weaknesses and to provide subjective interpretations of the data. You might want to discuss any possible explanations for your results when the results are unexpected. It is always good, in a political sense, to suggest the need for further research, although you should be specific about those areas of your study that need further evaluation. This section is often 12 to 15 pages, or longer. I would suggest that you have your instructor read this section in draft form. Many students miss important findings. Strong researchers can help you understand and locate findings that you may have missed.

6. **Implications:** Human service professionals should be grounded in the real world. The results of your study, however limited or small they might be, should have implications for some aspect of the work we do. In this section, you should try to connect the findings of your study to some real life problem, and you should discuss how it helps us better understand ways of dealing with that problem. As an example, doing a study of the prevalence of sexual harassment in the police department, the military, or any other large organization, should result in suggestions that can be used to generate needed change. While your writing should be controlled and objective, the seriousness of the problem and possible solutions should encourage you to be creative without being illogical or overly emotional.

The implication section might be as long as five pages and could include references from other studies, particularly when you discuss your findings and compare them to findings and implications from other relevant studies. This is a very important part of the study. If your findings fail to suggest a range of implications, then perhaps you haven't a good understanding of the meaning of your findings as they relate to your problem formulation. My experience is that students often miss an important opportunity to let their minds roam freely when discussing the implications of their findings. I would urge you to show this section, in draft form, to your instructor or to other researchers for additional feedback. The implication section should be the most exciting and enjoyable part of the research report, since you have the freedom to essentially say what you want to say, as long as it's rational and relevant.

WHAT TO INCLUDE IN A RESEARCH REPORT

Your instructor will probably have a suggested list to follow, but here is one you may find helpful in considering the essential material to include in the report.

1. **Title Page:** Title and author(s).
2. **Signature Page:** Signatures of the project supervisor or members of the thesis committee. This is more for a thesis and other more formal reports. You may not need a signature page for your project.
3. **Assigned Responsibilities Page:** For group projects only. I'm including an assigned responsibility page because some schools are picky, as they should be, about who did what and whether there was a fair distribution of labor in those research projects with more than one investigator.
4. **Abstract:** This should come next, and should be on a separate page. The abstract summarizes the report. It condenses what you did in the project and reports your major findings. The abstract should be about 150 to 200 words. Read the abstracts of published articles to get a sense of how this is done, but look at many articles since most published writers have the same problem explaining their work in 150 words that you might have.

   Professionals are often asked to condense ideas into a paragraph or two. While this is commonly the case in submitting papers for presentation at conferences, abstracts may also be used in the workplace as a means of submitting ideas, making suggestions, and asking for resources. Three brief abstracts are provided here as examples. In general, abstracts need to be carefully thought through since the precision of the language used is important.

   Example 1: The Role of Stress on the Health of Men
   This paper discusses male health trends and their relationship to stress and environmental factors. The data presented summarize statistical changes in health for men in the United States during the past 30 years (1976–2006) in such areas as prostate cancer; suicide rates; mental health problems; mortality rates related to homicide; alcohol and drug-associated health problems; blood pressure; cardio-vascular problems; the impact of smoking; and the increases in abusive behavior. Health data will be provided by ethnicity, age, socio-economic status, and by

geographic areas with an emphasis on differences between urban and rural environments. The presentation will provide reasons for shifts in data, some of them quite dramatic, and the work by the author on successful ways of communicating with men to ensure compliance with medical regimens. (137 words including the title)

Example 2: Abusive Male Behavior: A Threat to the Health of Women and Children

The goal of this paper is to share the findings of a study conducted by the author on the impact of male physical abuse of women and children. That impact includes severe health and emotional problems, which often continue on for considerable periods of time after the abuse. The paper includes the most current American data on the health-related effects of abuse and the treatment and social policy approaches favored by domestic violence workers to limit abusive behavior.

Findings from the study suggest that abusive men are a major threat to the health of women and children, and that prevention and treatment programs offer mixed benefits for both victims and perpetrators. Demographic data suggest that abuse is a problem in all ethnic and socio-economic groups. Treatment and prevention approaches that suggest effectiveness in reducing abusive behavior will be highlighted in the discussion. (154 words including the title)

Example 3: The Health Problems of African American Men

This presentation will consider the significant health problems of African American men. Those problems include high blood pressure, cardio-vascular problems, diabetes, problems related to substance abuse, and unusually high rates of colon and pancreatic cancers. The reasons for these health problems (many of them related to stress, diet, and environment) will be explored, and suggestions will be given regarding the treatment and prevention of health problems of African American men. Statistical data will be presented by age, socio-economic status, and income.

Responses to a study conducted by the authors on health choice patterns of Black males will also be included. These data show the importance of approaching African American males with health problems in ways that demonstrate cultural and racial sensitivity. A profile of the successful health-care practitioner will be provided, suggesting that African American males are more likely to follow medical regimens and to report satisfaction with workers who listen, show honest concern, and reinforce patient opinions about the best way to resolve a health problem. (175 words including the title)

5. **Table of Contents:** List the titles of each section of the report with the major headings and subheadings and the pages on which they will appear.

6. **List of Tables:** include page numbers.
7. **List of Figures or Illustrations:** (if any), include page numbers.
8. **List of Appendices.** This is a list of the names of each appendix. For example, Appendix A: Socio-Demographic Data Not Included in the Findings Section of the Report; Appendix B: Instruments; Appendix C: Human Subjects Forms.
9. **The Problems Formulation.**
10. **The Literature Review.**
11. **The Methodology Section.**
12. **The Findings Section.**
13. **The Implications Section.**
14. **References:** This section should be formatted according to the writing style you have been instructed to use. Most people in the social sciences use APA style. If so, you can check out chapter 5 in this book on APA style, and purchase one of the APA's style guides, available in your bookstore. Remember to use that style consistently throughout your report.
15. **Appendices:** Include your research instruments, consent and debriefing forms and statements, additional tables and data, and any permission letters allowing you to use an instrument or to do your study in a special setting. The letter from the Human Subjects Review Board approving your study should also be included (review the material in chapter 6 on Human Subjects Review Boards). You can include additional analysis of data that may not have been appropriate for the body of the report. A long list of verbatim responses from your open-ended questions might also be placed in the appendix, as well as additional analysis of data that are of secondary importance. Be sure to mention in the body of your report where the reader might find certain information (Appendix A, Appendix B). Assign each appendix an alphabetical letter and include only the information that logically should be included. For example, in one appendix, you might include verbatim responses from your study. In another appendix, you might include the instrument used.

ASSESSMENTS OF REPORTS

If you are working in a group, each student's contribution is usually assessed to the extent that it contributes to the entire project. Your individual and group contribution should be negotiated with your instructor before the project begins to avoid any problems when the report is completed.

Perhaps a written contract might be a good idea. The assessment of a research report is usually based on the following:

1. The clarity with which the research question is formulated.
2. How the research report provides insights into, develops, or expands our understanding of people, places, or events in the human services.
3. The breadth and depth of the literature review.
4. The appropriateness of the research methods in addressing the research problem.
5. The appropriateness of the statistics used.
6. The quality of the presentation of findings. Are they clearly written, accurate, and understandable to the reader?
7. The relationship of the implications of the findings to the research questions asked.
8. The overall presentation of the report including clarity of the writing, structure and organization, referencing, grammar, and spelling.

THE RESEARCH REPORT: AN EXAMPLE

The following is a short, fictional example of a research report using all six sections of the preceding outline to guide the report, plus an example of an abstract. While the issues discussed are serious ones, be advised that this is not an actual report but that data on the numbers of students who are male in social work and the prison population by gender are both accurate and current.

The Lack of Men in Graduate Social Work Programs

Abstract: Twelve (12) schools of social work were randomly visited to find out why there were so few male students in social work. The schools visited had a mean of 9.6% male students in their graduate social work programs, the approximate norm for the country. One hundred fifteen (115) participants (faculty, students, former students, and administrators) were interviewed in 12 focus groups composed equally of men and women. In general, the respondents failed to indicate concern for low enrollment rates of male students and said that men were not interested in social work as a career. When men *did* apply, they usually had lower GPAs, less work experience, far fewer good reasons for choosing social work, and seemed less willing to work with poor, disenfranchised clients than female applicants. The subjects in the focus groups did not believe that men had special abilities that would help troubled male clients and expressed a general sense that men were not likely to commit themselves to social work training until salaries were competitive with other fields.

Problem Formulation

The Council on Social Work Education (2006) reports that MSW programs in the United States have a male composition of less than 10%. This is troubling news for the many men who require the specialized help of a male social worker.

While the exact number of male to female therapy clients is unknown, we asked 15 randomly selected therapists in private practice selected from the yellow pages of the phone book and 15 randomly selected therapists from the out-patient departments of managed care facilities (HMOs) about the ratio of men to women in therapy. The consensus was that men constituted about 5% of the active participants in voluntary out-patient therapy, but had a much higher incidence of mental health problems leading to involuntary treatment for mental illness and addictions. Recent data from the U.S. Department of Justice indicate that men comprise 95% of the 2,193,798 incarcerated felons in American city, county, state, and federal jails and prisons (Bureau of Justice Statistics, 2005, December). One could argue that a reason for the high rates of male dysfunction leading to hospitalization or prison is that specialized services for men offered by trained male workers were not provided because of the small number of men in social work. If more men offering social work services were available, then men at risk would be less likely to be confined to hospitals, jails, or involuntary treatment settings for mental illness and addictions.

Hypotheses Guiding the Research Study

1. Men have limited enrollment in MSW programs because of a pervasive lack of concern for their inclusion in social work education.
2. Schools of social work are dominated by females who define social work as a female profession.
3. Men are discouraged from attending MSW programs because they are seldom recruited or offered the special incentives that define most underrepresented groups.
4. The lack of men in social work is an example of gender bias.

The Literature Review

Rather than do a complete literature review, the main elements of the review are summarized as follows: The literature review consisted of a computerized search using the help of the resource librarian at the University of North Dakota. The key words used in the literature search were: "social work, males in social work, social work admissions, social work education, and schools of social work." Government documents were reviewed as well as sources in EpscoHost and PsychInfo. Four hundred (400) abstracts (short summaries of the articles) were reviewed and 40 full articles from the abstracts were found to be of high quality and were read in their entirety. Thirty-five (35) full-text sources were included for this literature review.

The key findings of the literature review were as follows: thirteen (13) articles noted the general failure of social work journals to mention issues related to men. Six (6) articles suggested a female bias in the subject matter published in social work journals. Eight (8) articles suggested the need for more male social workers. Five (5) articles noted the preference men have for male social workers in treatment, while three (3) articles said that male therapists were neither better nor worse with male clients than female therapists. Fit of therapists, it was suggested, is more a class and racial/ethnic issue than a gender issue.

The Methodology

Twelve (12) randomly chosen schools of social work with graduate programs in the United States were visited. The total number of schools of social work with graduate programs is 150. One hundred fifteen (115) total participants were interviewed in 12 separate focus groups. The participants included faculty members, current MSW students, agency personnel and administrators, and admissions and recruitment coordinators in each school. The distribution of men to women was equal in the groups. The interviews were guided by a protocol (a list of questions scrupulously adhered to) to help discover why men were not being admitted to MSW programs in greater numbers, and what could be done to increase the number of men in MSW programs. Because the sample size was small and the use of focus groups is subjective in nature, the paradigm used was qualitative (a research paradigm that allows for more creative and flexible methodologies). However, there were three researchers involved in all of the interviews who collected data independently to provide objectivity. Consensus statements were developed for each question asked in each of the focus groups to further ensure objectivity. All questions asked in the focus groups had first been developed by a group of male and female social work educators working together at a national conference who had volunteered to spend a day at the conference developing the questions and discussing the research design.

Sampling

To randomly select the 12 graduate social work programs in America, a document listing all 150 current programs from the Council on Social Work Education was used. By choosing every 12th school starting with the 5th school on the list, 12 schools on the list in very disparate locations in the country were selected. These schools were equally divided among private and public, and large and small schools of social work. Letters to the deans of all of the schools selected were written and only one, in the midst of reaccreditation, declined. An alternative school was selected using the random selection process previously described.

One hundred fifteen (115) faculty members, students, administrators, former students, and admissions coordinators were interviewed, or approximately 10 subjects per focus group. Morgan (1997) indicates that the ideal size for focus groups is 10 to 12 subjects. Care was taken not to exceed or go lower than that number. Each group consisted of an equal number of students (2); faculty, including the dean and admissions director (6); and, agency personnel (2). The breakdown by gender was 50% male and 50% female. Race/ethnicity was also fairly evenly divided throughout the 12 schools with representation noted as: 50% Caucasian, 25% African American, 12% Latino, 10% Asian, and 3% Native American.

Maintaining Objectivity

Three colleagues accompanied the primary researcher on visits to all 12 schools of social work. One colleague videotaped each focus group to keep an accurate record of the proceedings and to use for later analysis. A second colleague helped develop consensus statements, and worked with the primary researcher in the interview process. A third colleague took careful notes of the proceedings, keeping track of any deviations from the questions asked or any attempts to manipulate answers. Upon completion of the study, all four researchers reviewed the tapes, question by question, and independently summarized their understanding of the answers to each of the 14 questions that comprised our protocol. When there were differences of opinion, the tape was viewed again and one of the four researchers helped negotiate an interpretation of the answers to a question that was acceptable to the other three researchers.

Findings

The responses to our 14 questions were remarkably similar in each of the 12 schools in which focus groups were held. Eighty-four percent (84%) of the respondents thought that it was wrong not to have more male social work students, but most (92%) noted affirmative action limitation on the use of color, creed, race or gender in the section process (this was particularly true of schools in California that operate under new laws eliminating affirmative action in state institutions). Eighty-five percent (85%) of the respondents said that men do not apply to social work programs in large numbers, but when they do, they usually cluster in the lower quartile of the applicants by GPA, experience, ability to write, and prior volunteer or paid experience in social work.

The focus groups were split almost evenly on whether recruitment would help increase the number of men, with half of the group members believing that low salaries were the greatest inhibitor to male enrollment. However, 73% of the sample admitted that little effort had been made to selectively recruit men and that race/ethnicity was still the primary concern in recruitment. Only 25% of the respondents felt that more men on faculty would serve to attract more male students, noting that 20 years ago, male faculty dominated social work education and that rates of male students were still very low. Seventy-eight percent (78%) of the respondents lamented the minimal numbers of articles about men in social work journals. There was general consensus that more research and scholarship about men was needed in social work. Finally, the consensus of the four researchers viewing the tapes was that the research procedures were adhered to closely, that the mood of the respondents was serious, and that there were no jokes or anti-male statements made by respondents in the focus groups. It was also thought that the similarity in responses across all 12 schools was an indicator that the opinions of the respondents could be generalized to other schools of social work not in the sample.

Discussion of Findings

Although the research hypotheses were not entirely proven to be either true or false, and perhaps the research approach wasn't exact enough to test all of the hypotheses, the findings suggest that qualified men are not applying to social work programs, and that schools of social work are reluctant to recruit men. The findings also suggest that men are a low priority in admissions and are not given the special consideration of other groups that allow entry into MSW programs because of special circumstances. While there is recognition of the need for more men in social work, schools have not recruited among the populations of men who might be ready to return to school, including those who are burned out in the business world and possess a strong social service interest. Many male social work students come from law enforcement, including probation and parole departments, but none of the schools had recruited these men. All schools visited had something in their literature urging women and students of color to apply to their school, but not one school included men in these statements. This is curious since women currently dominate student bodies in schools of social work and surely need not be urged to apply.

The lack of social work literature on men is also troubling. The sample was serious about the subject, but all four researchers who reviewed the tapes believed there was an absence of thoughtful consideration about the lack of men in social work and what it might mean to clients and to female students who might benefit from interacting with male colleagues. Men, it seemed to us, just didn't matter much to the respondents. This wasn't seen so much as an example of bias as it was a lack of ability to see an issue and deal with it. The existence of few men in social work seems to be a given, we felt, and was accepted by our respondents as a fact of life.

Implications

This study, although limited in its scope, seems to support concerns the researchers had about the willingness of social work programs to recruit, admit, and train men in social work. The data on the need for men in the helping professions seem fairly persuasive. We are not convinced by the studies that suggest that treatment fit is more a factor of social class than gender. It seems clear to us that the needs of young male offenders and gang members require the presence of male workers. We also believe this to be true of men who have committed sexual offenses against women, men in crisis who have had bad experiences in their personal lives with issues of intimacy, and a host of men who seem to be crying out for an understanding, supportive, and empathic male worker who might offer a substitute model of male behavior for the men whose fathers were absent during their formative years, often because they were abandoned. We think that more—much more—can be done to encourage males to enter the profession, and that recruitment efforts aimed at men who have a social service drive and are currently in jobs that have created high levels of burnout would result in considerably higher numbers of men in the field. The issue of salary, brought up so often, seems to us to be a capitulation to agencies that pay poorly and suggests that schools of social work are unwilling to fight for higher salaries for men or for women. We also think that such statements tie women in social work to long careers in the profession with limited prospects for decent incomes. We believe that much more can be done to attract men to the field, and we have submitted abstracts to national social work conferences where we will make that argument.

SUMMARY

This chapter provides an outline for writing a research report. It also offers an example of how an actual research report might be written. A guideline for the way a report should be presented is also included.

FIND THE MISTAKES

1. A literature review is your opportunity to include research that supports your argument. It's up to others to disprove your arguments with their own research review.
2. An example of an abstract might be the following: "This study sought the opinions of students in the human services about their writing skills and found that most didn't believe that writing is important."
3. Reports should always be written in a way that leaves unsaid what you actually believe. Just the facts are important.
4. Reports need to be politically correct to get a good grade (or to be published). One would never write a positive report on the behavior of men for an instructor who believes that men are the reason our society is in such difficulty. Political correctness is more than just using correct words to describe the behavior of people by gender, ethnicity, age, and race; it is actually sensitivity to what others expect from us by way of attitudes and beliefs.
5. In the implications section of a report you have an opportunity to imply anything you care to imply.

REFERENCES

Council on Social Work Education. (2006). *Annual report of the Council on Social Work Education*. Published by the Council on Social Work Education, Alexandria, Virginia.

Morgan, D. (1997). *The focus group handbook*. Thousand Oaks, CA: Sage Publications.

Bureau of Justice Statistics. (2005, December). Prison statistics. Bureau of Justice Statistics retrieved from the Internet March 2, 2007, at www.ojp.usdoj.gov/bjs/prisoner.htm

12

Requesting Money

At some point in your career, you may be asked to submit requests for money, equipment, materials, books, attendance at a conference, and many other types of funding that may help your career progress and make your life at work more productive. These requests may be competitive and usually require that you follow a predetermined outline and a very brief presentation of the results (or findings in a research report). In this chapter we will cover the most prominent forms of requesting funding: requests for research money; requests for attendance at conferences; and requests for equipment. Let's start with requests for research monies.

A REQUEST FOR MONEY: THE GRANT PROPOSAL

The well-done grant proposal should include the following:

1. *A well-formulated problem.*
2. Some unique aspects that entice the funding source. A proposal on a very current topic is usually enticing, particularly if it's a topic with little current research.
3. Findings that have important applications to problems in the human services.
4. The grant really does require special funding and cannot be done using common resources available in universities or agencies.

5. The proposal is based on the proven ability of the grant writer to get funding for prior projects.
6. Language that clearly explains what the grant will accomplish and the methodology used.
7. The proposal acknowledges other research that has been done in the field.
8. Evidence that the proposal is cost effective.

The following example is a request for funding limited to two pages. The competition included 45 other proposals with enough funding for five proposals. This one, fortunately, was funded. Let's consider the writing of the proposal and then the discussion suggesting reasons why the proposal was funded.

THE RESEARCH PROPOSAL: AN EXAMPLE

1. **Title**: "The Counseling of Abusive Men: A Preliminary Study Using the Practice Wisdom of Therapists."
2. **Abstract**: Male abuse of women and children is at an extremely high level. The literature describes this angry, often substance-abusing population as untreatable. This project is an attempt to determine the treatment approaches that actually work, which will be achieved by collecting and evaluating the practice wisdom of current practitioners who treat abusive behavior. As a result of this first step in finding effective treatment approaches for abusive behavior, the researcher hopes to attain additional funding to test the treatment approaches that appear most promising.
3. **Purpose**:
   a) To develop effective therapy approaches for treating male abuse of women and children.
   b) If successful, the project will offer the professional mental health community counseling and therapy approaches that may actually work in reducing subsequent abusive episodes.
   c) To test the treatment approaches identified as useful by current practitioners in a more ambitious long-range project. City, county, state, federal, and foundation monies will be sought for this additional phase of the research. Funding of this project will serve as seed monies to identify treatment strategies current therapists believe are effective with abusive men.
   d) Most of the researcher's current work relates to men, with particular attention to therapy and counseling strategies effective in treating male problems. Those problems include very high rates of suicide, substance abuse, violence to women and children, and destructive behaviors that lead to medical difficulties and early death. The project is a continuation of that interest and will, hopefully, add to the minimal literature on the treatment of social and emotional problems of men.

4. **Methodology**:
   a) Approximately 80 therapists in the Kaiser-Permanente Health Care System (the Fontana, California region) will be interviewed in eight focus groups. The group interviews will result in the development of vignettes of abusive situations involving men. The vignettes will then be sent back to the workers who will be asked to indicate the most appropriate and effective ways of working with abusive men. The returned answers will be evaluated using content analysis techniques to identify a core of practice behaviors most likely to reduce further abuse.
   b) Practice wisdom is seldom considered in the literature and will form a useful way of developing broad approaches to the treatment of abuse.
   c) The research will be conducted in the university's service area. Feedback will include data from diverse populations of therapists (by gender, experience, professional identification, and ethnicity) who serve a diverse client population.
   d) The project will be conducted during the current academic year. Geographic proximity to focus group participants and the cooperation of the host agency (see the attached letter of support) will permit timely completion of the project.
5. **Budget Narrative:** The researcher is asking for one released course ($3,500) to provide time to complete the research. Travel costs are limited to drives to interview sites in the Fontana Region of Kaiser ($300) and some limited state travel to share the conclusions of the research with colleagues at conferences. An additional $300 is requested to continue the search for research funding to do additional research. Supplies and services, including postage and questionnaire construction, will be limited to $300. A student assistant will help in analyzing the responses, in the further review of the literature, and in completion of the final report. At $8 an hour for 100 hours, this part of the budget will cost $800. Duplication expenses, including limited publication and distribution of the final report, will be $300. **Total request is for $5,500.00.**

Discussion

The primary reason the proposal was funded, according to the committee evaluating proposals, was that the topic was very timely. The O.J. Simpson case was in full gear and the subject of domestic violence was painfully current. The ability to help abusive men, while one reason for funding the proposal, wasn't the primary reason, however. It was felt that the proposal would lead to further funding on a larger scale and that this small request for "seed money" would lead to a substantial amount of additional funding for more research on work with abusive men, and it did. The grant also led to two book contracts (Glicken and Sechrest, 2003; Glicken, 2004) on the subject of violence, particularly, domestic violence.

In general, requests should be brief, clearly written, and include a strong emotional argument explaining why the funding is needed. Unemotional arguments may lead to funding, but even scientific requests that suggest the promise of important contributions do better than those written for the sheer desire to accumulate knowledge. As you will see in the following discussion, this small piece of research led to a number of conclusions, any one of which could be developed into a much larger and more expansive piece of research.

PROVIDING FEEDBACK TO FUNDING SOURCES

The following report was generated as a result of the prior research project. Note that this report was written for the funding source and, while academic in tone, the report explains the results of the study to a group who may not be familiar with the subject or the research approach used. The report also uses numbering of major points. Numbering is a good way to present complex information, but bullets may be as effective.

The Counseling of Abusive Men: Findings

In an attempt to establish the most effective treatment approaches for work with abusive men, the researcher met with 80 therapists from the Kaiser Permanente Mental Health Department in the Fontana, California area. Eight small focus groups of 10 therapists each were used to develop vignettes of abusive situations involving men. The vignettes were then sent back to the workers and they were asked to indicate the most appropriate and effective ways of working with the abusive men. Sixty (60) completed questionnaires were returned. The following summary of results is presented:

1. The most frequently utilized approach (45 of 60 subjects) by the subjects was anger management. This approach uses a cognitive-behavioral process in which men are taught "time-out" techniques to evaluate their perceptions of situations and to think through ramifications of an abusive act before actually responding. The cognitive-behavioral approach was coupled, as are many diversion project approaches, with the threat of jail time if clients continued the abuse.
2. Most respondents (38 of 60) believed that treatment of abusive men was most effective when done in groups composed of other abusive men. According to the respondents it is important to stagger the composition of treatment groups so that abusive men in treatment groups are at different stages in their recovery. More fully recovered clients help beginners to deal with abusive behavior and reinforce and support the therapist's work. Composition of the groups should be random and heterogeneity should be encouraged to provide the most impact from the group experience.

3. Respondents believed that a primary reason for the abusive behavior related to intense, irrational jealousy (52 of 60). All of those surveyed believed that abusive men are prone to serious misperceptions of female behavior and that treatment that fails to deal with these misperceptions is likely to have limited impact. While teaching abusive men to cope with jealousy is much harder than helping men learn to manage anger, it is a key component of successful therapy. Many therapists used the freeze framing approach that helps clients accurately check the situation that made them jealous against their over reactions.

4. Many workers (47 of 60) noted that while the physical abuse may be reduced during treatment, the emotional abuse continued and that its origins were usually associated with the man's perception of being taken advantage of by a wife or girlfriend. Some (23 of 60) workers even suggested that medication to control depression should be used since many of the men who exhibit extreme jealousy were also severely depressed. Workers (31 of 60) also favored controlled confrontations in supervised groups by women who had been abused (but not abused by men in the group) as a way of shocking abusers into recognizing the impact of their behavior and helping them become more empathic.

5. A number of workers (46 of 60) believed that abusive men know very little about women. Men who abuse are often at a low level of development in their ability to form relationships with women. In this population, relationships are frequently based on the belief that women are sexual objects and that one relates to them only in sexual ways. To help with this problem some workers (18 of 60) suggested the use of victim awareness techniques to sensitize men to the end result of their behavior including films and the use of novels, poems, and music (also known as Bibiotherapy). Other workers (12 of 60) suggested the need to include women in the treatment process as co-therapists to provide a female perspective to abusive men. A few workers surveyed (8 of 60), however, believed that women as co-therapists would very likely create discomfort and would only serve to increase drop-out rates among men who are already prone to disengage from treatment.

6. A few workers (6 of 60) discussed the inability of abusive men to use language that accurately represented their feelings during intense interactions with women and children. A suggested treatment approach by several of the therapists (8) would focus on teaching men a vocabulary to express feelings and to substitute appropriate language for force when dealing with situations that were likely to prompt abusive responses. Simulations and role plays could be helpful in this process. Videotaping group members in treatment was thought to be very important so that group members could watch and evaluate their attempts to use language as an alternative to violence.

7. Because many abusive men in treatment fail to change, some respondents (17 of 60) believed that the courts should maintain a registry of names of abusive men whose history would be available nationally and whose social security number would alert police in all jurisdictions that these

men have histories of abusive behavior. This approach would be similar to the one currently used in work with child molesters and rapists. Many of the workers (35 of 60) favored an immediate response to an abuse situation by urging the police to jail any man accused of physical abuse where there was clear evidence that he had caused physical injuries. These workers noted that in communities that use immediate incarceration, episodes of abuse had fallen dramatically. They also favored diversion projects in which perpetrators agreed to attend treatment sessions as a way of staying out of jail. Many of the same workers who favored diversion projects were skeptical about the effectiveness of treatment and wondered if abusive men who were forced to receive treatment would truly benefit (20 of 60).

8. Some respondents (20 of 60) had reservations about their ability to help abusive men and did not believe that we understand the way abusive men think or that we have the treatment technologies to change their behavior. These workers believed that abusers have antisocial personality disorders that lessen the probability of change. Many of these workers favored close monitoring of the abusive man by the courts and were reluctant to believe that treatment personnel had a role at all in the change process. Among the workers who saw little role for treatment personnel in work with abusive men, some (17 of 60) favored mandatory sentencing of abusive men, including night detention so that they might work and then pay for necessary help to victims of the abuse. They also believed that the men should pay for their own incarceration and supervision.

9. Among some of the workers surveyed (12 of 60), there was a sense that treatment should be saved for the victims. Treatment resources are scarce, they argued, and could best be used with the women and children who suffered most from the abusive behavior. These workers noted that victims are morally entitled to help and are likely to be more receptive than abusers. They also believed that abused women and children benefit because treatment would help them resist abusive relationships in the future.

10. Some workers (18 of 60) argued for a serious campaign to educate women in the dynamics of abuse so that they could stop it before it progressed in a relationship. These workers also noted that there was a need for resources to be made available to abused women and children, including safe shelters and other housing arrangements, so that they might remove themselves from abusive environments. Many workers (48 of 60) were particularly concerned that restraining orders should have teeth in them and that abusers should be jailed and fined if they violate an order. These workers also believed that if financial resources were made available to abused women, many would leave abusive situations on their own because financial dependency kept them in abusive relationships.

11. Some workers (11 of 60) discussed the need for abuse groups composed of abusive men and the women they abuse. Other workers (34 of 60) suggested the need for family approaches that treat the abusive system. These workers believed that abuse cannot be treated effectively unless the entire family is included, and that services limited to women or

children, or to the abusive men, are unlikely to produce real change. It should also be noted that while some workers favored this approach, many of the respondents (46 of 60) worried that it might lead to an escalation in violence when the couple or family returned home. Workers favoring systems approaches suggested the need to separate abusive men from their families during treatment to avoid further violence. In this approach men would live apart from their families and all contacts with families would be supervised.

12. Finally, some workers (23 of 60) argued for a more intensive therapy regime similar to those used with sex offenders, focusing on confrontation and cognitive restructuring. This approach would be patterned after similar approaches used in drug and alcohol rehabilitation programs in which residential treatment is used for a short intensive period of time to help give the client a crash course in impulse control and anger management. For these workers, abuse is only the overt manifestation of additional pathologies that can never be treated successfully without the intensive treatment provided in a structured residential setting. Given the prevalence of drug and alcohol problems in abusive men, these workers believed that treatment of substance abuse was also necessary before the physical abuse had any chance of being eliminated.

Discussion

As the reader will note, there is a great deal of information presented in the report that might lead to a larger research project and additional funding opportunities. Much as it was intended to do, this small piece of research led to a series of larger evaluations of programs treating perpetrators of domestic violence. It was also used to create several unique treatment programs for abusive men. The research design certainly wasn't complicated and the information attained was fairly ordinary. In truth, a literature review might have provided the same results. There is, however, something about asking experts their opinion that has a positive impact on funding sources. Furthermore, since the experts came from the private arena, the feedback was considered more reliable by funding sources than if it had come from the public sector.

WHY RESEARCH GRANTS ARE SOMETIMES NOT FUNDED

Jones and Bundy (2006, pp. 3–5) suggest a number of reasons a grant might not be funded. The following list of reasons is paraphrased from their work:

1. The question being asked is unclear, as are the outcomes and how one would judge success or failure.

2. The request fails to follow funding guidelines that include the purpose of proposals to be submitted and the type of information required. Along these lines, the grant may ask for more money than the funding source is willing to provide. Reading prior funded requests may help. Feedback from more experienced workers and researchers may also help.
3. The question being asked is illogical and ill-formed.
4. It isn't clear why the question is being asked or what the grant writers' motivation may be.
5. The proposal is routine, doesn't require special funding, and merely applies known techniques.
6. There is no clear application of findings to the human services.
7. There is little evidence that the grant writers will succeed where others have failed. To convince funding sources that you have a worthwhile idea you should: "(a) describe preliminary work you have done which shows that it is indeed a good idea; (b) include a list of publications, and perhaps include a short paper (preferably a published one) which gives more background, as an appendix" (Jones and Bundy, 2006, p. 4).
8. The grant writers claim a new problem is being studied but give too little information to judge the proposal's merit. This suggests that we give sufficient information to funding sources. If in doubt about what constitutes sufficient information, have others read your work who are unfamiliar with the grant to determine if they understand what you are proposing.
9. The grant writers are unaware of new research on the topic they plan to study and fail to include it in their proposal.
10. To hide the lack of an in-depth literature review, grant writers include too few references or only their own articles.
11. The proposed study has already been done or seems to have been done and the grant writers fail to mention this.
12. The proposal is badly written or incomprehensible to the funding source.
13. It is impossible to complete the study in either the amount of time or with the amount of money asked for in the grant proposal.
14. The proposal is much too expensive for the probable benefit. This should prompt all grant writers to be very frugal in their budget request, keeping the request focused on the study and not side benefits, such as attending a conference. Be realistic about what you can do with the funding you request and the time allotted. The rule of thumb is that it usually takes longer and costs more than your estimate.
15. The grant writers' organization should fund the study since the organization has available money and will benefit directly.

16. There is little evidence that the grant writers have sufficient expertise to complete the study. It might be a good idea to include someone in the request with specific expertise in the problem to be studied.

REQUEST FOR ATTENDANCE TO A CONFERENCE

The rules vary from agency to agency about how a worker requests funding. My experience is that the request should be very brief and contain only the salient information required. If more information is needed, management will let you know. I also include relevant information such as a quote on airfare and the conference brochure. You often have better luck getting funding if you have a paper accepted or plan to give a presentation to other workers about what you've learned when you return from the conference. Bringing back copies of papers (often available from presenters) and making them available to others in your agency is also a very good idea. Finally, anything you can do to save the agency money is certain to be appreciated, as in the following example:

To: John Davis, Executive Director
From: Jack London, MSW
Date: July 5, 2007
Re: Money to attend a conference

As you know, I have been using Alaskan huskies to keep older housebound clients company. They are very warm and empathic dogs, and the results have been gratifying. None of my clients with dogs to keep them company have required nursing home care, while clients who don't have dogs for company suffer a 50% nursing care rate.

I am requesting money to attend the Nome, Alaska, Annual Call of the Wild Conference to learn more about using dogs as an adjunct to providing social service assistance. Since my brother lives in Nome, I will not require money for housing or food. I am asking $500 for airfare and $250 for conference fees. I am willing to use vacation time to attend the conference since I believe that my attendance is vital for the work we do.

I have attached a conference brochure and a note from my travel agent assuring me that the airfare rate is the lowest available. I will bring back scholarly papers from the conference and I will give a two-hour presentation to other workers and to anyone else in the community interested in the subject.

I believe that having dogs as companions for many frail, elderly, and disabled people is an effective way of helping lonely and isolated people stay out of institutional care. I plan to write a major grant to further my research on the subject. Please let me know if you need any additional information about the conference or about my work. Thank you very much for your consideration of my request.

REQUESTS FOR EQUIPMENT

Requests for equipment should be specific with a very good reason supplied for needing the equipment. If the equipment is technical in nature, you should include a statement from technical support and an estimate from purchasing. If you have neither technical support nor a purchasing department in your agency, have your supervisor attach a note attesting to the need for the equipment requested. Also attach two or three estimates of costs, suggesting in your note which pieces of equipment will give the agency the most value for the money. For example:

To: Mike Manly
From: Jack Patrick, MFT
Date: July 14, 2008
Re: Request for a new computer

I am responding to the memo of July 13, 2008, seeking requests for equipment. I am requesting a new computer and monitor to replace my current but nonworking computer and monitor. I've attached a note from technical support verifying that neither piece of equipment works and that they are not repairable. The basic computer and monitor are, according to purchasing, available for $699. I've attached a memo from the purchasing department indicating the lowest cost available for a computer with the fundamental software needed to do my work. The computer is used for my reports, Internet searches to determine best evidence in research searches, and running SPSS for weekly statistical reports. It also contains programs that help me evaluate client progress and improvement. Since I do not have a working computer at present, I hope this request will provide me with the equipment necessary to do my job. Please let me know if I can provide additional information. Thank you for your consideration of my request.

SUMMARY

This chapter discusses how to write requests for money. Three types of requests are discussed: research money, money to attend conferences, and requests for equipment. Examples of each type of request are given. The research request includes not only the request for money but also the type of short report often required when money has been provided by a funding source.

FIND THE MISTAKES

1. I am writing to request $1,500 for a new computer. My current one is slow and a faster computer would make me more efficient.
2. I am requesting $3,000 to attend the annual conference of marriage and family counseling in San Juan, Puerto Rico. The brochure suggests many interesting workshops that will benefit my work.
3. The results of my study suggest the need for additional funds. I am therefore requesting $5,000 to continue this interesting and important line of inquiry.
4. The Institute for Personal Growth requests $50,000 to study the adjustment of men returning from service in the Middle East.
5. The impact of rape is often prolonged PTSD. We are asking $2,500 to do a pilot study of the impact of early treatment for women who have been raped and have gone to the local rape crisis center for help. We contend that early intervention will reduce PTSD.

REFERENCES

Glicken, M. D. (2004). *Violent young children.* Boston: Allyn and Bacon/Longman.

Glicken, M. D., & Sechrest, D. K. (2003). *The role of the helping professions in treating the victims and perpetrators of violence.* Boston: Allyn and Bacon/Longman.

Jones, S. P., & Bundy, A. (2006). Writing a good grant proposal. Retrieved June 11, 2006, from http://research.microsoft.com/Users/simonpj/papers/Proposal.html

13

Writing for the Popular Press

Human service professionals are often asked to write for the popular press. This may include magazines, professional newsletters, and newspapers. These opportunities to reach a mass audience should not be ignored because professionals can reach more people with an article or a story than they can in a lifetime of writing for academic journals or presenting professional papers.

The styles used for the popular press require the writer to move from the formality of the academic/scholarly style to a more flexible and informative style. An article for a mass media journal, two articles for newspapers, two letters to the editor, and two book reviews are provided as example of how to write for the popular media.

The first example was written for a popular mass market book I wrote called *Ending the Sex Wars: A Woman's Guide to Understanding Men* (Glicken, 2005a). The segment I've included here is called "Coffee House Wisdom" and forms the first chapter of the book. I wrote it to explain male behavior to a female audience I didn't think I could reach in a clinician-oriented book I had written (Glicken, 2005b) with similar content, but for a professional audience. I have strong feelings that men and women aren't doing well these days and I wanted to help move the dialogue along by writing a book that was sympathetic to men and to women but would also reach a mass audience.

The second article was written for a popular newspaper on the subject of men. While the newspaper may have expected a more scholarly piece, I wanted the reader to know what it felt like to be a divorced father with young children. I also wanted to counter the mean-spirited view of men so many people had when the article was published in the early 1990s.

The reader will note that the style in each article is crisp and fast moving, and that the articles sometimes include quotes from experts, but also from people who were interviewed for the articles.

If you are asked to write for a similar publication, I suggest that you read a number of the articles published in that publication so that you understand the format and style used. All popular publications have discernable styles. After reading a dozen or so articles, you will understand the style expected of you. When in doubt, seek assistance from the editors of the magazine, newspapers, or journals.

Coffee House Wisdom

Most mornings I go to a local cafe in Southern California for coffee. It's a sort of ritual for me. Sometimes I write checks for bills and organize my day or grade the accumulated papers I must read as a professor of social work at a California university.

The local men often walk by my table and nod in recognition. Sometimes they stop and talk to me about my articles in the local newspaper about men. These men are the workingmen of America; the plumbers and construction workers, the common laborers and retired railroad workers, the illegal immigrants from Mexico. Their trucks and beat up old cars line the restaurant parking lot.

I have come to value my conversations with these men. Many of them have done badly by women and children, and readily admit it. Some of them are extraordinary people who have done better than most of us. And there are always the men who sit and talk about women and you want to get up and ream them out. They sound like abusers. Worse, they sound like children in adult bodies.

I've learned a lot from listening and talking to these men in the morning. These men talk like real people. People with flaws. Human beings we all know in our daily lives.

When the wives and children of these men talk to me, you get a different picture of their behavior. They talk about abuse and neglect, about put downs and absences, and sometimes, about abandonment. They describe, in detail, how the insensitive behavior of their men affects the women and children who are trying so hard to love their husbands, boyfriends, and fathers.

Sometimes I get a chance to sit with the men and women and listen to them talk about the gender wars they have fought. The men often sit with their mouths open and ask, "Was I that bad?" Everybody nods their heads. The men have mellowed so it isn't easy for them to imagine that they've acted so badly in the past.

Sometimes the men hang around, after the women leave, to assure me that they weren't so bad, but there is an emptiness to their denial that rings hollow. Many times they walk away shaking their heads, angry at me for making them hear so much bad stuff about behavior they'd rather forget.

The men who interrupt me are ordinary men. Just regular "Joes" who need the sweet and tender loving of a woman. Men who are better when a special woman is in their life. Men who can hardly navigate the complexities of life and who depend on women in ways that are sometimes childlike.

Men like Roger, a plumber, who joins the early morning construction gang at my coffee shop. He sees me sitting in the back reading the paper and comes over to sit with me. Today he complains about his wife. She's too fat, he says. He's lost interest in her. I look over at Roger, who is perhaps 60 or 70 pounds overweight, and I ask if he's looked in the mirror lately. Does he know that his obesity is as off-putting to his wife as hers is to him? He mumbles something derogatory about my mother, but I see him everyday and he looks somehow, thinner. When I see him weeks later with his wife, they look nice together. Warm, maybe even tender in the way older men and women can be with each other.

He doesn't thank me for my advice or say how much his life has improved because of my simple suggestions. All he does is bring his wife over, an attractive woman in her forties. See how great my wife looks, his smile says? See what a hunk I must be to attract such a great looking lady?

Another guy, Richard, one of the few Black men who sit in the cafe, complains to me about the way his wife spends his money. "She's a shopping junkie," he says. "Ain't no way anyone can spend so much money."

He brings her in one morning, a nice, soft-spoken young woman. She talks to me about how difficult it is for a family to make ends meet, but Richard is a good husband and father and they make the money go a little further. Richard wants to buy me breakfast. He feels like dancing in the cafe. His wife has touched a part of his heart with love seeds.

How strange men must seem to women. How they talk so badly about the women in their lives but depend on them for everything. And how badly men do in giving women credit for what women do to make their lives easier and to help them in the small and large ways that men almost never regard as important or admit make a difference.

How absolutely contradictory male behavior must seem to most women. How men prance, and strut, and brag without end when inside they often feel as inadequate as anyone can feel and still they manage to get up in the morning and put their clothes on. And yet to talk to them, men seem on top of the world, kings of the hill, beyond pain.

Were it only so. If men were so secure, they wouldn't do the often terrible things they do to wives, girlfriends, co-workers and children. They wouldn't abuse and abandon their loved ones, or fly into jealous rages, or harass women in the workplace. If men were the winners in this war among the genders, they wouldn't fall apart in mid-life, or suffer the indignity of failing bodies that leave them old and emotionally wrecked because they don't take care of themselves, or see doctors, or limit their use of alcohol and drugs.

Just as I talk to the men when I have coffee in the mornings, I have come to cherish the time I spend talking to the women I see who come in for a quick cup of coffee before their impossibly long and complicated days begin. They are the working women of America, the unglamorous women who get up at 5 a.m. and care for their families before driving an hour or more to thankless jobs. I have come to think of these women as very special people. Though they are often war weary, they still have an optimism about the flawed men they meet, fall in love with, and marry.

They are the women like Betty Sue who, early one morning asks me what to do when a man loses interest in sex. As I begin to talk to her, some of the women in the coffee shop join us.

"He's a good man," she says, "and we used to have a great love life. I'm sure something is really wrong."

One of the women in the group sitting at the table says, "Why not just say to him something like, 'Honey, it sure used to be nice how we'd spend our time in bed. It would sure be nice to have that again.' Why not give it a try?" Betty Sue looks over at me and I nod in support.

The next day she comes back with a big smile on her face. All of the ladies at the table rib her until she says, "He thought I wasn't interested anymore. He thought maybe I was with another man, and it was making him crazy."

"How could he think something like that?" someone asks, and one of the ladies says, "Because, he's a man. That's the way men think."

Another time, Denise, a woman perhaps in her late thirties, is going through the early stages of knowing that her marriage is all but over. "I don't understand it, doc," she says to me. "We were such good friends. We really liked being together. But now, he just always seems like he's in another world. When we talk, it's always about the house or the car, it's never about how unhappy we are together."

It's very early in the morning but Denise has been up for hours and her bloodshot eyes suggest that she's been crying in the car on the way to the coffee shop. "It's tough," I tell her, "when a man shuts down. Have you asked him if something is wrong at work or in his personal life?"

She shakes her head. "He always tells me when something is wrong," she says. "He's not one to keep things inside."

We sit in silence for a while and watch the regulars walk in, many of them still sleepy from nights too short to make up for the hours of driving and the hard work ahead of them. I look at Denise and gently touch her hand. "Maybe there's something wrong, Denise, that's so troubling to your husband that he can't discuss it with you. Men often find it hard to talk about really personal problems. Try asking him tonight and stay with it. Don't let him push you away or avoid talking."

Denise looks at me with a look I've seen all too often. The moment comes in a relationship when you've tried everything and you've unconsciously begun to give up. It's the moment of being emotionally divorced. Denise looks up and nods her head, her shoulders slumped. "O.K. doc," she says, "I'll try for you, but I don't think it's gonna work."

A week goes by and Denise hasn't come in for coffee. I'm ready to blame myself for bad advice since failure is an occupational hazard we live with in the helping professions. But one morning she comes in with her husband. They find their way over to my booth and after introductions and handshakes, Denise and her husband, Ed, sit for a while and drink their coffee while we make small talk. Finally, Denise tells me what's happened in the past week with Ed watching, a serious look on his face.

"I didn't want to do it, doc, but I knew you'd be hurt if I came to you for advice and didn't use it. So I waited until Ed was sitting in his chair after dinner and I made the kids go outside so we could talk. I said to Ed how he seems to be unhappy all the time and that I don't think we're gonna make it. And he says back to me that he's fine and that it's my imagination. But I won't let it go, doc, and I keep at it until he finally says to me that he thinks he might lose his job and he doesn't think I'll stay with him if he doesn't have a job." I look over at Ed and he's nodding quietly as Denise tells the story.

"Where did he get that crazy idea?' I asked him, and he says, 'From you, Denise, from you.' I argued with him about that but he reminded me of the many times I've said, sarcastically, that I'd never take care of a man. And it's true. I've said it a lot but I didn't mean *my* man. But of course, that's the way he took it. We talked most of the week about the situation and we got it straightened up. We didn't think we could because there were so many other things that were going wrong, but we did and it's so much better now I can't even believe it was possible. I thought that Ed was like most men and that he couldn't talk about the really tough stuff. He fooled me, though. Once I reached out a little, he could talk just fine."

I've had hundreds of conversations like this with the men and women of the coffee shop. Not all of them end so dramatically or well, but I think that men and women are much better together with a little gentle guidance, some good information, and some timely help.

I think men and women hunger for better times. No one wants to be in a constant war between the sexes. When relationships between men and women improve, we all gain. And since love is everything it's cracked up to be, nothing in this world beats the wonder of two people in love.

So here goes. Let's discover what we can about men to make your life just a little easier and maybe in the process, their lives, as well. (Glicken, 2005a, pp. 1–6)

Discussion of "Coffee House Wisdom"

The reader can see that I wrote this piece in a very nonacademic way. I learned this style by writing a number of articles for the Dow Jones publication, *National Business Employment Weekly*. When you have only 1,000 words to inform people, you need to be very brief and descriptive in your presentation. This can be done by writing short, sequenced, descriptive paragraphs that are informative and interesting to others. It is probably the most difficult writing you will ever do because there is so little space to develop ideas. After you've done it a while, however, you will be able to summarize major ideas and understand what will interest the reader. A suggestion that has helped my writing is that the title is the most single useful way to start an article. Getting the title right gives you a clear idea of what to say in an article. That, and the understanding you and the editor have about what is to be included in the article. Clear directions from the editor can save you a great deal of rewriting later on.

In this piece, I thought the personal experience I was having with the men and women in the coffee shop would be much more dramatic than the statistics and quotes I use in academic articles and books. There is something very touching about the problems people have in relationships that grab a reader's interest immediately. I also thought the setting would appeal to many working women who often experience difficulty in relationships because of the overwhelming amount of pressure on them and on their husbands. I am, after all, a social worker and the stress on working people concerns me. I grew up in a blue-collar home and I wanted to write about the people I care about: working people who make too little money to thrive; husbands and wives who have few support systems in their lives; the disgraceful way we ask families to do so much but seldom help them by offering low-cost health care, low-cost transportation, and other forms of help to strengthen families. These are the people who concern me the most because of my personal and professional inclinations. Writing about them was motivating to such an extent that the book wrote itself in a month.

A NEWSPAPER ARTICLE: SINGLE MEN AND THEIR CHILDREN

The second example is a newspaper editorial (Glicken, 2005a) written to change people's way of thinking about issues. The reason I wrote the article was to make the topic as personal as possible. Most readers aren't only interested in information, they also want to relate that information to their own lives. In this article, written after my divorce, my experiences with divorce were melded with those of other men. Hopefully, this approach had a more powerful impact on the reader than a more professional and less personal article with data and quotes from experts.

Single Men and Their Children

In the summer, the divorced men of America shuttle their children back and forth across the country for the annual ritual of summer vacation with their children. If you are in your middle years and your children are in a growth spurt, meeting them at the airport can be disarming. One minute a child looks like a child and the next minute they are young men or women asking to drive the car.

For the lonely single men in America, summer with their children makes life sweet again. Someone laughs at your bad jokes and listens to your fears, your hopes, and your dreams.

This annual ritual of summer vacations is not without its painful side. You get used to having someone in the house, but once they leave, the loneliness you feel is like a knife in your heart.

Many of the single men I know feel as if their lives are over. They know that they will never experience family life again or the sweet and tender moments of love. Their experiences as single men confirm their growing belief that the single women in the core group they date will only complicate and reduce their lives. It is a profound sorrow for most of them.

The men I know wish they had been better husbands and fathers. If they knew at 30 what they know at 50, they would have worked very hard to keep their families together.

These single men in their middle years often fear commitment and relationships with women more than anyone can know. It is a fear so steeped in the pain of divorce and the dislocation of loved ones that they shy away from love and tenderness just as they claim it is the very thing they want.

When these men re-marry or find someone to share the good moments of life, they so hold back emotionally that wives and lovers inundate the counselors of America to understand how best to deal with them. It is a difficult task, dealing with men who can't love or trust, and second and third marriages often end in divorce.

Those of us who are interested in the lives of men know how afraid men are to self disclose, how they almost never seek help when they are in turmoil. We know that they turn to alcohol and drugs and, when all else fails, suicide to resolve hurts so deep that even a good therapist can only scratch the surface.

The wives and lovers of many men paint dismal pictures of their lives together. They increasingly view men as children and often use terms like *child* and *baby* when they discuss their husbands or lovers.

As one listens to them, it becomes clear that many of these men are alone, preoccupied, and lost in an inner dialogue that makes them seem inaccessible.

But during summer vacation these lonely and emotionally aloof men reach inside for the love and intense pride they feel for their children. If they are very lucky, and if their children care deeply about them, it is a summer of discovery and joy.

But if the uncompromising and rigid nature of their thoughts keep them distant and aloof, the summer is one more indication to their estranged children of the unloving and mean-spirited nature of their fathers.

We live in hope and we hope for the best, but from where I sit in the detached and aloof way people live in Southern California, where fathers see children who live a mile or two away once or twice a year (or not at all), it looks as if many fathers have abdicated their roles and abandoned children.

I hope not. I haven't. Other men work hard to keep the lines of love open with their children. Perhaps it is just the single men I see in restaurants with children, vacant-eyed and silent, who make me feel so pessimistic and sad (Glicken, 2005a, pp. 99–100).

(This article has 664 words including the title)

Discussion

I received a number of requests to reprint this editorial. Many women called or wrote to tell me that their ex-husbands were good men and that they hated the male bashing they were witnessing; male bashing, they told me, had a bad affect on their male children. But I also received a number of negative calls and letters saying that I was representing men in a much too positive way. Men, these callers and writers noted, emotionally and financially abandon their children and they should be publicly chastised for their bad behavior.

Both sides of the argument were welcome. In an editorial, you're trying to make people think. Personal reactions are a sign that you've touched a nerve. If you are asked to write for a newspaper, prepare yourself for the response you might get. It's the nature of the mass media to inform a large, diverse, and sometimes antagonistic population. Many of the political and social positions human service professionals hold are out of the mainstream, so writing for people who have very different worldviews can be challenging. Pick your subjects well, be sensitive to other positions, and use approaches that not only inform, but also try to change opinion, as I tried to do in this article about men.

AN EDITORIAL FOR A NEWSPAPER

The following editorial was written to tell readers that older people are still full of life, creativity, and wonder. I've written about the same subject in my professional books. I tried to keep the article about 800 words long, since prior articles in the newspaper I'd hoped to publish it in were roughly that length. I also tried to use the format of short paragraphs that I saw in prior articles. Newspapers print in columns, so short sentences and paragraphs are always best. Finally, I thought it might be interesting to compare myself to someone many of the readers would know. By showing the difference between someone who is successful but, perhaps, not terribly happy, and myself, perhaps I could show the obvious differences between us. Of course, setting someone up as a straw man (an easy target) whom you blow over in your writing is a little obvious—still, I think it works here.

On the Joys of Being an Older Published Author

My significant other and I went to the Skirball Cultural Center in Los Angeles to hear my fellow writer, Christopher Hitchens, talk about the war in Iraq. I count Mr. Hitchens as a colleague because I've published eight books in the past three years, although none have made any money and no one has invited me to speak about anything.

Mr. Hitchens was brilliant and entertaining. I could learn a lot from him about being a successful writer, like wearing a white suit, drinking wine during the lecture, using words that would make my sainted mother blush, and fingering a cigarette so longingly that even though I don't smoke, I wanted to grab it out of his hand and smoke it for him.

Mr. Hitchens is wildly successful. I, sorry to say, am not. I put my heart and soul into my books. While they are admired in certain arcane academic circles, they haven't sold enough copies to buy me a cup of coffee. I knew this would happen when I wrote the books.

You write to please yourself. I'm 67 years old and I have two more books coming out in the next year; good books, books that make me proud when I read them. I'm almost done with a mystery novel, my third one (unpublished, of course).

Sixty-seven. Who would have guessed at this age that I would feel better physically and emotionally than I've ever felt in my life, and who cares, anyway, if my books sell or if the people know who I am?

One of my books is about men, but it's really about my father and the tough and tender immigrant people I grew up with in that least Jewish of places—North Dakota. Another book is about psychological resilience, but it's really about my daughter and members of my family who struggle with illness and every imaginable setback, and yet come out of that struggle stronger than ever. Another book is about Positive Psychology, an approach to helping others that focuses on what's right about people. I wrote it in the mountains of Utah, and every day, deer and moose would come to my door and watch me write. No one could ever put a money value on that magical experience.

The book I wrote about men has amazing stories from men who have achieved in life, although the odds were certainly against them. I wrote it because men are being bashed, and bashing, like racism, is mean-spirited and ugly. It makes me proud to know that I can write what I believe, and that someone else might be touched by what I've written.

My daughter, Amy, has contributed to many of my books. This is what she wrote about her juvenile onset diabetes: "After having diabetes for 14 years, it has become more than a chronic disease for me, more than a steady companion; diabetes is very much a part of who I am. Diabetes is not a burden, nor is it a crutch. It is just a disease that I, and millions of others, live with every moment of every day. When we face the fact of surviving with diabetes, as many have to face the fact of surviving with cancer or heart disease, we find strength in our uniqueness; we find strength in our ability to share our knowledge with others; we find strength in our ability to control our illness rather than letting it control us. I live with diabetes as though it were my troubled child—a lot of work and occasionally painful, but in the end, oddly beautiful and uniquely mine." Who wouldn't want to write books when you can include such beauty?

Mr. Hutchins has the knowledge that he's read by millions of people and that his positions, which sometimes seem deeply cynical, are influential, while mine are not. But the one thing I can say that perhaps he can't is that everyday I write, it's like a love poem. The words I write feel thrilling and I feel blessed to be able to do what I've always wanted to do—to be a published writer and to understand, in my daughter's words, that our task, "is simply to discern what our gifts are and to utilize them. Because, in the end, we are each our own Tooth Fairies, taking what has been lost and giving gold in return."

Morley Glicken is Professor Emeritus in Social Work at California State University, San Bernardino, and lives and writes books on mental health in Los Angeles.

(Word count: This editorial is 750 words long)

LETTERS TO THE EDITOR

I've been writing letters to the editors of newspapers and magazines since I graduated from university. Many of the letters are about issues that resonate with me, but I've also used letters to explain new agency programs and to promote my organizations. Letters should be brief with short paragraphs of no more than two sentences. Make the writing interesting and get to the point quickly. You'd be amazed at how many people read letters and how influential they can be. The first letter I've included is one I wrote describing a new program for men initiated at an agency I managed. Rather than publish the following letter on the services my agency provided to men, the newspaper interviewed me and it led to a front page story. The second letter (also unpublished) is about the mess the Red Cross made of using the money given after Hurricane Katrina devastated New Orleans.

A Letter to the Editor about a New Service

I am writing to tell men in our community about a new program offered by Jewish Family Service of Greater Tucson that might have prevented the tragic problems experienced by John Ferguson that ended in his suicide. (*Tucson Star*, June 2, 2007).

Jewish Family Service offers short-term consultation to men having concerns about work, their relationships, or in other areas of their lives that cause stress.

Consultations are with an older trained licensed male social worker who has many years of experience in helping men with practical life problems. Usually, one or two meetings are sufficient, but if you'd like to spend more time talking to your consultant, that's perfectly O.K.

Some examples of the reasons men come for consultations might be an unappreciative employer or work setting; children and spouses who aren't as caring as you'd like them to be; not knowing when you'd like to stop working, or when a good time might be to change jobs or careers; work that isn't satisfying; feelings that seem different from how you usually feel, and other common experiences men have that respond well to brief consultations.

All information provided to our male worker is confidential. Evening and weekend hours are available to accommodate your schedule. Grants permit us to offer the first two consultations at no cost. Further meetings are based on what you can afford.

Many times it's hard to think through the best way to handle a tough life problem. Please contact Jewish Family Service at (999) 583-6127 if you think you need help. We invite men of all religions, races, and ethnicities to be part of this program.

Dr. Morley D. Glicken
Executive Director
Jewish Family Service of Greater Tucson

(Word count of the letter is 284 words)

A Letter to the Editor about Charitable Giving

To the Editor: Dec. 19, 2005

Several stories in the *Los Angeles Times* (December 14 and 16, 2005) about the problems experienced by the Red Cross in the Katrina crisis prompt me to encourage readers to make certain they know how nonprofits like the Red Cross use their money.

The Red Cross has had numerous problems throughout the years. The organization is dominated by an old boys'/old girls' network of board members who have done a dismal job of overseeing the agency. I give my money to a cluster of agencies that include the Salvation Army, Jewish Family Services, and Catholic Charities. I know from experience that they do an excellent job and that people get helped.

The next time you give to a charity, and I hope you give as often and as much as you can, check to see how much of your money goes directly to client services. If it's not the bulk, you're paying for inflated administrative and advertising costs, and you're helping to sustain a badly functioning agency.

Dr. Morley D. Glicken, DSW
My address and phone number

(Word count for the letter is 183 words)

THE BOOK REVIEW: TWO EXAMPLES

Many of you will write book reviews for your classes while others will advance to writing for publications. The following steps for writing a good book review are suggested by Escales (1997):

1. Provide the author, the title of the book, the cost, and publisher information.
2. Indicate the subject matter and the type of book (fiction, nonfiction, professional, academic, etc.).
3. Explain the major theme(s) of the book.
4. Provide enough background information to help the reader know about prior work done by the author or the overall themes of the author's work.
5. For fiction, review the story line, but only briefly, and be certain not to give the book's ending away or anything that will lessen the reader's suspense. Movie critics have a tendency to do this to such an extent that it often ruins a film.
6. Describe the book's story, major arguments, and themes. Give your own opinion of the book by indicating if you liked it, agreed with the author, or thought the issues raised were important ones.
7. Are there other authors who do a better job of covering the same material?
8. Did the book affect your point of view, personal agenda, or worldview?
9. Conclude by summarizing the major themes and ideas of the book. Provide an opinion suggesting whether you recommend the book and whether you believe it is worth reading.

I began writing book reviews for the *Minneapolis Tribune* shortly after I received my MSW degree at age 24. The books I reviewed were usually self-help books or books about psychology, mental health, or social policy. The style I used was condescending and superior. Readers loved the style, but it makes me a little sick at heart now that I've been writing books. Reviewers are like judges. They should be fair and not enter their own biases into the review. They should read the book carefully and thoroughly, something I've begun to suspect is rare in book reviewing. Writing book reviews requires the reader to trust the reviewer's honesty, good judgment, and fairness. In the end, however, it also requires an opinion. Here's a self-review of a book I wrote on resilience (Glicken, 2006).

Learning From Resilient People: Lessons We Can Apply to Counseling and Psychotherapy

by Dr. Morley D. Glicken, Sage Publications, $39.95

It may seem odd to ask the author of his own book to also be the reviewer, but who best to tell readers what's right and wrong with a book than the author? Authors always know whether a book is good or bad, and they should be trusted to give an opinion. This is mine.

Learning From Resilient People (Glicken, 2006) is about the ways resilient people navigate the troubled waters of life's traumas and how we can apply that information to counseling and psychotherapy. While a number of researchers believe that resilience is the key to understanding how people successfully cope with traumatic life events and why they often come out of a crisis stronger and more certain of their goals and directions in life, the concept is still fairly new in the research literature. Although we think we know what it means to be resilient, we know far less about why some people are resilient, or how their resilience functions across the life cycle and through multiple life events.

This book continues the development of ideas found in two other books I've written: one on the strengths perspective (Glicken, 2004), and the other on evidence-based practice (Glicken, 2005c). Much of what I've found in researching both books leads me to believe that knowing how resilient people cope with traumas and applying these successful approaches to the helping process will lead to a breakthrough in the way we conduct psychotherapy.

The process of gathering stories about resilience for this book needs to be explained. I asked people at professional and social functions, friends, colleagues, and people I met randomly who had stories of resilience to send them to me. The stories were to contain the traumas experienced by the storyteller, when they were experienced, what they did to cope with the traumas, and why their coping approaches seemed to work. The stories would then be compared to the existing research to confirm or disagree with current beliefs about resilience.

Like many of us who grew up in families that were overwhelmed with life problems, I learned about resilience from my blue-collar, immigrant parents. They dealt with illness, lack of finances, social isolation, and the bigotry of people against immigrant Jews in ways that modeled resilience. But being resilient and surviving serious life problems, while still achieving at a high level, isn't done without a price, and the reader will note throughout this book that resilience is defined as successful social functioning. Some readers will take exception to this belief, feeling that truly resilient people must necessarily be happy and self-fulfilled.

Even though the book was written for professionals in the human service field, the reader interested in mental health issues will hopefully appreciate the book for its many touching stories and for the accumulation of research data on resilience. The book also contains information on resilient communities and paints a loving and vibrant picture of the way people in my hometown of Grand Forks, North Dakota, coped with a devastating flood in 1997. It also discusses resilience in people we often don't think of as being resilient: the mentally ill, older adults, the very ill, and those who abuse substances.

I came out of writing the book with a sense of optimism about people, even if I feel somewhat pessimistic about our country and its future. I worry that readers will find the book too sunny and positive, and that it could make some people think that morally superior people are resilient, and that everyone can be resilient if they only try.

That isn't true, of course. Not everyone is resilient. I hope readers will remember that many among us suffer because of the harm done to them by others. They include the abused and neglected; the homeless and the hungry; the victims of terror; the immigrants who suffer indignities to the body and to the spirit; the children who grow up with violence; and, finally, far too many of our fellow citizens who live with unimaginable social and emotional pain. Their anguish should motivate us to open our hearts and minds and, in Bertrand Russell's words, to have "unbearable sympathy for the suffering of others."

Dr. Morley D. Glicken is the Executive Director of the Institute for Personal Growth in Los Angeles and Professor Emeritus in Social Work at California State University, San Bernardino. He is the author of eight books and two more in process.

(Word count for this review is 767 words including the title and information about the reviewer)

A Book Review With Questions: The Sibling Society

Book reviews are very powerful ways of influencing a large readership. Often people read a book review and never read the book itself. For that reason, book reviews can be very influential in the way people think about issues. The following is a book review that discusses issues that are relevant today even though the book was published in 1996. Please read the review, decide how you feel about the issues it raises, and discuss the questions posed at the end of the review with classmates or colleagues in a small group of five or so.

In his book, *The Sibling Society* (1996), the American poet Robert Bly suggests that a new generation of Americans has lost its ability to function as responsible citizens. Rather than being trained for the responsibilities of adulthood, children are now being trained for eternal adolescence. As adolescents, they lack responsibility to anyone, including the families that raise them. Characteristics of members of the sibling society are lack of a work ethic, an inability to treat others with care and consideration, a feeling of entitlement, and an inability to accept, or discharge, their responsibilities to society.

Guided by the need for pleasure and by an endless belief that they are entitled to be irresponsible, members of the sibling society provide convenient excuses when its citizens fail. There is an excuse for every failure and Bly argues that over time, the responsible few begin to take care of the irresponsible many. Often the responsible few are immigrants and their first-generation children, or the children of healthy parents who provide their children with a strong work ethic. The sibling society lives off the hard work and the social concern of this diminishing minority. Where once college students fought against the war in Viet Nam and racial injustice, the sibling society riots when beer privileges are taken away from them on high-profile campuses.

Bly believes that the sibling society invents excuses for failure that affect our legal system. The issue is no longer guilt or innocence, or whether the trial was fair, but a series of excuses that justify, explain, absolve, and ultimately encourage its citizens to act out again.

Bly argues that the continuation of the sibling society will create adults incapable of dealing with the responsibilities of a democracy. Citizens of the sibling society will be so disassociated from the necessities to think of the community, to exercise restraint in daily living, or to act for the greater good, that Americans will permit the nation to slip into an autocracy because adult members of the sibling society are unwilling to vote, to know issues, to understand the democratic process, to be activists, or to speak out when there are injustices.

Bly believes that welfare and unemployment will mark the sibling society because its members lack motivation to care for themselves and feel certain that others will take care of them in any eventuality.

Bly sees the American parent as a partner in the sibling society. Instead of providing values and moral lessons that assist the society in dealing with new social and economic problems, Bly believes that American parents want a partnership with their children. Such a partnership blunts the lines between parent and child so that children find it difficult to accept moral messages, when given, because the messenger is their buddy, their companion, their playmate, and not their parent.

As evidence of the existence of a sibling society, expectations in universities have dwindled. American business can no longer find enough American-born workers to fill its requirements and depend, increasingly, on immigrant labor. And while we suffer from intense xenophobia (the fear of immigrants) in America, the reality is that hard-working immigrants propel the economy and permit us to live in a high degree of affluence. Much as Rome depended on slave labor, the sibling society depends on its immigrants to do the many tasks it is unwilling to do for itself.

Bly believes that the American mass media and the liberal philosophies of the helping professions are largely responsible for the creation of the sibling society. As the power of the American media affects other societies, he believes that the sibling society will become a worldwide reality, and that national agendas will be determined by a sense of entitlement and narcissism. The end result, according to Bly, bodes badly for the future of our planet.

(Word count for this review is 642 words)

Questions

1. Do you agree with Bly's argument that we are becoming a sibling society? Give compelling arguments either for or against the notion.
2. Do you believe that immigrants do for the society what most native-born Americans will not do for themselves? Also provide compelling arguments for or against this notion.
3. Do you believe that the children you know personally (your own children, the children in your extended family, the children of friends, and the children you work with or come in contact with on a daily basis)

have the characteristics of the children of the sibling society? Give examples of the personal characteristics of those children and whether they match the characteristics of children in the sibling society.

SUMMARY

Writing for the popular media can be one of the most satisfying, powerful, and informative types of writing any professional can do in his or her career. Not only does writing for the mass media reach a large audience and has the power to influence people, but it also brings out a side of professionals they may not know exists: their creative side. If you have an idea for a creative piece and you want to try your skills, contact any of a number of journals, newspapers, and magazines, find out their editorial policy (some even pay), and give it a try. What, after all, do you have to lose?

FIND THE MISTAKES

1. **A Letter to the Editor:** "To the Editor: The article by Garcia in the Sunday Times made me sick. Who does he think he is, anyway? Suggesting that we should be thankful for immigrants who come to America and work hard for low wages? What kind of argument is that? Only Americans should work hard for low wages."
2. **A Letter to the Editor:** "To the Editor: Immigrants are hard working, loyal and responsible people. The article by Garcia is an example of how we should think about immigrants—people who come to America and work hard without asking very much in return except a safe home life. Were it up to me I'd have an open border and get rid of those useless border patrol who only enjoy rounding up poor Mexicans so they can feel superior to them."
3. **An Editorial:** "20% of all Americans suffer some form of emotional dysfunction serious enough to require professional help according to NIMH. But we have to few human service professionals to meet those needs and many of us fear that unserved Americans with emotional problems will become a serious problem effecting crime, homelessness and unemployment; we need to give out more scholarships to human service students and pay higher wages to encourage more people to become social workers, psychologists, and counselors."
4. **An Editorial:** "As a counselor working for the mental health clinic, I am writing to complain about the cuts in our budget prompted by a reactionary group of county commissioners who believes that good mental health is ensured by going to church. I know lots of unhealthy

people who go to church but still have problems. Going to church, while commendable, is no substitute for professional mental health services offered by trained personnel of the kind we have at the county mental health clinic of which I am a proud member."

5. **A Book Review:** "Glicken's new book on writing is an absurd, silly, and altogether useless display of putting words together which has no meaning and which suggests that Glickens Godless liberalism is the sin of thinking that you know more than anyone else, and is the same snotty, arrogant junk that human service books suffer from. For once I'd like to see a book that tells people how to write without using jargon and meaningless plap that is not only insipient but also suggests a third-rate mind."

REFERENCES

Bly, R. (1996). *The sibling society.* Boston: Wesley-Addison Longman.

Escales, M. (1997). *Steps for writing a good book review.* Retrieved Sept. 13, 2006, from St. Cloud State University's Literacy Education online web pages at http://leo.stcloudstate.edu/acadwrite/bookrev.html

Glicken, M. D. (2004). *The strengths perspective in social work practice.* Boston: Allyn and Bacon/Longman.

Glicken, M. D. (2005a). *Ending the sex wars: A woman's guide to understanding men.* Omaha, NE: iuniverse.

Glicken, M. D. (2005b). *Working with troubled men: A contemporary practitioner's guide.* Mahwah, NJ: Lawrence Erlbaum Associates.

Glicken, M. D. (2005c). *Improving the effectiveness of the helping professions: An evidence-based approach to practice.* Thousand Oaks, CA: Sage.

Glicken, M. D. (2006). *Learning from resilient people: Lessons we can apply to psychotherapy and counseling.* Thousand Oaks, CA: Sage.

14

Writing Course Outlines, Professional Workshops, and Brochures

Professionals are often asked to teach courses, workshops, or to give educationally oriented presentations. Course outlines are helpful to the professional and to his or her audience, because they spell out the relevant issues of the course, including content, a class schedule, assignments, and the course objects. Education is increasingly outcome-oriented. The course outline becomes the document by which others may judge the quality of the plan to present educational material.

The course outline examples for workshops and brochures I've included in this chapter will hopefully provide you with an understanding about how each is written. Remember that the outline forms the contract between the instructor and the students. In any misunderstanding or grievance, the outline binds the student and the instructor to the terms presented in the outline. For that reason, be particularly certain that your language is clear and appropriate. Let students know the penalties for late papers and how assignments will be graded. It's their right to know.

Course objectives usually include three types of objectives: knowledge, skills, and values. Knowledge objectives refer to the material students need to know to gain skill. This might include theory and ways of understanding certain issues. Skill objectives refer to the behaviors students need to be able to master to help clients. These might include the ability to write accurate client assessments or to develop treatment plans—skills limited to what we normally do in class. Values refer to the underlying ethical base needed to guide professional human service practice with clients. Learning objectives must be behavioral. That is, there must be a way to determine if they have been achieved.

To help you better understand the words used in constructing course objectives and the meaning of those words, the following list of major categories of educational objectives (Gronlund, 1970) is provided with commonly used words for each objective.

1. **Knowledge:** Knowledge is defined as the ability to recall relevant material, including facts, complete theories, and divergent points of view. Before one can practice helping approaches with actual clients, there is a body of information learners must know. These are knowledge objectives.
   a) **What this means:** The learner knows common terms, specific facts, methods and procedures, basic concepts, and principles.
   b) **Words used with knowledge objectives**: Knows, understands, remembers, defines, describes, identifies, labels, lists, matches, names, outlines, produces, selects, states.
2 **Application (Skill):** Application refers to the ability to use learned material in new situations. This may include the application of rules, methods, concepts, principles, laws, and theories.
   a) **What this means**: The learner can apply concepts and principles to new situations; apply laws and theories to practical situations; solve practice-related problems; develop competent treatment plans; and demonstrate correct usage of a method or procedure.
   b) **Words used with skill objectives**: Changes, demonstrates, produces, shows, solves, and uses.
3. **Values:** Values are concerned with the ability to judge the importance and accuracy of material for a given purpose (in our case, anything related to providing service to clients and agency life). Valuing best evidence in practice would be considered a value since its purpose is to provide clients with the best possible assistance based on concrete research evidence. Values also describe ethical behaviors students must possess and be able to apply to be considered a professionally competent practitioner. Professional values are found in professional codes of conduct, licensure laws, legal statutes, and agency policies.
   a) **What this means:** The learner can judge the logical consistency of written material; the adequacy with which conclusions are supported by data; the importance of professional ethics; the acceptance of certain beliefs as they apply to gender, ethnicity, age, race, and religion (for example).
   b) **Words used with value objectives**: Values, appreciates, accepts, concludes, justifies, and supports.

The following are examples of how learning objectives might be applied to a course on domestic violence. Upon completion of the course the student will be able to:

- **State** strategies that abused women might use to protect themselves from abuse.
- **Describe** the way abusive men are influenced by feelings of jealousy.
- **Relate** the practice approaches most supported by best evidence for work with abusive men.
- **Explain** children's rights in criminal and family court.
- **Compare** different types of testimony such as eyewitness testimony, confessions, and hypnotically produced evidence.
- **Appreciate** the impact of domestic violence on families.
- **Value** the need for prevention strategies to protect victims from domestic violence.

A COURSE OUTLINE: VIOLENCE IN THE FAMILY

Course: Social Work 581

Dr. Morley D. Glicken, Instructor
Mondays 6:00 PM–8:00 PM
Spring 2008
E-mail: mglicken@msn.com
Room E330

Violence in the Family

I. Course Rationale
[Explains the reason the course is offered and what students will learn.]

SOCWRK 581, <u>Violence in the Family</u>, is designed to provide students with an introduction to the knowledge, skills, and values utilized in direct social work practice with victims and perpetrators of family violence. The major objective of the course is to prepare students to apply appropriate practice interventions, including the strengths perspective and evidence-based practice, within a setting in which professional social work is practiced. In this course, students are expected to:

A. Demonstrate an understanding **(knowledge)** of, and a capacity **(skill)** to apply **(skill)**, the dual focus of person(s) and environment that underlies all social work practice with issues related to violence in families.

B. Demonstrate a value base **(value)** consistent with the professional values that guide social work practice when working with the victims and perpetrators of domestic violence.

C. Demonstrate a commitment **(value)** to effective social work practice with diverse populations that takes into consideration ethnicity, race, age, gender, and the underrepresented/undeserved who require special considerations, both as victims and perpetrators of domestic violence.

D. Develop the capacity **(skill)** to evaluate one's own practice in order to maintain a high degree of competence and effectiveness.

E. Develop the capacity **(skill)** to utilize knowledge from a variety of resources to continue the educational process required for maintaining competent practice when working with the victims and perpetrators of domestic violence.

F. Understand **(knowledge)** that social work practice requires the application of a variety of alternative strategies/techniques in order to meet the needs of clients in their social environments.

II. Learning Objectives
[These objectives should be evident in the course outline, assignments, and readings and should be tested in the classroom.]

Students will demonstrate that appropriate learning has taken place by:

A. Developing **(skill)** a frame of reference when working with the victims and perpetrators of family violence that focuses on the interactive nature of person(s) and environment.

B. Demonstrating the capacity **(skill)** to integrate the knowledge and values that underlie the social work process and are necessary for effective practice in the area of family violence.

C. Understanding **(knowledge)** the principles of effective communication and the application **(skill)** of those principles to intervene with client systems.

D. Identifying and applying **(skills)** the requisite components of professional relationships with perpetrators and victims of family violence.

E. Demonstrating **(skill)** a genuine awareness and appreciation of the varying qualities and values **(Value)** of all individuals and groups when providing direct and indirect services to victims and perpetrators of family violence.

F. Developing **(skill)** the beginning capacity to analyze one's own practice and to make relevant adjustments to maintain practice effectiveness with victims and perpetrators of family violence.

III. Content Related to Gender, Ethnicity, Diversity, and Issues Pertaining to Cultural Difference

SOCWRK 581, <u>Violence in the Family</u>, is strongly committed to training students for effective work with all clients. Of particular concern is providing educational experiences that lead to effective social work practice with people of color, the elderly, ethnically diverse populations, women and men, the young, and other groups whose lack of economic, social, and political viability creates serious vulnerability to social, economic, and emotional difficulties. To achieve this goal, the course will use a number of learning opportunities including assigned readings, use of case studies, values clarification exercises, written assignments, role plays, class discussion, critical analysis of practice situations, and lectures. The focus of these learning opportunities is to help students achieve the following:

A. Learn **(knowledge)** about and develop an appreciation **(value)** for the unique qualities of diverse groups and populations at risk.

B. Demonstrate the ability **(skill)** to develop special approaches in practice with identified vulnerable groups who are the victims of family violence.

C. Through the use of exemplars, reading, exercises, class discussion, and values clarification, become sensitized **(values and knowledge)** to practice issues that relate to working with diverse groups.

D. Develop competencies **(skill)** related to ethnically sensitive work with diverse client populations.

IV. Course Requirements and Assignments
[This section shows how learning objectives will be evaluated.]

Students are expected to read all assigned readings and to be prepared for graduate level discussion. The following are the graded assignments for the quarter:

A. A take-home examination discussing the Rebecca Bartlow case available on Blackboard. The case is due 03-31-08 and is worth 25% of your grade. **Late papers will be docked 5 points for each late day. Length should be 8–10 pages, using 1.5 line spacing, and a 12-point font.**

B. A small group presentation of one hour on a special topic related to family violence. See the instructor for some additional ideas, but several possible presentations might be: (1) women as perpetrators of family violence; (2) parent abuse by children; (3) abuse of older adults by their adult children; (4) the impact of emotional abuse on children; (5) the relationship between child abuse and early onset violence in children; (6) family violence and ethnicity or social class; (7) dating violence; (8) mandatory arrests for domestic violence; (9) anger management and empathy training as alternative treatments for perpetrators of family violence.

The presentations will be on 4-21 and 4-28-08. Presentations will be worth 25% of your grade (20% for your individual presentation and 5% for the group presentation).

C. A final paper: 50% of the grade. The paper will be a minimum of 14 typed pages, 1.5 line spacing, 12-point font. You will be asked to develop a treatment plan for a client (imaginary, real, or someone you know but are not working with directly), and to justify your treatment strategies with research data from the literature. The paper is due in class May 5, 2008. **Late papers will be docked 5 points for each day late. See the questions for the assignment at the end of the course syllabus.**

D. Students are expected to attend all classes and participate in classroom discussion. Failure to do so will result in the lowering of grades as described in the MSW Handbook on pages 16 and 17.

V. Grading
The grade for the course is based on a maximum of 100 points for all assignments. Grades are assigned according to the following schedule:

100–90 points = A
89–80 points = B
79–70 points = C
69–60 points = D
59 points and below = F

Readings:

The following books and readings are required for this course:

Glicken, M. D. (1995). *Understanding and treating abusive male behavior: A research report.* Unpublished manuscript (55 pages). Referred to as Abuse Monograph. Available on Blackboard.

Mignon, S. I., Larson, C. J, & Holmes, W. M. (2002). *Family abuse: Consequences, theories and responses.* Boston: Allyn and Bacon Publishers.

Selected chapters from books by Glicken and Sechrest (2003), Glicken (2004) on violent young children, Glicken (2004) on the strengths perspective and other sources on selected subjects, all available on Blackboard.

Selected articles will also be available on Blackboard.

Course Schedule:
[It should be clear to students and others that the course content, readings, and their order in the schedule all relate to the course objectives.]

01-14-08: Goals; objectives; course expectations; historical perspective; definitions: legal, psychosocial, and psychotherapeutic. The actual amount of family violence from the U.S. Justice Department.

01-21-08: Martin Luther King Day. No class. Please join the faculty, staff, and your classmates for a walk to the state capitol in recognition of human rights.

01-28-08: Dynamics of families with violence; role of early childhood abuse; substance abuse.

Readings: Glicken, M. D. (1995). Understanding and treating abusive male behavior: A research report. Referred to as Abuse Monograph. Available on Blackboard.
Mignon, et al., Chapters 1 and 3.

02-04-08: Why partners stay in violent relationships; co-dependence; economic factors; video on co-dependence.

Readings: Mignon, Chapter 7.

02-11-08: Physical and emotional harm done by family violence to adults. Case study: Seana Fernandez in Glicken, M. D., & Sechrest, D. K. (2003). *Treating the victims and perpetrators of violence.* Boston: Allyn and Bacon/Longman Publishers, Chapter 6. The case is available on Blackboard.

Readings: Mignon, et al., Chapters 2 and 4.

02-18-08: Presidents' Day. No class.

02-25-08: Physical and emotional harm done by family violence to children; hypervigilence; the probability of future abusive behavior.

Readings: Glicken, M. D. (2004). *Violent young children.* Boston: Allyn and Bacon/Longman Publishers. Sections of a chapter on the relationship between child abuse and early violence in abused children. Found on Blackboard.
Glicken, M. D. & Sechrest, D. K. (2003). Chapter 5: Child Abuse. Available on Blackboard.
Mignon, et al., Chapters 3 and 6.

03-03-0: Sexual abuse; date rape, sexual violence.
Readings: Mignon, et al., Chapter 5.
Glicken, M. D. & Sechrest, D. K. (2003). Chapter 6: Sexual Violence. Available on Blackboard.

03-10-08: The dynamics of abusers and victims.

Readings: Mignon, et al., Chapters 9 and 10.

03-17-08: Spring Break. No class.

03-24-08: Treating perpetrators. Cognitive therapy; empathy training; perpetrator groups; mandatory arrest; macro-system change; video. Case study on Blackboard: Rosalie Myron (Glicken & Sechrest, 2003) chapter 4. **Take home case analysis is due in class.**

Readings: Mignon, et al., Chapters 11 and 12 (Treating victims and perpetrators).
Scott & Wolfe (2000). Treating batterers. Available on Blackboard.
Davis, et al. (1998). The deterrent effect of prosecuting domestic violence perpetrators. Available on Blackboard.

03-31-08: Treating perpetrators continued.

04-07-08: Treating victims: Case study on Blackboard: Rebecca Bartlow (Glicken & Sechrest, 2003), Chapter 4.

Readings: Abel (2000). An empirical review of treatment approaches for battered women. Available on Blackboard.

04-14-08: Treating victims continued: Survivor Therapy with adult victims of family violence (video). Take home examination is due the start of class.

04-21-08: Small group presentations.

04-28-08: Small group presentations.

05-05-08: Summary, feedback, and suggestions for future classes. **(Final papers are due.)**

Questions for the Final Paper

1. Describe a client with whom you are working, an imaginary client, or someone you know who is the victim or perpetrator of family violence. Give a history of the current situation in the client's life for which they are seeking assistance from a human service practitioner. (15 points)

2. Provide any relevant "family of origin" issues that may have contributed to the problems, such as dysfunctional family interactions, prior abuse as a child, alcoholism, abandonment, co-dependence, etc. Show any connections

between that prior behavior in the family and how it is now affecting your client. (20 points)

3. Based on the accumulated data you have reported, give your diagnostic impression of the client and his/her problem. In other words, what seems to be the primary reason(s) for the problem? Also provide social and emotional strengths that might help in the resolution of the problem such as high motivation to change, a supportive spouse, etc. (15 points)

4. Based on your diagnosis, go to the research literature related to the diagnosed problem and find research articles that propose ways to help the client change. Describe the research in the articles and indicate whether you think the quality of the research justifies using the data generated to treat your client. Five or more articles that show uniform agreement with one another must be cited. (30 points)

5. If your client is a victim of domestic violence, provide social policies and community efforts that might protect your client from further violence and permit the client to heal emotionally and physically. If your client is a perpetrator, provide community efforts and social policies that would prevent your client from doing more harm. Use the assigned literature or additional literature to justify your answer. (20 points)

Please Note: Past experience with this assignment suggests that minimum length should be 14 pages space and a half with a 12-point font, with additional pages for references. APA style is required. The paper is due May 5, 2008, in class. You are required to bring at least two drafts of your paper in for review and feedback prior to submitting your final paper for feedback. Final papers will not be accepted without submitting two prior drafts (*Reader: This is not only to improve the quality of papers but to stop plagiarism*).The paper is worth 50% of the course grade. **Late papers will be docked 5% per late day. No exceptions.**

VI. Bibliography
[Include an up-to-date bibliography in your course outline of mostly new (within the past five years) articles, books, papers, and monographs. Important articles and research older than five years are always desirable to include.]

AN EXAMPLE OF A WORKSHOP OUTLINE

This is the type of workshop outline many of us use for one-day workshops for human service professionals. As you can see, the outline is very brief and focuses on the schedule and workshop content. Often, organizations sponsoring these types of workshops must first gain approval from curriculum committees who make certain that objectives and course content actually meet standards set by the organization and, in this case, the state licensing board for counselors and social workers. I'm including two workshop examples: one on child abuse and a second on legal and ethical issues, a mandated course that all licensed clinical social workers (LCSWs) and marriage and family therapists (MFTs) must take to maintain their clinical licenses in California.

Child Abuse: Identification, Assessment, and Treatment
PSYC 1002
April 22, 2008

Dr. Morley D. Glicken, Instructor

Description: This course on child abuse and neglect includes content related to the identification of child abuse and neglect, in all forms. The course also includes treatment interventions for victims and perpetrators, the laws governing child abuse and neglect in California, the role of mandated reporters, and prevention strategies.

Workshop Objectives
1. Provide current, evidence-based information about child abuse and neglect and its impact across the lifespan.
2. Increase awareness of cultural diversity with regard to child abuse and neglect.
3. Provide the current laws about reporting child abuse and neglect, and problems with quick responses by public organizations.
4. Increase knowledge of the various forms of child victimization and the appropriate interventions and prevention strategies.
5. Increase knowledge of repressed memory syndrome in childhood sexual abuse.
6. Recognize the signs of child abuse and neglect.
7. Increase awareness of less obvious forms of child abuse, including Munchausen's by Proxy and emotional abuse.
8. Develop an understanding and appreciation for prevention of child abuse and protection of children.
9. Understand the need for the uniform application of existing laws and changes, when necessary, in the way those laws are enforced by existing child welfare agencies.

Workshop Schedule

Time	Topic
8:30–9:00:	Introductions and Perspectives on Child Abuse and Neglect: State and National Data

9:00–10:00:	California Child Abuse and Neglect Laws Definitions of Abuse and Neglect Penal Code 11164-11174.3 Mandated Reporters Helping Organizations
10:00–10:15:	**Coffee Break**
10:15–10:45:	Recognizing Child Abuse (Video and Graphics)
10:45–12:00:	Sexual Abuse (Video)
12:00–1:00:	**Lunch Break**
1:00–2:15:	Physical Abuse and Neglect
2:15–3:30:	Treating the Impact of Child Abuse and Neglect Treatment Approaches With Children Treatment Approaches With Adults Treating Emotional Abuse Repressed Memories
3:30–3:45:	**Coffee Break**
3:45–4:15:	Munchausen's by Proxy (Video)
4:15–5:20:	Prevention of Child Abuse and Protection of Children
5:20–5:30:	Feedback and Evaluations

Presented by Dr. Morley D. Glicken, former dean of the Worden School of Social Service in San Antonio; founding director of the MSW Department at CSU, San Bernardino; past director of the MSW program at the University of Alabama; the former executive director of Jewish Family Service of Greater Tucson; author of eight nationally recognized books on mental health and resilience.

A SECOND WORKSHOP OUTLINE EXAMPLE

The following workshop on law and ethics is mandated by the state of California. The state board overseeing licensure of social workers and counselors just says that a 6-hour course must be given, but says nothing about the content. I was asked to create a course for a local university. This is what I developed. I will refine it as I get feedback from the committee reviewing the material at a local university.

Law and Ethics: A Licensure Workshop for LCSW and MFT Professionals

Description: Law and Ethics is a 6-hour required licensure course by the California Board of Behavioral Sciences for LCSWs and MFTs applying for or renewing their licenses. The course covers the codes of professional conduct in both fields; practical issues related to the codes of professional conduct; understanding state confidentiality laws; ethical issues that can lead to loss of licensure; legal responsibilities to clients; the HIPAA laws that require professionals to fully disclose their policies and procedures for sharing information with others; appearing in court to provide expert testimony; ethics exercises; laws and policies regarding sexual harassment and workplace violence; ethical practice and the role of the worker in teaching clients ethical and legal behavior.

Objectives

1. To understand the need for professional ethics and codes of conduct.
2. To understand and apply the MSW and MFT codes of professional conduct and ethics.
3. To understand state confidentiality laws.
4. To know the ethical violations that can result in loss of licensure in California.
5. To know the laws pertaining to sexual harassment and workplace violence.
6. To know the HIPAA laws pertaining to privacy and the sharing of confidential client information with others.
7. To understand the role of professional testimony in court and the California laws pertaining to privileged communication for LCSWs and MFTs in certain settings.
8. To understand the role of professionals in modeling legal and ethical behavior for clients.
9. To recognize that diversity requires special sensitivity to people of color, women, those with disabilities, and others who may experience discrimination in their lives.

Course Schedule

8:30–9:00: Introductions; workshop objectives.

9:00–10:00: The codes of professional conduct and ethics for LCSWs and MFTs. How these codes are applied in actual practice situations.

10:00–10:15: Break

10:15–11:00: State of California laws covering confidentiality and those providing privileged communication in certain settings.

11:00–Noon: The federal HIPAA laws covering privacy and client rights.

Noon–1:00: Lunch

1:00–1:30: Sexual harassment and workplace violence laws: practical examples of how those laws work.

1:30–2:00: Violations of ethical conduct that can result in loss of licensure in California.

2:00–2:45: Modeling ethical behavior for clients.

2:45–3:30: Expert testimony: professional conduct when testifying in court.

3:30–3:45: Break

3:45–4:45: Sensitivity to diverse populations.

4:45–5:00: Feedback; evaluations.

Presented by Dr. Morley D. Glicken, former dean of the Worden School of Social Service in San Antonio; founding director of the MSW Department at CSU, San Bernardino; past director of the MSW program at the University of Alabama; the former executive director of Jewish Family Service of Greater Tucson; author of eight nationally recognized books on mental health and resilience.

PROFESSIONAL BROCHURES

From time to time, you may be asked to develop a longer workshop for a specialized audience. I developed the following brochure for a workshop in Mexico. A brochure does more than inform. It also tries to market (sell) the workshop. I actually had another several pages in the brochure but since I'm not trying to sell you anything, I removed them. If you would like to see the brochure as it appears on my website with color pictures, go to www .morleyglicken.com and look for the link that says "Workshops."

WORKING EFFECTIVELY WITH NEWLY MIGRATED MEXICAN NATIONALS: A PROFESSIONAL WORKSHOP HELD IN GUANAJUATO, MEXICO

July 13–27, 2008

The Workshop
The purpose of this two-week workshop is to help human service professionals and students learn about contemporary Mexican life so that they can improve their understanding of the social and emotional needs of Mexican Nationals immigratng to the United States. The workshop will be offered **July 13–27,**

2008, at the Academia Falcon Educational Community in Guanajuato, Mexico, often called "The Most Beautiful City in Mexico."

Using knowledgeable and experienced Mexican professionals as guest lecturers and Dr. Morley D. Glicken, a well-known social work educator and author, the workshop will provide 45 hours of course content in the following areas: ethnically sensitive work with Hispanic clients; relevant family and gender issues; the political, religious, historical, legal, and socio-economic context of life in Mexico; Mexican/U.S. relations; the Mexican educational and health systems; folk healing; Mexican literature and what it tells us about contemporary Mexican life; and Mexican approaches to life that will sensitize participants to contemporary Mexican life and the ways of viewing the world held by newly migrated Mexicans. By offering the course in Mexico, participants will develop a broad awareness of the reality of Mexican life and the experiences that shape the lives of Mexican immigrants in the United States.

In addition to the workshop, participants will take 40 hours of immersion Spanish, live and take meals with a Mexican family, have an opportunity to visit a number of interesting and often astonishing archeological and cultural sites in and around Guanajuato, and meet other professionals from around the country.

Workshop Leader

Your workshop leader is Dr. Morley D. Glicken, DSW. Dr. Glicken is an internationally known social worker and author. He is the former dean of the Worden School of Social Service in San Antonio and the original director of the MSW program at California State University, San Bernardino. Dr. Glicken is currently the executive director of the Institute for Personal Growth: A Training, Counseling, and Research Cooperative in Los Angeles. He is well known for his books on evidence-based practice, working with troubled men, social research, resilience, and the strengths perspective. Dr. Glicken taught a similar workshop in Mexico several years ago.

About Guanajuato

Guanajuato (pop. 90,501; alt. 6,724 ft.) is considered by many to be the most beautiful city in Mexico and owes its fame and fortune to the rich veins of silver and gold discovered by the Spanish many centuries ago. Like other silver cities of Mexico, Guanajuato has beautiful cityscapes and architectural treasures. The 16th-century mining boom led to the construction of fine town houses, beautiful haciendas and romantic plazas, for which the city is famous. Clean and beautifully preserved, Guanajuato should be high on anyone's list of places to visit in Mexico.

Immersion Spanish

Participants will take 40 hours of immersion Spanish during the 2-week workshop. Placement examinations will help determine your level of Spanish so that you can be placed in an appropriate class. Spanish is taught Monday through Friday from 9:00 a.m. to 1:00 p.m. by experienced instructors in classes of no more than five students. Spanish conversation classes for professionals are also

A Quick Glance at Your Schedule (2 Weeks)

Sunday	Monday	Tuesday	Wednesday	Thursday	Friday	Saturday
Field Trips to Various Cultural Sites in and Around Guanajuato 9:00am –9:00pm	Spanish Class 9:00am–1:00pm	Spanish Class 9:00am–1:00pm	Spanish Class 9:00am–1:00pm	Spanish Class 9:00am–1:00pm	Spanish Class 9:00am–1:00pm	Field Trips to Various Cultural Sites in and Around Guanajuato 9:00am–9:00pm
	Optional Conversational Spanish 1:00pm–2:00pm	Optional Conversational Spanish 1:00pm–2:00pm	Optional Conversational Spanish 1:00pm–2:00pm	Optional Conversational Spanish 1:00pm – 2:00pm	Optional Conversational Spanish 1:00pm–2:00pm	
	Optional Independent Study Program With Dr. Glicken 2:30pm–4:00pm	Optional Independent Study Program With Dr. Glicken 2:30pm–4:00pm	Optional Independent Study Program With Dr. Glicken 2:30pm–4:00pm	Optional Independent Study Program With Dr. Glicken 2:30pm–4:00pm	Optional Independent Study Program With Dr. Glicken 2:30pm–4:00pm	
	Professional Workshop 4:00pm–8:30pm	Professional Workshop 4:00pm–8:30pm	Professional Workshop 4:00pm–8:30pm	Professional Workshop 4:00pm–8:30pm	Professional Workshop 4:00pm–8:30pm	

available from 1:00 p.m.–2:00 p.m. daily, increasing the number of hours participants can take in Spanish to 50 hours. Immersion Spanish means that only Spanish is spoken in class.

Living With a Mexican Family
You will live with a wonderful Mexican family during the workshop. Workshop fees cover your room and board. By living with a Mexican family, you will learn about family life, practice your Spanish, and experience family gatherings, celebrations, and family interactions. The fee you pay is based on double occupancy.

Fees
- **$1,158:** Includes registration, Spanish language instruction, room and board with your host family, Spanish textbook, two weekend field trips, and a fiesta. This fee is paid directly to Academia Falcon Educational Community.
- **$300:** The professional workshop fee, which is paid directly to Dr. Glicken. Fees must be paid no later than June 15, 2008.
- **Total Workshop Fees: $1,158 + $300 = $1,458**

Contacts for Further Information
- For information about the professional workshop, please contact Dr. Morley Glicken at: mglicken@msn.com or call him at 1-123-768-9199 Information about the workshop is also available at www.morleyglicken.com
- Many of the questions pertaining to Academia Falcon Educational Community can be answered by accessing their website at: www.academiafalcon .com

SUMMARY

This chapter discusses course and workshop outlines and the professional brochures we are often asked to develop. Examples are provided. Three types of learning objectives are noted with the meaning and words associated with those objectives provided. Action words are also included to give the reader an understanding of how one might write learning objectives in the human services. Learning objectives are always behavioral in nature and are, therefore, measurable.

FIND THE MISTAKES

1. The course outline is a contract between the student and the instructor. If the student accepts the course outline it means that the instructor is required to only teach what's in the course outline.

2. A value objective obligates you to believe whatever the instructor says you'll believe as presented in the course outline.
3. It's always wise to use very recent references in a course outline instead of older references. Older references (more than 5 years old) are too dated to be useful.
4. A knowledge objective means to know and be able to apply knowledge. Knowing the mechanics of a client assessment and being able to write one would be a good example.
5. The course outline is also a contract between the instructor and the college showing that the instructor has the knowledge, values, and skills to teach the course.

REFERENCE

Gronlund, N. E. (1970). *Stating behavioral objectives for classroom instruction.* Toronto, ON: Macmillan Company.

15

Using the Internet and the Laws Governing Privacy (HIPAA)

Can and should the Internet be used for professional functions? This chapter discusses the use of the Internet for clinical and agency supervision and e-therapy, and the writing issues one might face using the Internet. There are privacy issues at stake using the Internet, and this chapter will also look at a major federal privacy law known as the Health Insurance Portability and Accountability Act (HIPAA).

USING THE INTERNET FOR PROFESSIONAL FUNCTIONS

Stofle and Hamilton (1998) believe that chat rooms can be used for certain professional functions including supervision: (a) when confidentiality can be maintained by the use of code words; (b) for discussions of team functioning; and (c) to discuss new approaches to treatment. The authors believe that online supervision can be an acceptable substitute for face-to-face supervision when distances are great, as in rural areas, or when students are placed in agencies far removed from a central agency or educational site. They caution that online supervision requires a solid, trusting relationship, and motivation. The authors agree, however, that a serious problem with using the Internet for supervision is the inability to see the nonverbal behavior of workers or of the supervisor, but they have devised a simple code to indicate emotions. Some examples are:

:)	Smile
<g>	Grin
:(	Frown

;)	Wink
:	Disappointed
:O	Shocked
?	What?/Explain/Why?

Gainor and Constantine (2002) found that web-based supervision experienced the following problems: (a) the lack of nonverbal cues to correctly perceive behavior in web-based groups made it difficult for supervisors to identify group members who were having difficulty with complex issues, including their attitudes toward diversity; (b) Ladany, Hill, Corbett, and Nutt (1996) found that a third of the students being supervised in their study using face-to-face supervision failed to disclose racial or ethnic bias against clients, and that this number could increase in non-face-to-face supervision, such as web-based groups; (c) Robson and Robson (1998) suggest that although computer technology can be used for intimate communication, impersonation (assuming someone else's identity) and impersonalization (not relating to someone in a sensitive manner) may increase barriers to intimacy; and (d) Gainor and Constantine (2002) report that other researchers have also had positive expereinces with web-based supervision. For example, Myrick and Sabella (1995) indicate that school counselor trainees and practicing counselors reported more advantages than disadvantages to web-based supervision, including more accessible assistance and encouragement from supervisors, a feeling of openness in most interactions, the ability to read and review at one's convenience, and exciting interactions with others.

Stofle and Hamilton (1998) summarize the advantages and disadvantages of using the Internet for supervision as follows:

Disadvantages: (a) lack of nonverbal cues; (b) technical problems such as the server being busy or getting bumped off; (c) poor typing skills that take time from the process or confuse meaning; (d) space limitations that prevent the sender from sending the entire message and the receiver from responding to the entire message; (e) silence or inactivity between typed sentences can be interpreted as others not paying attention or as disinterest; and (f) distractions such as conversation from other people nearby and outside noise.

Advantages: (a) simplicity; (b) convenience, since group supervision can be done anywhere at any time, including when workers are at home; (c) some things are easier to write than to say, particularly if you sense that others in the group will disapprove in face-to-face group conferences; and (d) the meeting is permanent since it can be saved and referred to in the future.

E-THERAPY: A CONTROVERSIAL APPROACH FOR HUMAN SERVICE PROFESSIONALS

Online therapy seems to be flourishing with many hundreds (or thousands, judging by an Internet search) of therapists offering therapy online with general client satisfaction (Alleman, 2003). Although Alleman and others wonder if Internet therapy is ethical and whether it actually helps clients resolve emotional problems, he worries that if we don't take Internet therapy seriously and begin to deal with it in licensure and certification processes, those doing therapy on the Internet will be the ones left over, who don't have professional affiliations and other credentials—in other words, generally the less qualified therapists. Alleman points out that despite many of the criticisms of Internet therapy (that it lacks proof of client honesty and that therapists can't gauge affect as they would in face-to-face contacts), people fall in love every day using the Internet and meet online and create bonds of friendships before they ever meet in person. It is also true that many people who use the Internet for dating and friendships are sorely disappointed when they actually meet in person and complain about discrepancies in age and personal information. Not a few married people use the Internet for dating and fail to inform those online.

However, even with these and other concerns, Alleman believes that online therapy is a fact, and while it raises many questions, it also offers us an opportunity to provide cost-effective services to many clients who might otherwise not have access to treatment: those who are homebound; those who live in very remote and isolated areas that lack therapists; the elderly or immobile who have difficulty traveling to a therapist's office; and those who are too shy and embarrassed for face-to-face therapy.

Fenichel (2003) takes a critical view of Internet therapy. He wonders if we have any idea of the difficulty of doing therapy when we can't gauge client honesty or affect. He points out that people sometimes assume other personas on the Internet, as is the case in some chat rooms where otherwise meek people assume very assertive identities and ways of communicating that are distant from their usual ways of behaving. He also indicates that many clients are much clearer when they speak, have problems expressing themselves in writing, or read and comprehend written language slowly. Fenichel believes that visual cues are of major importance. Without seeing the client, therapy is very difficult to do effectively. However, he concedes that there is growing evidence that cognitive assignments and online treatment have been effective in addressing social anxiety, and that group dynamics in chat rooms and message boards are said to have improved people's awareness and social skills. Still, he is uncertain that what we experience as gain in online treatment actually takes place in reality.

Smith and Reynolds (2002) suggest the following benefits and liabilities of Internet therapy:

Benefits: (a) Internet therapy allows us to reach clients in remote areas with limited available mental health services; (b) it gives us the ability to schedule sessions at times that are convenient to the client and therapist that might otherwise not be possible; (c) it allows us to establish a permanent record of all therapeutic communications; (d) clients have the ability to seek psychotherapists who have specialized training in specific problems, read their resumes, see their pictures online, and determine if they have training in Internet therapy; and (e) clients self-disclose more than might be possible in face-to-face sessions. The authors admit, however, that there is little evidence of the effectiveness of e-therapy when compared to face-to-face therapy.

Limitations: (a) confidentiality issues; (b) the inability to appropriately identify cultural nuances; (c) the handling of crises such as health emergencies or suicide attempts (because we are not dealing with a person face-to-face, we don't really know who they are. If there's an emergency, we may be unable to find out who they really are and provide needed help; (d) it's possible we're dealing with imposters since anyone can log on to an e-mail address if they have access; and (e) what we say may have liability issues because the client has a record of all e-mail conversations.

My feeling about e-therapy is that it seems very unlikely that it's actually therapy. I see it as much like personal (or life) coaching. While the distinctions between personal coaching, brief psychotherapy, and crisis intervention are vague, personal coaching is often thought of as a brief, goal-oriented way of problem solving that generally works on a specific problem with healthy people. It is performance oriented and is only interested in resolving a single specific problem unlike therapy where the development of insight or broader application to other areas of life are important. Clients are generally people who have intrusive problems requiring quick solutions. Work-related problems, job changes, divorce work, and relationship problems may all be issues that respond well to personal coaching. However, the aspects of e-therapy that *may* be very useful are:

1. The use of online or e-mailed articles and research studies sent to or made available to clients that reinforce treatment.
2. The ability to quickly respond to clients when problems need discussion.
3. The fact that many people are more comfortable writing than speaking and may be more elegant in their communications and insightful use of the Internet to communicate than in face-to-face therapy.

4. The use of e-therapy has great potential for ongoing work with clients who may have chronic problems or require long-term support.
5. Chat rooms that function as self-help groups have considerable potential for helping people. Finn (1999) studied the content of messages sent by people with disabilities using the Internet as a form of group therapy. He found that most correspondents wanted to talk about their health and about specific issues of treatment and quality of care, but that overall, the correspondents acted as a support group helping one another cope with emotional, medical, and social issues. The issues included everything from "highly technical descriptions of medications, procedures, and equipment to subjective accounts of treatment experiences. There also was considerable discussion of interpersonal relationship issues such as marital relationships, dating, and sexuality" (p. 228). Finn (1999) notes that many disabled people are homebound and that the Internet becomes an important part of the communicating they do each day. This is particularly true for homebound people who may also have difficulty speaking or hearing.

CASE STUDY: THERAPY USING THE TELEPHONE AND E-MAIL

The following case describes the use of the telephone for therapy, with e-mails to supplement treatment. Some of the following material first appeared in a book I wrote on the strengths perspective (Glicken, 2004).

A technique that some workers describe as effective is having clients write summaries after each session and then sharing those summaries with the worker so that issues to explore during the next session can be identified. A colleague of mine who had just begun therapy with a therapist he liked very much used this technique. After nine sessions, just as they were beginning to progress in treatment, my colleague accepted a new job in a small community thousands of miles away. Because of the absence of therapists in the new community, the original therapist and my colleague decided to continue treatment by telephone. The day after the first telephone session, my colleague began to send the therapist an e-mail outlining what he'd learned during the telephone session, what he intended to do about it, and the issues he wanted to discuss during the next session. If there was a need to interact with the therapist, or vice versa, e-mail was used to clarify points, ask and answer questions, and propose new topics for discussion. He said that in many ways, the work they did together on the telephone was much more powerful and relevant than the face-to-face work he had done with the therapist.

"First of all," he told me, "it *is* possible to do therapy on the phone. I had to be very focused, but since I was in a room with no distractions, that was easy. Then, we had to have a sense of where we wanted each session to go or we would misuse the time. Therapy seemed to last longer on the phone, because,

I suppose, there were no distractions. In my prior sessions, we must have spent a lot of time warming up because I'd leave feeling half done. In our conversations on the phone, I felt as if we'd covered the material in a much more concise and usable way. The day after the first telephone session, I began to write about a page or two summarizing what I'd learned from the session, what I was going to do about it, and what I wanted to discuss in the next session. Then I'd e-mail the material to my therapist.

"It started a process I found extraordinarily helpful. Of course, the therapist was terrific and, after a session or two, I think we both knew that something pretty special was taking place. The other thing about our phone calls was that I took a more active role in my treatment. I began to read everything I could find about mid-life depression and loneliness. What I found was a very strong literature that was really helpful. I discussed medication with my therapist and then went to see my physician about it. In the end, they didn't recommend medication because of the side effects, but my goodness, I felt as if I was being consulted and cared for in an extraordinary way even though my therapist was thousands of miles away.

"I should add that one of my sessions was held the day of the World Trade Center bombings. We were both in such a troubled state of mind because of the horrible loss of life, that the session was electric. I still can't quite believe how powerful it was, or how touched I was that my therapist was in her office waiting for my call when she had family members in New York who may have been harmed by the bombings." (p. 56)

LAWS OF PRIVACY

There are many important privacy concerns about the use of web-based supervision and e-therapy. Robson and Robson (1998) wonder if inappropriate people might access confidential information, particularly when others have access to computers used by clients or supervisees (as in university or public library computer labs). The authors also point out that some people have very limited knowledge of computers and that confidential information may inadvertently be sent to others. How many of us have done this in our personal lives? I certainly have when I'm in a rush.

The possibility of computer hackers accessing private e-therapy and supervisory sessions seems considerable. Employees often take confidential information home, raising the possibility that it might be lost or stolen and that a breach of confidentiality might occur. Even though the HIPAA provisions of 1996 obligate organizations with employees who work with confidential material to be trained in the rules of privacy, the training doesn't seem to have deterred many employees working with very senstitive material from using it in illegal ways. In 2006, for example, a Veterans Affairs employee took a laptop home that was then stolen from the worker's home. The computer contained confidential material on many men and women in the military. The fallout was enormous, with concerns that hundreds of thousands of cases of identity theft would result. The agency had a rule that confidential information about clients should not be removed from the agency but it was removed anyway. Laptops and other digital storage media substantially increase the possibility of theft or loss.

To ensure that clients' privacy rights are protected when material related to health and mental health issues are exchanged among providers (insurance companies, physicians, clinicans, agencies, and government), the federal act known as HIPAA (U.S. Office of Health and Human Services, 1996) provides the following privacy rights:

1. **Access to Medical Records:** Patients are generally able to see and obtain copies of their medical records including those pertaining to mental health treatment, and to request corrections if they identify errors and mistakes. Health plans, doctors, hospitals, clinics, nursing homes, and other covered organizations and individual providers must generally provide access to these records within 30 days and may charge patients for the cost of copying and sending the records.

2. **Marketing:** Providers are not allowed to use client information to market services. If client information is used for scholarly reasons (research studies, for example), clients must be given consent forms to sign and must be fully apprised of the nature of the study. Clients cannot be forced to participate in studies.

3. **Notice of Privacy Practices:** Covered health plans, doctors, and other health-care providers must issue a notice to their patients indicating how providers may use personal medical information and the client's rights under the new privacy regulation. Doctors, hospitals, and other direct-care providers will generally provide this information on the patient's first visit. Patients are asked to sign, initial, or otherwise acknowledge that they have received this notice. Health plans must mail the notice to their enrollees if the notice changes significantly.

4. **Limits on the Use of Personal Medical Information:** The privacy rule sets limits on how health plans and covered providers may use individually identifiable health information. To promote the best quality care for patients, the rule does not restrict the ability of doctors, nurses, and other professionals to share information needed to treat their patients. In other situations, though, personal health information generally may not be used for purposes not related to health care, and providers of services may use or share only the minimum amount of protected information needed for a particular purpose. In addition, patients must sign a specific authorization before a provider of service may release their medical information to a life insurer, a

bank, a marketing firm, or another outside business for purposes not related to their health care.

5. **Confidential Communications:** Under the privacy rule, patients can request that their doctors, health plans, and other providers of services take reasonable steps to ensure that their communications with the patient are confidential. For example, a patient could ask a doctor to call his or her office rather than the patient's home, and the doctor's office should comply with that request if it can be reasonably accommodated. Providers are allowed to fax medical information or to use other means, including e-mail, as long as it's on a secured line.

   This area of the law is often badly handled. For instance, a friend with diabetes asked that the doctor only call her home. Instead, the doctor called my friend's work number and left a message about her diabetes on the agency's line where four or more people heard, for the first time, that she had diabetes and that her condition was worsening. Soon, the entire agency knew about it and she was told to see the director who was concerned that she might be too ill to continue working. From what I gather in my normal discussions with friends, this isn't an unusual example.

6. **Written Privacy Procedures:** The law requires service providers to have written privacy procedures, including a description of staff that has access to protected information, how it will be used, and when it may be disclosed. Providers generally must take steps to ensure that any business associates who have access to protected information agree to the same limitations on the use and disclosure of that information.

   As someone who has supervised students placed in medical facilities, I'm told they have open access to patient files, and that these patients sometimes include faculty members and fellow students. The records also contain mental health information. This gives rise to legitimate concerns about privacy, and students need to know that they should not look at the files of anyone other than the clients with whom they are working. Students must also have permission from their supervisors to read client files. Students who disobey this rule are at jeopardy of violating the rights of others and may face disciplinary action by their universities.

7. **Employee Training and Privacy Officer:** Providers must train employees in their privacy procedures, and must designate an individual to be responsible for ensuring that procedures are followed. If providers learn an employee has failed to follow these procedures, they must take appropriate disciplinary action.

8. **Sending Private Information Over the Internet:** When sending private information over the Internet it is wise to have a statement at

the end of the message indicating that the information is for private use only and asking the recipient, if not specifically entitled to the information, to discard it. A privacy statement attached to all outgoing e-mails might read as follows:

> This message is a PRIVATE communication. This message and all attachments are a private communication sent by a social agency and may be confidential or protected by privilege. If you are not the intended recipient, you are hereby notified that any disclosure, copying, distribution, or use of the information contained in or attached to this message is strictly prohibited. Please notify the sender of the delivery error by replying to this message, and then delete it from your system. Thank you.

SUMMARY

This chapter discusses the use of the Internet for supervision and therapy. It suggests many benefits and liabilities in the use of the Internet for professional functions, and briefly outlines the privacy policies noted in a federal law known as HIPAA. That law provides for client privacy and directly affects the way we communicate with others in our professional capacities.

FIND THE MISTAKE

1. It would be perfectly fine for a human service professional to call a client at work and leave a message, even if the client hasn't specifically said it's OK. The need of the client overrides the client's privacy rights, according to HIPAA.
2. The great thing about e-therapy is that you can reach people who don't live near a real therapist.
3. HIPAA allows you to tape a client session without the client's knowledge if the tape is kept confidential and is only used to help the clinician provide better service.
4. One of the strong points in using the Internet for group supervision is that workers who feel uncomfortable in face-to-face supervision may now feel able to communicate without anxiety.
5. HIPAA allows therapists in private practice to use verbal testimonials from clients without asking the client for permission as long as the client's name is not used.

REFERENCES

Alleman, J. (2003). Proving psychotherapy over the Internet. *Psychiatric Time*, XX(7).

Fenichel, M. (2003). Online psychotherapy: Technical difficulties, formulations and processes. Retrieved February 14, 2006, from www.fenichel.com/technical.shtml

Finn, J. (1999). An exploration of helping processes in an online self-help group focusing on issues of disability. *Health & Social Work*, 24(3), 220–231.

Gainor, K. A., & Constantine, M. G. (2002). Multicultural group supervision: A comparison of in-person versus Web-based formats. *Professional School Counseling*, 6, 104–111.

Glicken, M. D. (2004). *Using the strengths perspective in social work practice.* Boston: Allyn and Bacon/Longman.

Ladany, N., Hill, C. E., Corbett, M. M., & Nutt, E. A. (1996). Nature, extent, and importance of what psychotherapy trainees do not disclose to their supervisors. *Journal of Counseling Psychology*, 43, 10–24.

Myrick, R. D., & Sabella, R. A. (1995). Cyberspace: New place for counselor supervision. *Elementary School Guidance and Counseling*, 30, 35–44.

Robson, D., & Robson, M. (1998). Intimacy and computer communication. *British Journal of Guidance and Counselling*, 26, 33–41.

Smith, S. D., & Reynolds, C. (2002). Cyber-psychotherapy. *Annals of the American Psychotherapy Association*, 5(2), 20–22.

Stofle, G., & Hamilton, S. (1998). Online supervision for social workers. *New Social Worker*, 5(1).

U.S. Office of Human Services. (1996). Summary of the HIPAA privacy rule. Retrieved from the Internet March 2, 2007, at www.hhs.gov/ocr/privacysummary.pdf

16

How Writing Can Change Our Lives

Creative writing can help us become much more self-aware because it opens hidden doors and helps us remember the past in ways that may surprise us. Through our writing we may find out why we feel the way we do about our parents, our families, our work, our partners, our spirituality, and about an infinite number of issues and experiences that make up the human condition. Creative writing is not only cathartic, but it opens us to new ways of viewing the world. These are very important considerations for the human service professions where self-awareness, empathy, and introspection often help us become better clinicians.

In several studies of the impact of writing about one's problems, Smyth, Stone, Hurewitz, and Kaell (1999) report that researchers at North Dakota State University took a sample of subjects with asthma. Although each group's level of distress was the same, 47% of those who wrote about the stress of their disease showed clinical improvement, compared to 24% in the control group. Both groups received exactly the same medical treatment. Lung functioning in the group of subjects who wrote about their problems improved by 19%, while the control group showed no improvement. In the same article, researchers found that arthritis patients who wrote about their physical and emotional health problems experienced a 28% reduction in the severity of their symptoms. Writing about ourselves appears to have positive health benefits.

In this chapter, we will discuss the importance of two approaches that specifically use writing: bibliotherapy and story-telling. To help you use writing for self-discovery, I have provided examples of creative writing and writing exercises that may help in this process. Let's consider it a form of self-therapy.

To begin self-discovery through writing, take a few minutes to schedule some private time for yourself. Decide where you will write (writers can be very superstitious about the place where they write and believe that good Karma helps in the process). Use a computer if you'd like because it makes revising your writing so much easier. I know some of you dislike computers because the feel of words on a piece of paper in longhand is almost sensual, but trust me, computers are your friend and, in the long run, your writing will improve by using one.

THE USE OF STORIES

Discussing the importance of stories in the lives of people, Zuniga (1992) writes "Stories inspire people to address complex issues they would not ordinarily consider. Moreover, stories enable people to have sudden insights" (p. 56). Stories serve as an ideal way of helping people to remember important life events and identify themes in their lives that may continually be repeated. Stories also serve to explain definitions of masculinity and femininity that may help us understand related problems.

In an example of the importance of stories, after being asked to write about his father in a therapy group because he found it so difficult to talk about his father in group, a male client read the following to the group:

> My father was an FBI agent. Very macho, you know. The strong one. In fourth grade he took to driving me out into the country and telling me how useless his life was. At these times he would take his gun out and put it to his temple. "If I had the guts," he'd tell me, "I'd pull the trigger." He never did, you know, until I was in 10th grade. By then he'd lost his job because of his drinking. We never did know what the trouble was, it was so deep inside. By the time he killed himself, I wasn't surprised, I was relieved. I vowed that I'd never be the wimp *he* was and here I am at 38 with the same preoccupation with death and the same pain inside I can't explain. (Glicken, 2005a, p. 108)

The group tried to help the client understand the source of his pain. In time, it became clear that at a very early age, the client was required to rescue his father from his suicidal inclinations. Failing at that, the client became a therapist. As a therapist, he repeatedly failed to prevent similar problems with his own clients. Connecting his failure to prevent his father's suicide and the sense of failure that followed him as a therapist became a theme in his life and helped to explain his choice of an occupation that caused him such sorrow. The group asked him to continue writing about his father and, in one piece of writing he read to the group, he said:

The peace officer with a gun to protect others cannot use it to protect himself or, for that matter, his son, who now has the same preoccupations with death and failure that his father did. The weapon is no longer an object for protection; it is a metaphor of destruction just as I see therapy as a metaphor of destruction. I can't be a therapist until I overcome the sense that helping others ends in hurting them. Until that feeling goes away (it re-creates my feeling when I felt helpless to save my father), I shouldn't do it anymore. I feel sad about not being a therapist, but I know as I gain understanding of myself that all the desire I have inside to help others will lead me to a good place. (Glicken, 2005a, p. 109)

BIBLIOTHERAPY: THE USE OF NOVELS, POETRY, FILMS, AND MUSIC

In another example of the importance of writing, many therapists use bibliotherapy to facilitate the therapeutic process. Myers (1998) defines bibliotherapy as "a dynamic process of interaction between the individual and literature, which emphasizes the reader's emotional response to what has been read" (p. 243). Pardeck (1995) offers six goals of bibliotherapy: (1) to provide information; (2) to gain insight; (3) to find solutions; (4) to stimulate discussion of problems; (5) to suggest new values and attitudes; and (6) to show clients how others have coped with problems similar to their own. "Bibliotherapy provides metaphors for life experiences that help clients verbalize their thoughts and feelings and learn new ways to cope with problems" (Myers, 1998, p. 246).

Poetry can be particularly useful in helping clients see situations in ways that elicit strong memories of prior events. A poem used in treatment with a husband who could not accept the rape of his wife is a particularly poignant example (MacLeod, 2000).

> After six months,
> I'm told about the oily green basement couch,
> the muffled evening news upstairs,
> and the two hands grabbing the back of her head,
> forcing it down to his crotch.
>
> And I can't hear this.
> I just want to drink beer and talk
> about the weekend or Raymond Carver
> or any other damn thing, but here I sit
> feeling my fingers rake flesh from my thighs.
>
> She thought that if she just went along—
> if she could have just made herself want to—

> it wouldn't have been what it was. But no one
> pulls that off and after walking past her parents,
> she fell to her knees and vomited on their porch.
>
> Then her voice trails off and I start in.
> I stand up and say to her, **say** to her,
> because I'm not yelling yet, what's his name?
> But she shakes her head and she
> just wants to forget. Forget it all.
>
> We are not doing any forgetting tonight.
> I punch the bookcase, knocking novels and poetry
> to the floor. I take her arms so she can't ignore me
> and yell things at her that I won't remember later and
> I feel strong and goddammit, somebody is going to bleed.
>
> Her look sobers me.
> I shut up and let go.
> Softly, she picks up her keys and walks out,
> leaving me to melt deep into the cracks of the couch,
> pale and shaking,
> like him.
> (Jason Michael MacLeod, "The Two of Us")

After reading the poem, the husband broke down and cried, telling the worker that it was just impossible for him to accept his wife's rape. While he felt responsible to be loving and sensitive to wife, he also felt repulsed. These opposite feelings were driving him away from his wife. Although he knew these feelings were terribly hurtful to his wife, he also felt, irrationally, that his wife was to blame and that she had somehow encouraged and enjoyed the rape. The poem helped him get back in touch with the recognition that terrible things can happen to any of us, and it started a long, slow reconciliation with his wife who had felt rejected and demeaned by her husband's behavior toward her since the rape.

Interestingly, it wasn't the content of the poem that prompted the client to reevaluate his feelings about the rape, but rather the suggestion of powerlessness in the phrase, "Leaving me to melt deep into the cracks of the couch." The poem didn't touch the client at a literal level. Instead, it described, through the metaphor of melting into the couch, the client's feeling of powerlessness at not being able to prevent the rape. The client believed that he should be an understanding and sensitive husband and support his wife, but what he actually felt was anger, self-recrimination, and the urge to blame her. The confusion over this collision of feelings made him feel powerless, and the metaphor in the poem allowed him to discuss these significant feelings with the clinician.

WRITING CONVEYS HIDDEN MESSAGES

Writing is often a voyage into forgotten memories. What we write about, the choice of subjects and the characters, the settings, the plots, the style we use, and the stories we want to tell come from a place within us that is sometimes inaccessible when we speak. The story itself is often the script we began to write for our lives in childhood.

Let's consider the way forgotten memories and messages sometimes enter into our writing and examine what they might mean. I'm going to show you some of my own writing. I'll tell you what it means to me, although you may have an entirely different opinion. That's perfectly OK. There are no hard and fast rules in creative writing. Throughout this chapter I'm going to provide examples of writing. I'll let you know what I think the writing means, and then I'd like you to do the same by writing down your interpretations, impressions, and observations. Here is a short piece I wrote about my father after attending a writer's workshop where we were asked to write about the parent we admired the most.

A STORY: "A RIDE ON THE STREETCAR"

The following story (actually a vignette) was published in a book I wrote on resilience (Glicken, 2006), but it was originally written for the Sunday magazine of a major newspaper. I thought it was a bit too personal at the time and elected not to have it published until, years later, it became one of many life stories I included in my book. In this vignette, the issue of a sick mother who has become hospitalized and the child's feelings of abandonment are explored. The literary form gives the child's experience a power it might not have if it were written as a professional article. You be the judge.

A Ride on the Streetcar

I am eating breakfast with my father, listening to him describe the Cossacks and the retreat of the White Russian Army during the Russian Revolution. It is very early in the morning, well before the birds start singing. My father is dressed in his long underwear and has pieces of toilet paper covering cuts on his face from a used double-edged Gillette razor.

"You should have seen the women," he tells me. "They were more beautiful than you can imagine." I am maybe five years old. It sounds nice to listen to my father talk about beautiful women. I imagine that they all look like Mrs. Cooper down the street who everybody considers to be very beautiful, although she seems mean and unfriendly to me.

My mother, who used to be beautiful, lies in a hospital ward with an illness no one can explain. She is still a young woman but she looks old and wrinkled and

I try not to think of her when my father talks about beautiful women. In a while, we will take a streetcar to see my mother in the hospital. I don't want to go.

"We could hear the Cossacks hours before we saw them," he says, as he flips over the eggs and the kosher salami we will eat together for breakfast. "The horses—and there must have been thousands of them—made a noise like an earthquake."

My father adds a little coffee to my hot milk. It makes me feel grown up. I am his confidant in these early morning chats before he goes off to work for the railroad. I am unsure of what he does on the railroad, but his leather jacket looks dashing and I imagine that it is something important. Maybe he drives train engines, or blows the whistle on the morning train I watch alone from our house near the railroad tracks.

"We all walked out of our houses and watched the Cossacks pass through our town," he continues, putting the fried eggs and salami on my plate. He never ruins the eggs and I can always dunk toast into the yolk and watch it run down the bread. "We were poor people and my mother told us not to watch them or one of the Cossacks would put a sword through our stomachs, but we couldn't help ourselves. We watched them for hours. They were covered with frost and they had menacing looks in their eyes."

My father walks to the window and looks outside. Even though it's still dark outside, he is certain the day will be mean. "I hate the rain," he says. "I hate this endless warm weather. I miss the snow and the cold." I'm not sure about snow since I've never felt it, but from my father's description of the Cossacks in winter, it sounds wonderful to me, maybe like soft melting ice cream or fluffy feathers.

I am too young to have developed any animosity toward my father. Like so many sons and fathers, that will come in time. But in this moment—this perfect moment before the dawn—before anything else intrudes on his time, I listen to his Russian stories and I am in love with him. I love the way he shaves and the way he smells after his shower. I want to be just like him—driving trains through the city and blowing the engine whistle to let everybody know I'm coming.

I help my father put away the dishes from breakfast and then dress for my trip to see my mother. When the apartment looks decent enough, as decent as it can look with a working father taking care of a young son, we walk down the block to catch the streetcar. The first light of dawn is just coming through and the city looks lovely to me. It is all that I have ever known and the smells mesmerize me, call out my name, talk to me.

I don't want to take this ride with my father. I'd rather sit at home and listen to his stories about Cossacks. But we board the streetcar anyway so that my father can see my mother before work begins. I never want to go and use every excuse I can muster. My father looks hurt when I tell him my excuses. Secretly, he doesn't want to visit her either. My little fibs just confirm his own feeling that my mother has given up and that the rides we take to the hospital on the streetcar are pointless. Often we ride together in brooding silence watching the people on the street and smelling the strange smells of foreign cooking that float through the open windows of the streetcar.

Sometimes on our rides to the hospital, my father tells me stories about the way he and my grandmother and aunt walked across Russia to escape the communists, but I look out the window and try not to listen. The fact is that my mother has abandoned us and I don't want to give up my five-year-old anger for one second.

Once in a while, on our rides to the hospital, a lady smiles at him. He doesn't know what to do and smiles back, making sure that he waves his wedding ring so the ladies will know that he's married. It's such a half-hearted effort that it only encourages them more. Not a few times on our way to the hospital, he moves away from me and sits next to one of the ladies on the streetcar. It seems to me that he has every right to be friendly with other women. His woman has given up on us. I secretly wonder what some of the ladies would be like as mothers. Better than mine, I'll bet.

The streetcar leaves us off a few blocks from the hospital. The neighborhood is full of people who aren't like us at all. They speak different languages and seem happy and carefree. In our neighborhood, people keep to themselves and seem secretive about everything. My grandmother, who lives on the next block, says that we shouldn't talk to strangers and that we should keep our troubles to ourselves, but these people seem like they'd be happy to listen to a five-year-olds' troubles. Once in a while we stop at a bakery and have a pastry before we go to the hospital. I know my father is delaying the moment we have to visit my mother, but I don't care. We can stay here forever as far as I'm concerned.

The people in the bakery all speak another language, but the pastries are delicious and the people are nice to us. Sometimes they give me a cream soda and talk to me in their language. I don't know what they're saying, but I like the way the words sound and the way their faces seem so animated and full of life when they talk. I want to wait for my father in the bakery, but he says my mother would be hurt if I didn't come. I don't care.

We walk in silence to the hospital. Inside, the hospital smells of disinfectant and I want to leave as soon as we walk into the lobby. But we climb up the dark old stairs to the third floor where my mother lies in a charity ward. I'm not sure what a charity ward is, but it seems to me that all the women in the ward have sad looks on their faces, looks of hopelessness and desperation.

My mother sits up in bed when she sees us. She tries to smile, but the effort is so great that her body slumps. I know that she is 28 years old but she looks as old as my grandmother. Her hair has turned white. I hardly know what to say to her. She kisses me and I pull away, afraid, I guess, that I'll catch whatever she has. If she notices, I can't be sure. I have become an expert at reading the signs of hurt in people. It is a burden to be five years old and worry so much about other people's feelings.

My father gives her a perfunctory kiss and begins to tell her about work and the gossip from our street. I watch the ladies in the ward and focus on a little girl sitting next to her mother. She is probably my age and has a very innocent look on her face. She is holding her mother's hand for all she is worth. Her mother, like the rest of the ladies on the ward, looks ill beyond repair. Little tears trickle down her mother's face, which the little girl wipes off with a tissue. The little girl has the same look of bewilderment I must have on my face.

I don't know why, but I start to sob just looking at her. My father looks distraught and puts his finger over his lips, but I can't stop. The tears pour down my face and I feel ashamed to be causing such a scene.

One of the nurses comes over and speaks to me. She says that I'll have to leave if I don't stop crying, but the tears gush out of me and I sit on the chair next to my mother's bed and weep. The nurse takes me downstairs and makes me sit in the lobby next to the information booth. I want to stop crying, but I can't. The nurse tells the lady at the information booth that I'm a naughty boy and that if I can't stop crying, they won't let me see my mother anymore. I just want to be back in the bakery having a cream soda and eating warm pastries. I want someone to fuss over me and treat me like I'm five instead of an adult.

On the way home, my father puts his head down and covers his face with his hands. I want to hug him, to give him a kiss, to let him know that I'm sorry his wife is sick and that he has to take care of me all by himself. But he just sits there in the streetcar with his head down and says nothing. Maybe he's hurting too, and we ride together, silently, keeping whatever is in our hearts to ourselves. (pp. 191–195)

Discussion

This is a story about a child's reaction to abandonment. Professionals write about the same issue everyday in the professional reports they share with other professionals. But for a mass audience, the short story format felt as if it would have more impact than a professional article for a journal. Not everyone can write short stories, but if you compare a professional paper on abandonment with this short story, you will hopefully feel the power it has for a mass audience.

Writing creatively requires a connection to the inner person—the hidden person who collects the hurts, the disappointments, and the sorrows of life. It means that the writer must be willing to self-disclose and to believe that no topic is ever too personal to share. However, creative writing isn't stream of consciousness writing because poems and stories have structure and discipline. The rewrite of this story took two months and perhaps 50 edits before I found it even close to being acceptable. While the basic idea was always clear, it took time and effort to clarify the conflicting ideas about the story and their meaning. Was it to be about abandonment? Was it about a boy's relationship with his father? Was it about early hostility to his mother that had implications for his future relationships with women?

In the end, I wanted to say that out of a sense of abandonment, children develop deep feelings of anguish. Those feelings may be irrational, but they are deeply felt. The experiences described here might result in severe conflict for the child as an adult. And so, the story begins quietly. A father and son are having an early breakfast together. The father is talking about a subject, beautiful women, inappropriate for a five year old, but clearly a subject to capture the father's own sorrow about his wife's absence from the home.

The streetcar conveys time and place. The little boy's inability to understand many of the events swirling around him captures the confusion and the trauma of early childhood trauma. The hospital is a place of despair, lost dreams, and fear. As a result of his mother's illness, the child knows that his childhood is over and that he has begun the process of becoming an adult to help his family deal with a crisis.

As I wrote and rewrote this story, I felt my father's presence. He was always in my heart, but describing the impact he had on me was complicated. He could be difficult, competitive, discouraging, illogical, and overwhelming. At the same time he was fun, exciting, endlessly fascinating, and outrageous in his views. How does one capture these complex and contradictory elements and understand the impact they might have on us as adults?

I've written about my father a great deal. Each time I write about him, I love him a little more. As I've learned to love him, I've begun to love myself, as well. That is the power of writing and its ability to reinvent the people and the events in our lives. This story is the idealized version of my father; the child's notion of what he was like. To be sure, he could be this way from time to time, but to help in my own growth as a man and as a father, I've chosen to write about my father by using the good memories and eliminating most of the bad. The unconscious desire to have a good father is very strong in me, and I've progressively written about him in ways that are positive because they make me feel much better about myself. It's difficult to like one's self while actively disliking a parent.

In a way, we all have a fantasy of how we would like our lives to be. This make-believe world we create often holds the key to many of our beliefs and values, and fantasy becomes the transmitter of our dreams and aspirations. Consider this example of my fantasy about love that forms the prologue to a romance novella I wrote entitled *Remembering Zion* (Glicken, 2005b).

PROLOGUE TO A ROMANCE NOVEL: AN EXAMPLE OF FANTASY

Remembering Zion

Sometime in the night, a vision came to me. It was a vision of Zion National Park and the beautiful towers of granite and sandstone that rise from prehistoric oceans and form the enchanted sacred walls of that beautiful place. I had been there many times before, but in my vision it looked different in ways that dreams make the commonplace slightly surreal.

I saw many splendid things in my vision, but the most wonderful of all was the birth of a child. I did not know whose child it was, but I can remember that I wept when she was born. In my dream it felt like the rebirth of the world when I saw her tiny body.

And then she grew up before my eyes and it was my Jennifer, suddenly a grown and beautiful woman. She beckoned to me and I touched her hand. It was warm and soft to the touch. She held me and we listened to someone preach from the sandstone formation known as the Pulpit, which is in the Valley of the Patriarchs.

I do not remember the person who spoke, but his words ring true to me, even now. He said, "Do not grieve for loved ones who are no longer with us. Each day brings with it the possibilities of new love. Permit your heart to be receptive, and do not discount life's opportunities. Love is like a mighty river. It cannot be stopped, but flows through us and goes its own course."

His majestic voice surrounded everything and hung from the tops of the canyons and filled the Valley of the Patriarchs like thunder.

"Be appreciative of every opportunity God presents us. Never turn those away with whom you may truly find happiness. Be gentle as the spring wind with those who are dear to you."

It is strange that I can remember what he said in the dream as clearly as if he'd said it this very minute. Perhaps I remember the dream so vividly because it is what I believe. Perhaps the speaker in my dream touched my heart and fashioned his sermon from my thoughts and feelings. I do not know. But when I am very sad, when things go badly and I feel so lonely that it is like a knife inside my heart to go on with another day, I hear the words of that secret preacher, and they soothe me.

I worship at the alter of love. I praise God for giving us such a sublime experience. I hope, with all that is within me, that it will happen again and again until I am too old to love, and then I hope it will happen to me then, as well.

We are so afraid of love. We have a bad love and we would do anything not to repeat the pain. And yet, love is wonderful beyond measure when it is right and true, and we crave it just as the religious fanatic craves the caress of God.

In many ways, I feel like a wanderer in time and space. I am here with everyone, but my heart and soul are elsewhere. They are with the special women who captured my heart and made life more bearable for an aging man.

For them, and for all the women in the world who reach out and touch the hearts of men, I write this experience of the heart and spirit. There isn't a man alive who is not susceptible to love, and all men who experience the sublime feel of a woman's touch are better for it. (pp. 3–4)

Discussion

Should grown people fantasize about relationships the way I do here? What do *you* think? Is it healthy to have such an idealized view of love? I think so, but what about you? Should we be grounded in the reality of relationships? Should we believe that relationships are destined to become predictable and boring, or should we agree with the Bard that love knows not good, nor bad, but goes where the wild heart leads? It's clear to me that I think love is exciting, wacky, unpredictable, and terrifically wonderful.

Maybe that's why I've been single so long, or maybe it propels me to keep up the search until the ideal woman, the Czarina of the Heart (to use Robert Bly's expression), comes along and walks, trots, flies me into old age on the wings . . . yes . . . on the wings of a snow white dove.

Were I to give this piece to any therapist, they would probably tell me that my notion of love is destined to bring me heartache and pain, and that it is probably unachievable. But is it? Should I expect anything less? And if I do, will it make me miserable? How about you? What do you wish for in relationships? Does this piece touch you? Does it describe how you feel about love and relationships? How *do* you feel? Why not write 250 words right now about your fantasy for love. Let's see what *you* have in mind for yourself.

ACCESSING FORGOTTEN MEMORIES THROUGH YOUR WRITING

I want to encourage you to write about important episodes in your life, process your writing with others (or by yourself once you get the hang of it), and then rewrite each story, poem, or vignette until the meaning begins to emerge and you can confidently understand the piece in more detail. Once that has happened, you should rewrite the piece to determine the additional insights you have about your work until you have closure. Closure comes when you understand the work and its meaning sufficiently to use it for additional self-understanding and, perhaps, more stories.

Forgotten memories may be at play when your creative writing has one theme or when a specific character is repeatedly used. This suggests that the hidden issues in your writing are still unclear. You may be able to resolve those issues by writing new endings to a piece or by changing descriptions of a character. Give it a try. Instead of writing about something in a negative way, try writing about it in a more positive way. See if that attempt to change the tone and voice of the piece doesn't lend itself to some change in your view of the issue, person, or event.

One effective way to access forgotten memories is to think about something you would like to write before going to bed at night, and then write it immediately after you wake up. Something happens during the night—let's say the unconscious begins to unfold—and you may be able to write the piece effortlessly. Dreams are a key to lost memories, as are repetitive behaviors that may be self-destructive. Often, we move into relationships that have disaster written all over them because they replay the confusing relationships we had with our parents as children. This is particularly true when parents were abusive or abused substances, and we became their caretakers. Although we know the relationship can't possibly be good for us, we enter it anyway. Something about it is familiar and predictable. It may cloud our perceptions and judgment. That's the unconscious at work. Trying to understand the unconscious is what most writing is really about.

WORKING IN SMALL GROUPS

One way to help you in your writing is to work in a small group of three or four people. It's better not to work with people you know. Take half an hour to write your story, and another half an hour to read it and get feedback from the group, followed by a half hour to revise your work using the feedback from the group. If you would like to work on the story during the week between group meetings, that's fine. In the following session, you will meet back with your group and you can read them your revisions. Here is a guide to help you provide feedback to the members in your group, which I included in chapter 1 (Julagay, personal correspondence, April 22, 1998). You don't have to follow it absolutely, but it might help.

GROUP FEEDBACK PROFILE

1. Can you identify a main point (thesis) or purpose in this story?
2. Does the subject matter and the style of writing reflect depth, fullness, and complexity of thought? Indicate any areas that need improving.
3. Does this story demonstrate a clear, focused, unified, and coherent organization? Indicate any areas that need improving.
4. Are there enough details in the story to identify the person, place, group, or event being written about? Make note of any sections that are vague, or any general statements that fail to hold your interest. Indicate at least two examples of vivid detail. How appropriate are the details in this story?
5. Evaluate the mechanical aspects of the story. Look for grammar, punctuation, paragraph formation, variation, and the use of transitions. Indicate any obvious areas needing improvement, but do not spend an excessive amount of time on this aspect.
6. Is the information presented in a way that makes others want to listen, but is also easy to follow? If not, what suggestions would you offer to make it more interesting or easier to follow?
7. Reread the beginning of the story and decide whether or not it is effective. Did it capture your attention? Is there any quotation, fact, or anecdote elsewhere in the story that might make a better opening? Did the opening adequately represent the rest of the story?

WORKING ALONE

You can work alone on these exercises if you would like, although I think that it's best to work in the group, initially. Once you get the hang of it, you can certainly do your writing and revising as you wish. I've given you some guidelines to help in the evaluation of the writing, but you can do the same for yourself once you understand the process.

A WRITING EXERCISE

Here are some suggestions to help you access hidden feelings and memories:

1. Think about a fantasy you're having. It can be any fantasy. There are no rules here.
2. Write the fantasy down and don't worry about what other people will think or how the writing looks.
3. Once you've written the fantasy, immediately read it to your neighbor, no holds barred.
4. Discuss what you think the fantasy means to you and why you are having it **NOW**!
5. What is the theme of your fantasy? Is it about freedom, boredom, excitement, romance? What inhibits you from acting on the fantasy?
6. Try to think of something happening in your life that may have prompted the fantasy. Describe it to your neighbor.
7. Was there a time in your life when you actually *did* what your fantasy is about? Tell your neighbor about that time and why you stopped doing whatever you did.
8. Rewrite the fantasy using the new information you have to expand the work.
9. Has the fantasy given you any insight into current emotions and behaviors?
10. Remember, all creative writing is about fantasy. Feel free to fantasize. It will lead to creativity and creativity is what we're looking for in this experience.

SOME FINAL WORDS

While I hope I've helped you become a better writer, I also hope I've encouraged you to think of writing as an important and creative form of expression.

Many people discover the gift of writing late in life. It's never too late to use writing in its most creative forms to express intense beliefs and emotions. You may be surprised at how powerful words are and how moved you will be by what you've written. It isn't always easy, and it doesn't always work out the way we expect it to, but in the end you will think of writing as I do: much like your troubled child—a lot of work and occasionally painful, but in the end, oddly beautiful and uniquely your own.

SUMMARY

This chapter discusses the use of creative writing to help us understand our behavior. Several examples of creative work I've written and my analysis are provided. Readers are encouraged to write creatively to help them understand complex issues in their lives that may lead to better awareness. The significance of stories and the use of metaphors are also noted.

FIND THE MISTAKES

1. I remember my father as being willful, abusive and demeaning. His behavior led to my becoming an alcoholic and an assortment of other dysfunctional behaviors. He is the cause of my misery.
2. My experiences with women make me think that my mother was very seductive and used subtle forms of manipulation that were quasi-sexual in nature.
3. Metaphorically speaking, it's better to be rich than poor.
4. I asked the client to tell me a story about his father. I thought it would probably tell me more about him and his role as a man than it would tell me about his father.
5. It doesn't matter what you write, so long as you put words down on paper. Sooner or later you'll see connections between issues in your life and their origins.

REFERENCES

Glicken, M. D. (2005a). *Working with troubled men: A contemporary practitioner's guide.* Mahwah, NJ: Lawrence Erlbaum Publishers.
Glicken, M. D. (2005b). *Remembering Zion: A spiritual love novel.* Omaha, NE: iuniverse.
Glicken, M. D. (2006). *Learning from resilient people: Lessons we can apply to counseling and psychotherapy.* Thousand Oaks, CA: Sage.
MacLeod, J. M. (2000). "The two of us." *Grinnell Review,* 16, 49–50.

Myers, Jane E. (1998). Bibliotherapy and DCT: Co-constructing the therapeutic metaphor. *Journal of Counseling & Development,* 76(3), 243–251.

Pardeck, J. T. (1995). Bibliotherapy: An innovative approach for helping children. *Early Childhood Development and Care,* 110, 83–88.

Smyth, J. M., Stone, A. A., Hurewitz, A., & Kaell, A. (1999). Effects of writing about stressful experiences on symptom reduction in patients with asthma or rheumatoid arthritis. *Journal of the American Medical Association,* 281, 1304–1309.

Zuniga, M. E. (1992). Using metaphors in therapy: Dichos and Latino clients. *Social Work,* 37(1), 55–60.

Index

Effectiveness Matters, 145
e-therapy, 213; benefits of, 214; chat rooms, 215; limitations of, 214; privacy issues, 216; as useful, 214–15. *See also* Internet
Evidence Based Resource Center, 144

Faulkner, William, 22
Federal Depository Library Program (FDLP), 146
Find Articles, 145
formal writing: business letter, 107–8, 121; business letter, samples of, 108–11; committee minutes, 116–17; committee minutes, examples of, 118–19; committee minutes, guidelines for, 117; complaint letter, 111–12, 121–22; complaint letter, samples of, 112–15; reference letter, 119–20; reference letter, example of, 120; referral letter, 115–16, 121
funding, 169, 170, 171; feedback to, 166; forms of, 163, 172; requests, for conference attendance, 163, 171, 172; requests, for equipment, 163, 172; requests, for research money, 163, 172

Google, 142
government documents, 146–47
grammar rules, 38–46; subject and verb, agreement of, 39–40; tenses, 38–39
grant proposals, 163–64
Guide to Clinical Preventive Services, 145

Health Insurance Portability and Accountability Act (HIPAA), 211, 216; privacy rights of, 217–19
Health Technology Advisory Committee, 144
Health Technology Assessment (HTA) Database, 144
Hemingway, Ernest, 2, 22, 27, 37
Holocaust survivors, 101, 102, 103
Horney, Karen, 102

human services writing, 2, 3, 13, 41, 46; bureauspeak in, 61, 62; foreign phrases in, 58–59, 62; generalization in, avoidance of, 41; humor, use of in, 43–44; language use in, 40; meaningless words in, 44–45; metaphors, use of in, 42; misused words, 50–57; psychobabble, use of in, 59, 60, 62; redundant words, 57–58, 61; slang, usage of in, 59–60, 62; spelling in, 49
human subjects committee, 82; debriefing statement, 83, 89; informed consent statement, 83, 89
Hurricane Katrina, 16, 184

informed consent statement, 83, 89; example of, 86–87; guidelines for, 85–86
Infoseek, 142
Internet, 219; academic writing resources, 147; chat rooms, 211, 215; computer viruses, 141–42; e-therapy, 213, 214, 215; group therapy, as form of, 215; online supervision, 211, 212; privacy issues, 211, 216; research search, 140, 141; social work resources, 147; virtual libraries, 141; websites on, 143–45. *See also* e-therapy

Julagay, Cecilia, 8, 9

Laux, Dorianne, 2
Learning from Resilient People (Glicken), 187
libraries: research, 142
life coaching: e-therapy, 214
literature review: libraries, 142; quality of, 138, 140
The Little Red Writing Book (Royal), 53
Lycos, 142

MacLeod, Jason Michael, 223–24
McCarthy, Cormac, 1
misdiagnosis, 92

Narcissistic Personality Disorder (NPS), 92
National Health Service, 144
National Library of Medicine, 144; Health Services/Technology Assessment Text (HSTAT), 144
National Research Register, 144
Netscape, 142
NHS Economic Evaluation Database (NHS EED), 145

objective client assessment, 91, 104; example of, 96–101; contract, 100–1; diagnostic statement, 98–100; strengths perspective approach, 96, 103; treatment plan, 100; writing of, 94–95

Parker, Yana, 123
Patient-Oriented Evidence that Matters (POEMS), 144
plagiarism, 79, 89; citations, use of, 80, 81; consequences of, 78; data, falsifying of, 81, 82; as defined, 77; Internet, 77, 78; as rampant, 77
poetry: forgotten memories, 223, 224
popular press: book reviews, 185–89, 191; letters to editor, 184, 185, 190; newspaper articles, 180; newspaper editorials, 182, 190, 191; styles of, 175, 176, 179; writing for, 175, 190
positive psychology: strengths perspective, 138
posttraumatic stress disorder (PTSD), 14, 15, 16, 37
Pound, Ezra, 11
Primary Care Clinical Practice Guidelines, 145
professional writing, 4; psychobabble in, 2; slang in, 2
pseudo-transference, 92
Publication Manual of the American Psychological Association (APA), 2, 63, 74, 78
punctuation, 8, 34; colon, 37; comma, 1, 34, 35; dash, 37; exclamation mark, 34; paraphrasing, 36;

parentheses, 37; period, 1, 34; question mark, 34; quotation mark, 35, 36; rules of, 33–38; semicolon, 36

racism: and misdiagnosis, 92
RehabTrials.org, 145
Remembering Zion (Glicken), 229
reports, 13; audience of, 19; information, availability of, 17–18; expertise, 19; outlining, 23; as relevant, 18–19; sources for, 135–38; special meaning toward, 17; time constraints, 18; topics of, 17
research abstracts, 143
research articles, 139–41
research proposal: example of, 164–65
research report: assessments of, 155–56; design and methods, 150; examples of, 153–54, 156–61; findings, 150, 152; hypothesis, 151; implications, 152–53; introduction, 149; literature review, 149–50; material in, 153–55; outline of, 149–53; parts of, 149; problem statement, 149
resumes, 123, 134; examples of, 125–29
resume writing: tips on, 123–25
Royal, Brandon, 53

Scott, Bill, 63, 75
Scribe, Doc, 63, 75
search engines, 142
September 11, 14, 15
The Sibling Society (Bly), 188
Statistical Package for the Social Sciences (SPSS), 150
storytelling: importance of, 222; as self-therapy, 221
SUMSearch, 145

telephone therapy, 215–16
Terrorist (Updike), 33
Thompson, Hunter S., 23
Tschabrun, Susan, 79

About the Author

Dr. Morley D. Glicken is the former dean of the Worden School of Social Service in San Antonio; the founding director of the Master of Social Work Department at California State University, San Bernardino; the past director of the Master of Social Work program at the University of Alabama; and the former executive director of Jewish Family Service of Greater Tucson. He has also held faculty positions in social work at the University of Kansas and Arizona State University.

Dr. Glicken received his bachelor's degree in social work with a minor in psychology from the University of North Dakota and holds an MSW from the University of Washington and MPA and DSW degrees from the University of Utah. He is a member of Phi Kappa Phi Honorary Fraternity.

Dr. Glicken published two books for Allyn and Bacon/Longman Publishers in 2003: *The Role of the Helping Professions in the Treatment of Victims and Perpetrators of Crime* (with Dale Sechrest), and *A Simple Guide to Social Research*; and two additional books for Allyn and Bacon/Longman in 2004: *Violent Young Children* and *Understanding and Using the Strengths Perspective*. He published *Improving the Effectiveness of the Helping Professions: An Evidence-Based Approach to Practice* in 2005 for Sage Publications and *Working With Troubled Men: A Practitioner's Guide* for Lawrence Erlbaum Publishers in 2005. In 2006, he published *Life Lessons From Resilient People* and *Social Work in the 21st Century: An Introduction to Social Problems, Social Welfare Organizations, and the Profession of Social Work*, both published by Sage Publications.

Dr. Glicken has published over 50 articles in professional journals and has written extensively on personnel issues for Dow Jones, the publisher of the *Wall Street Journal*. He has held clinical social work licenses in Alabama and Kansas. He is currently professor emeritus in social work at California State University, San Bernardino, and director of the Institute for Personal Growth: A Research, Treatment, and Training Institute in Prescott, Arizona, offering consulting services to non-profit agencies. More information about Dr. Glicken may be obtained on his website: www.morleyglicken.com and he may be contacted by e-mail at mglicken@msn.com.